CREATING THE CUSTOMER-DRIVEN LIBRARY

Building on the Bookstore Model

JEANNETTE WOODWARD

AMERICAN LIBRARY ASSOCIATION
Chicago

In Association With

Ess Ess Publications
New Delhi

Creating the Customer Driven Library:
Building on the Bookstore Model

ISBN: 978-81-7000-562-9

Rs.875/-

First Indian Imprint 2009

Published by:
Ess Ess Publications
4837/24, Ansari Road,
Darya Ganj,
New Delhi-110 002.
INDIA
Phones: 23260807, 41563444
Fax: 41563334
E-mail: info@essessreference.com
www.essessreference.com

in arrangement with

American Library Association
50, East Huron Street,
Chicago, Illinios 60611
United States of America

Printed and bound in India at Salasar Imaging Systems.

To, Chris, Laura, and Lowell with much love

CONTENTS

INTRODUCTION

Have you taken a good look recently at your local bookstore? That's probably a silly question because, as book people ourselves, we tend to lock up the library in the evening and head for the bookstore to relax. Next to the library, bookstores are our very favorite places. There are some things that they will always do better than we can, and we wish them well. In fact, every time a bookstore closes, we mourn.

Bookstores have become enormously popular places where customers can do many of the same things that librarians once viewed as their exclusive province. Unlike bookstores of the past, modern "superstores" encourage people to read and spend time just as they would in a library. They have been highly successful in attracting customers, and there is even some evidence that bookstores are taking customers away from libraries.

You may remember that a few years ago, a heated battle raged on the pages of several library journals about whether libraries should imitate bookstores. Looking back on those articles and the angry letters they generated, I wonder if we didn't somehow miss the point. Sure, bookstores have done a great job of increasing their customer base and yes, it is probably true that some people are choosing to visit their local bookstores rather than their public libraries. However, that surely doesn't mean that libraries have less to offer. Isn't it possible that we can cherish all the things that make libraries wonderful and vital to our society while at the same time learning from the bookstore's success? In other words, can't we be better than a bookstore?

Focusing on Success

Although each library type has different goals and priorities, most libraries, whether they are public, school, or academic, can all be more successful by focusing on ways to attract customers and better satisfy their needs. In our contemporary society, businesses have developed sophisticated techniques to attract customer attention. Despite the many services they have to offer, libraries may seem boring by comparison. With tight budgets, librarians may feel that they cannot afford the time and money needed to lure customers. In fact, the lack of both funds and focus may eventually result in our libraries taking on a down-at-the-heel look that repels all but the most determined customers.

Of course, bookstores exist primarily to make money. It should be made clear from the start that this book is not encouraging libraries to sacrifice their own identities or imitate bookstore values. Libraries are focused not on profit but on their mission to support a democratic, information-literate society. This is a distinction that cannot be emphasized too strongly. Libraries are dedicated to producing knowledgeable citizens who can make well-informed decisions about their lives and the world they live in. You could say that libraries are focused not on making money but on making a difference. We provide services to the people who need them, not just the people who can pay for them.

However, bookstores have much to teach us. Since broadening library use and making the library more relevant to its community are central to our mission, we cannot afford to ignore the bookstore's success. Librarians all across the country are taking note of bookstore innovations and using the model to develop new and innovative library services. With quite limited resources, they are expanding their scope to include functions that were scarcely dreamed of a few years ago. When you get right down to it, libraries offer products and services that are far more desirable than any bookstore. Now they must find ways to toot their own horns.

Looking Ahead

In chapter 1 we will be taking a tour of a typical bookstore. If you have visited a "chain-type" bookstore recently, you may have noticed that it attracts many more people than does your library. You are likely to see a broader spectrum of customers strolling through the aisles or enjoying their espresso in the bookstore café. Although librarians are active supporters of diversity, we must confess that our libraries attract a rather narrow, homogeneous group of people. Only in children's services do we usually find anything that begins to approach true diversity, and even here, parents and children often come from mainly white, middle-class households.

Although bookstores rely heavily on this group, they attract many people who are scarcely aware of the library's existence. For example, they have been quite successful in attracting older teens. If these people were to become regular library users, the library's customer base would increase dramatically. If, in addition to this bookstore-customer group, the library were able to attract other new users for whom the bookstore's wares are too costly, then library support would skyrocket.

Likewise, since statistical studies indicate that only a small fraction of the population uses libraries, the library is at a disadvantage when it comes to funding. Since most libraries, whether public, school, or academic, are publicly funded, limited use translates to a low priority when it comes time to allocate budgets. When local economies are in decline, libraries may be among the first to experience cuts. If decision makers have the perception that the library is a luxury enjoyed by a small minority, then, naturally, they are more expendable than other public services.

Let's Hear It for Libraries

What we sometimes forget is that bookstores have prospered largely by imitating libraries. They have discovered that we have something very alluring that is worth copying. Many of the innovations we associate with modern bookstores are simply library services. Take, for example, the new emphasis on relaxing in a comfortable chair and just reading a book. What could be more central to the library experience? Where did they get the idea for children's story hours? From us, of course! Some bookstores are even hosting book discussion groups—an obvious steal if there ever was one. Look at the decor. What we often see is a recreation of a nineteenth-century library, complete with imitation oak paneling and bookcases, leather chairs, and dark, gleaming library tables. We have both a heritage and an identity that bookstores envy. If they can market our wares so successfully, shouldn't we be doing the same?

All Libraries Can Learn

Before going further, I would like to make it clear that this book is not just for public libraries. There is no library, no matter whether school, special, or academic, that can't be more effective by appealing to a wider population. In some cases this is obvious, but in other situations it may be less evident. Take, for instance, the large research library. Glitz is definitely not a high priority for the director of a research library. Instead, he or she must daily struggle with the overwhelming problem of how to acquire and house a significant portion of the world's knowledge. Many are struggling with reduced operating budgets, delayed building programs, and too many materials squeezed into a space intended to hold only a fraction of the current collection.

What we have been observing in recent years, however, is that no one wants to spend time in these libraries. First, undergraduates fell by the wayside. As instructors gradually reduced the number of library assignments, college students found ways to avoid the library. Librarians reasoned that this was perfectly understandable. Inexperienced students were intimidated by the hallowed halls of learning, so undergraduate libraries were built to better serve their needs. Now many of those undergraduate libraries have seen better days. Though once trendy and attractive, they have been neglected. The library's responsibility to the research community has been placed ahead of its obligation to beginning students.

Although research libraries have focused on the collection needs of advanced students and faculty, they have assumed that such scholars will automatically take advantage of their resources. This has not been the case. Increasingly, all students, whether neophytes or doctoral students, are doing much of their research from home and taking advantage of online databases. They dread coming into the central library because it tends to be an unpleasant experience. The staff, much reduced in size by budget cuts, is available only on the main floor. The remainder of the vast building is crammed with stacks, but one can find very few library users. Whole floors, though stuffed with dusty records, are totally devoid of even one living, breathing human being.

Academic libraries are going through a difficult and uncertain period. With new databases appearing daily, many faculty and administrators assume that the university library is dead or soon will be. This conviction is reinforced when, on a rare visit to the library, they find themselves in a dingy, uninhabited warehouse. Is it any wonder that they do not view the library's budget as a high priority?

Special libraries have yet another set of problems, and very possibly these are the more difficult to address because of their invisibility. Whether medical, legal, or corporate, these libraries interact most with clerks, secretaries, and entry-level staff, who have little or no input into decision making. When the boss asks for an article or report, they produce it, often without even mentioning the librarian who spent several hours searching for it. Thus, when budget cuts are being considered, high-level managers are almost unaware of the library's productivity. They will be much more aware of the efforts of the secretary who merely put in a phone call than the library staff who practically turned cartwheels to produce their report.

Marketing skills and customer-service expertise are, therefore, just as important to the special library as to the public library. Special librarians must somehow get to those decision makers, presenting a positive, inviting image of the library and the library staff. They must somehow communicate the message that the library is vitally important to the success of the organization.

The Library's Mission Comes First

I should mention that there may come a point when you as a librarian will need to say "Stop! Whoa! This is as far as we go!" For most of us, this will probably never occur because we have such a lot of work ahead of us. There are libraries, however, that have taken their image in their communities very, very seriously. Like bookstores, they have looked at their user populations and asked what they might do to become the center of activity, the hub around which the community revolves. Unlike the bookstore with its commercial focus, however, they have no clear way to measure success, no obvious bottom line. Step-by-step, they have brought new groups into the library by providing interesting programs, cozy ambience, and popular materials. They have tried to become all things to all people, and to an amazing degree they have succeeded.

What's wrong with this? Nothing! Nothing, that is, until they cross an invisible line and cease to be real libraries. Instead, they become community centers with some library services tacked on. In such libraries, goals and priorities have been turned upside down. Once the library sought to attract users who would, in turn, live more satisfying, more information-literate lives. Now its focus is entirely on numbers. Either the library or its parent organization has come to perceive the library's success in terms of a popularity contest. Major funding is diverted from collection development to programming. The library hosts every razzle-dazzle event, whether or not it contributes to cultural and educational goals. With space at a premium, reading and study areas are invaded. In fact, films, concerts, receptions, forums, and children's programs gradually expand beyond the capacity of the library's meeting space and take over much of the library. Patrons wishing to sit quietly and read find that this activity is no longer encouraged. Staff are unable to catalog books or answer reference questions because they are now running a three-ring circus.

Modern technology has contributed to this confusion about the library's role as well. For example, purchasing, repairing, and upgrading public computers and computer software may become so costly that the materials budget is decimated. Reference staff find their time consumed with computer crashes, viruses, and e-mail glitches, while technicians casually and often inaccurately answer reference questions.

As more people are encouraged to use the library for their own special interests and activities, some of them come to feel a sense of ownership. Why not hold a committee meeting at one of those nice tables in the reading room? In fact, why not close the library altogether for the big reception? That way no uninvited undesirables will line up for refreshments. Even library boards and volunteers occasionally view the library as their own personal domain where everything can be adjusted to suit their personal tastes. It does not seem to dawn on anyone that such high-handedness is a violation of the library's mission. The library should not exist for any privileged inner circle, and it may not exclude the "have-nots" who may need library services far more than more affluent patrons. In addition, the library was not designed for such functions. Such in-groups never pause to consider the burden that catered luncheons place on the library's custodial staff or the rodents that will enjoy the leftovers as their main course, with rare books for dessert.

When people begin seeing the library as an extension of their living rooms, when they use it to entertain their friends and associates and to exclude undesirables, then it's time to call a halt. In the same vein, children's programs are wonderful, attracting large numbers of children to the library and to the world of books. However, when the library becomes an unlicensed day-care center, things have gone too far.

The mission of the library, whether public, academic, school, or special, is as relevant now as in the past. In fact, we may quite honestly say that the world needs libraries more than ever. It is our responsibility to show the world, or at least our own library communities, what a real library can be. A real library is responsive, empowering, and inviting. A real library is able to reach out to its community and attract customers from every segment of society.

Before moving on to the first chapter, I feel, gentle reader, that I must issue a warning. You may be learning more about the great state of Wyoming than you care to know. As a new resident of the nation's least populated state, I have become entranced by both its libraries and its bookstores. If I ever needed convincing, Wyoming has reassured me that our libraries are in great shape. Despite a multitude of problems, they are making a real difference in the lives of young and old, rich and poor. Whether serving the 200 souls who call the hamlet of Pavillion, Wyoming, home or the 600 residents of the bustling metropolis of Shoshoni, they are reaching out to their communities and improving the quality of life for everyone. Because of the willingness of librarians to cooperate and communicate, distance from cultural meccas is no longer a handicap to anyone seeking information. Although they may be living a thousand miles from a major research center, writers, researchers, wildlife biologists, Park Service naturalists, and genealogists can satisfy their information needs almost as easily as if they were residing on a large university campus. What we as librarians have to offer is indeed precious. Because it can make a difference to so many people, we must do a better job of spreading the word. That is what this book is all about.

chapter 1

Why Bookstores Are So Appealing

Since we will be comparing libraries to bookstores, perhaps it would be a good idea to take a closer look at one of the chain bookstores in our neighborhood. If you have your seat belt on, let's drive out to a suburban shopping center. Of course, there are still small, privately owned bookstores here in town, maybe on the square or squeezed into storefronts on quieter side streets. However, newer chain bookstores are so large that they require warehouse-type accommodations. Not only are they as big as warehouses but their construction is similar. Most are large building shells.

We found the address easily in the yellow pages of our phone book. The display ad listed the hours of operation and also provided brief directions. Of course, it would be hard not to know about the store and its location. Newspaper advertisements and bulk mailings are all too numerous. The bookstore's book signings, live-music schedule, and children's programs are always prominently listed in the newspaper's "What's Happening" section.

Location, Location, Location

Look up ahead. The bookstore is easily visible from the busy highway, and we can see it from quite a long distance away. The bookstore's large, distinctive signs attract our attention while we still have time to slow down and change lanes. A great deal of money and research has been invested in finding the best location, and considerable effort has also gone into determining the most efficient way for vehicles to enter and exit. Large bookstores are usually located along or just off major thoroughfares. They assume that nearly all their customers arrive by car and so make little provision for pedestrians. We would find a large, urban bookstore on one of the city's nicest streets near bus lines and other public transportation. Once again, easy access is the prime consideration.

Now we're approaching the vast parking lot. The bookstore management knows that to attract customers, it must provide ample and convenient parking. It cannot assume that customers will somehow find a parking spot on a side street or walk a couple of blocks from the parking garage that charges by the hour. Although the lot is pretty full, there are still spaces available. Notice that the surface has been repaved recently, and the white lines dividing parking spaces are sharp and easily seen. If this were a snowy day, the lot would be plowed frequently because potential customers might not stop if they feared they might slip on the ice. Corporate headquarters also frowns on icy parking lots because of the possibility of lawsuits.

Figure 1-1 Parking is readily available at this Calabasas, California, bookstore.

If this were evening, the parking lot would be brightly lit, making it easier for customers to reach the store without turning an ankle and making it more difficult for car thieves and other criminals to do their worst. Seen from a distance, the brightly lit parking lot filled with cars conveys a sense of excitement to passing motorists. The bright circle of light on a dark night is infinitely appealing. This is where the action is. When potential customers see many other people choosing to spend time at the bookstore, they wonder what they're missing. Maybe this is where they too can spend an enjoyable evening.

The Welcoming Bookstore

As we approach the entrance, we can see that a lot of effort has gone into making it attractive. Pots of flowering plants and benches herald the pleasant experience to come. There is ample space in front of the entrance for drivers to drop off passengers on rainy days or pick up Christmas shoppers loaded down with heavy packages. Well-polished glass doors provide a glimpse of the treats that await the customer. (I haven't specified a particular day or time for our visit, but the bookstore is probably open. Most of the larger ones are open seven days a week and rarely close before ten at night.) Corporate headquarters has conducted extensive research to find out when customers do their shopping. Their research has made it clear that most people are otherwise occupied during normal business hours. Both men and women are working at full-time jobs, and with the exception of a quick errand during lunch hour, most do their shopping evenings and weekends.

Once inside, the customer is immediately confronted by a colorful, artistically designed display of merchandise. Although lots of professional expertise has gone into the displays, it is the books and media packages themselves, displayed to best advantage with their endless variety of arresting covers, that provide much of the visual excitement. One display leads to another and yet another until the customer is "hooked," or completely immersed in the bookstore's offerings.

If, however, the customer is looking for a specific book or subject, help is at hand. One or more service points are readily visible from the door. Service desks are not numerous, however. In fact, newer stores rarely have staff available in every department. I'm reminded of the venerable Foyles in London, which seems to go up higher and higher, one creaking stairway after another. At each landing a service desk with highly trained staff awaits the panting customer. Here in our suburban bookstore, staff are considered expensive, no matter how meager their salaries, and modern stores owned by large corporations are ever focused on the bottom line. Managers usually make the most of staff resources by assigning more employees for busy periods and fewer for slow ones.

Staff assistance, however, is rarely needed. Signage is both attractive and effective, located precisely where customers are most likely to need help. That's because such signs have been designed by signage professionals who have carefully researched the best size, fonts, and locations; the most visible color combinations; and the most desirable arrangement of signage elements to avoid confusion and clutter. Bookstore managers and chain owners have determined that good signage is well worth the financial investment. Not only does it reduce the number of clerks needed to direct customers but it gets people quickly to the areas where they are most likely to find materials that interest them. If customers find what they're looking for before their energy flags, they are more likely to make purchases.

Observing Customer Service

Let's stop at the checkout desk and ask a question. If staff are busy, they may send us to the information desk. If no customers are waiting, they will probably answer our questions themselves. I have tried this at several bookstores and have come to some tentative conclusions. Nearly everyone I have approached has tried to be helpful. There doesn't seem to be a great deal of difference between the expertise of staff on the two desks. It may be that info-desk staff are a little more familiar with stock, and checkout staff quicker on the cash register. Neither group possesses the expertise of a reference librarian, but both have been fully trained to answer customers' frequent questions. Of course, longtime employees know more, and newer ones less, but all have received standardized training in customer service. Midwestern staff may smile more broadly and chat more easily, while New Yorkers are less chummy. However, on only one occasion during these recent sorties have I met with indifference and never with actual rudeness.

Layout and Signage

Finding a particular book or CD is not usually difficult. Large signs lead to the right section of the store, and smaller signs indicate broad subjects like American history or writing. Within these categories, books are arranged alphabetically by author, CDs by performer or composer. Larger chains are now providing computers, similar to library OPACs, that allow customers to look up particular titles, but it is usually just as easy to go directly to the shelves. Of course, items are sometimes misplaced, just as they are in libraries.

Note that quite a lot of attention has been paid to traffic patterns. The bookstore obviously expects to play host to a large number of customers, so careful consideration has been given to moving them through the store without bumping into one another. Main aisles are wider, and routes have been planned almost like a highway system. Aisles are wheelchair accessible, and only the ones off in corners or near the periphery are likely to be as narrow as library aisles. In contrast, most libraries maintain a standard aisle width of thirty-six inches (if they are ADA compliant), no matter whether the aisle is used constantly or infrequently traversed.

The New Bookstore Model

If we'd like to sit down and read, there are comfortable chairs available for this purpose. That's actually a fairly recent phenomenon. Years ago, most bookstore owners discouraged readers from blocking the aisles to peruse a book or magazine for any period of time. The idea was that if customers could read a book in the store, they wouldn't buy it. That is no longer the prevailing philosophy, and visiting a modern bookstore has become a much more enjoyable experience. In fact, often, when people are pondering the question of how to spend an enjoyable evening, the bookstore is one of their more attractive options. They might spend half an hour or so perusing the new books, curl up with one that especially appeals to them, listen to a few tracks from a new album, and then stroll over to the bookstore café for dessert and a nice cup of espresso. Maybe there's even a jazz trio playing, and, of course, there's no cover charge for the entertainment. It's all part of the package. On most Friday and Saturday nights, there is usually quite a crowd, and they appear to be in no hurry to leave. That's fine with the bookstore because the longer customers wander and read and sip, the more likely they are to make purchases.

If you look very closely at the building, you will discover that it is very much like a big barn. *However,* a lot of effort has gone into preventing customers from noticing this. Walls are lined with attractive bookcases, posters, and other large graphics. Displays are so eye-catching that they effectively take the place of expensive architecture. Most of what gives the bookstore its trendy look can be changed easily. A daringly painted wall, some new signs and displays, and voilà! The store has a fresh, up-to-date look.

Let's continue down this aisle and take a good look at the children's department. It's surprising how much it looks like a children's library. The puppet stage with tiered seating is used frequently. Story hours are common. Children's furniture is sturdy and meant to encourage younger customers to enjoy the books and other merchandise on display. Of course, these are new books. They are not torn, dirty, chewed, or written in.

Story hour is about to begin. My, what a mob! I see that the manager is dealing with the situation by transferring a staff member from the information desk. She seems a little flustered, but now she's marshaling her troops and leading part of the group to an adjacent area. No, storytelling is not her regular job, but she's become adept at changing hats when a children's program is unexpectedly successful. I think it's fair to say that the bookstore does not approach such services to young readers with the same professionalism as a children's librarian. Again, the aim is not really education but sales. Nevertheless, even to knowledgeable library spies like us, programs seem very similar to those presented by the library.

Food, Drink, and Entertainment

Now let's take a look at the café that is so often talked about. It probably occupies a space that is separate from the sales floor but clearly visible. Maybe a low wrought-iron railing or a few steps separate it from the merchandise. Customers are standing at a counter ordering from a menu of light snacks and an endless selection of coffees. Instead of the carpeting that covers the floor in the rest of the store, customers are probably standing on hard-wearing vinyl or ceramic tile. Tables may look like real wood, but they are protected by heavy coats of polyurethane.

Look at that woman taking her espresso to a table piled high with books. We cringe, confident that the espresso will soon be soaking into the pages of those shiny new books. In fact, this will probably not happen. Most of the books will either be purchased or returned to the shelves in good condition. It's true that the bookstore environment is somewhat different from a library. After a few perusals by coffee-sipping customers, many of those books will probably leave the bookstore forever (and they will take their microorganisms with them).

While books are residing on our library shelves, they may be protected from the occasional coffee spill. However, our goal is (or should be) to send those books *home* with customers as frequently as possible. Once our patrons have returned home, it is not long before they brew a pot of coffee similar to that served in the bookstore and curl up to read. In other words, popular library books are probably exposed to food and drink even more often than books sold at the bookstore.

But let's get back to our tour. Over in the corner, we notice a piano and sound system. A few times a week, local musicians might play a set or two. Note that they're usually not just any musicians. They're chosen to enhance the bookstore's image as a happening place. In many areas, the bookstore's customer base is heavily weighted toward the over-fifty crowd. In other locales, trendy young singles may dominate. Both groups are known to respond to sophisticated jazz, folk, and light classical fare. Bookstores that consider themselves music stores as well and seek to attract an even younger crowd may lean more toward rock. You may not hear a lot of rap in bookstores unless their marketing departments have identified a sizable market segment that considers it hip or cool. Bookstores know that music preferences are closely linked to socioeconomic status and are interested mainly in customers who have money to spend on their wares.

Well, *tempus fugit,* and we must move on to our next destination. Let's take these books to the checkout or cashier's desk. It's easy to identify the line; we simply follow the path, often marked by theater ropes and displays of popular items.

On the average, customers in a large bookstore probably spend more time in the checkout line than they might in a library. However, the bookstore's attendance figures are also much higher than the library's. Also, since customers can browse best sellers and coffee-table books while they wait, it may not seem quite as long.

Theater ropes are still a new development in libraries; often, customers still mill around the desk, uncertain which line they're in or which checkout stations are open. Such a confusing situation heightens anxiety, and just one experience with a fellow customer who pushes in front and demands service can sour the entire library visit. Purchasing a few stanchions, ropes, and display racks is an inexpensive way to transform the customer experience.

Leaving the Bookstore

Notice as we're leaving that the bookstore has a security system very similar to the ones in use at most libraries. Why didn't we notice it as we were coming in? If we look carefully, we will probably discover that our attention was occupied elsewhere. Our eyes were drawn to the colorful displays, which lined our path and moved us efficiently into the "store proper." There's no getting around the fact that a security system is off-putting. Going through a gate or metal frame puts a bad taste in our mouth, and a little of our enthusiasm dies. Even though bookstores are usually much more security conscious than libraries, their security measures seem to be less in evidence. They have taken care to provide surveillance equipment and security personnel without drawing attention to them.

When libraries become aware that their materials are disappearing, they show none of this finesse. They station security guards at the entrance who paw through patrons' book bags and pocketbooks. They install security gates that are rarely serviced and so sound off loudly at inappropriate times. Of course, the truth is that bookstores commit some of these same indignities, but usually only departing, rather than entering, customers are aware of it.

Once outside, we deposit our purchases in the car. Shall we do a bit of shopping while we're here? Bookstores are usually located near other stores and can frequently be found in shopping malls. Once again, location is important. The more reasons customers have to visit this part of town, the better. Corporate headquarters know that they will increase sales if they ease the inconveniences associated with the trip and increase the payoff awaiting customers upon arrival.

As we've sauntered through the bookstore, you've probably been getting lots of ideas for your library, and you've been able to congratulate yourself that the bookstore could take some tips from you as well. Although there are a lot of important differences between the two, there are even more similarities. These similarities are even more noticeable to our customers, most of whom know little about the library's heritage and goals. They merely respond to what they see.

Well, let's move on now and take a look at a nice neutral library—not yours or mine or any with which we're personally familiar. In truth, it will really be an amalgam of different libraries, just as the bookstore we just visited could be a Borders or a Barnes & Noble. It might be in Kansas City or in Kalamazoo. Our library will be just as nebulous, but in many ways, it will be all too recognizable. Let's see how it compares with the bookstore.

RESOURCES

Fialkoff, F. "Mimicking the Library." *Library Journal* 124 (February 15, 1999): 136.

Kazdan, S. "True Confessions of a Bookstore Addict." *Feliciter* 44 (November/December 1998): 8.

chapter 2

Comparing Libraries and Bookstores

We're probably in agreement that our bookstore tour was most enjoyable, although our belts may feel a trifle tighter after the gourmet bagel we "inhaled" with that cup of rich espresso. What we need now is some exercise to walk off those calories. That means we're ready for the second half of our tour. No, it's not another bookstore. This time we're heading for a typical library. Of course, that's a misnomer. There really is no such thing as a typical library. Unlike chain bookstores, which are the result of a corporate formula, libraries are born (and grow) in their communities, whether local or academic. Each has a unique personality that has evolved over many years, and each, to some extent, mirrors its community.

Nevertheless, libraries and bookstores have a lot in common, so for the purposes of our tour, I'll try to put together a picture of one not unlike those we most frequently encounter. It could be a school library or the one that serves the local community college. When many people think of a library, however, the picture that often comes to mind is their neighborhood public library. Let's start there.

The Library's Location

Where is it, you may wonder? Let's stop and ask that woman standing by the bus stop. "Library?" She's not sure. Maybe it's that big building on Third Street. She apologizes, obviously feeling a little guilty that she doesn't have a clue. She hasn't visited the library since she was a child. Didn't she read something about the library moving to a new site? Actually, the last library building project was fifteen years ago. It's possible, of course, that a similar random query about the bookstore might also yield no information. However, few local residents are usually unaware of the location of a Borders or a Barnes & Noble superstore. In fact, it would be difficult to ignore the television commercials, the full-page newspaper ads, and the huge signs. When you consider that the library is intended to serve the entire population and the bookstore consciously sets out to target only certain demographic segments, the library's anonymity is even more troublesome.

Well, when all else fails, we paw through the glove compartment, sending candy wrappers and charge card receipts flying, and pull out the map. While the bookstore was planned to be as accessible as possible, the library's location resulted from a variety of factors. Although the superstore is a recent innovation, many libraries have been at the same spot for as long as a hundred years. During that time, several neighborhood transformations have taken place. Libraries that were once nestled in residential neighborhoods may now be surrounded by industrial blight. Libraries once accessed via quiet neighborhood streets may now be hemmed in by on-ramps and cloverleafs. Even worse, library neighborhoods where children once played have become so dangerous that parents no longer allow their children to visit the library unaccompanied.

The locations of newer libraries were the result of other circumstances. Branch libraries, like bookstores and community colleges, have followed residents into the suburbs. Although they are often much more convenient than those in urban centers, decision makers sometimes fail to consider bus routes or proximity to schools and shopping centers. Instead, decisions may be made on the basis of which piece of property the county or municipality happens to have available. In contrast, the site of the bookstore was most likely determined only after an expert analysis of demographics and traffic patterns. Unfortunately, library locations are more often the result of happenstance.

The importance of selecting the right library location cannot be stressed strongly enough. It is true that, to some extent, the decision may not be up to the library or its board, and a location may be chosen by people who are not really involved with the library. However, it is too easy to place the blame on others. All too often, the library board and director must assume the lion's share of the blame, especially if they failed to clarify the library's needs or desperately embraced any piece of property that presented itself.

Building on publicly owned land is not always a bad idea. If, for example, the county or municipality already owns a piece of property, the cost of a building program will be reduced. This may mean that funds are available for a larger or better-equipped structure. Maybe it also means that some luxuries not otherwise within the library's reach can be included in the plans. If it is possible for the library to have its cake and eat it—in other words, if you can have both a good location and a more costly building—then the decision is a sound one. If, however, the library builds a palace complete with every service and convenience but loses customers because of an inconvenient location, then the library has made a fatal mistake.

Let me tell you a story, not about a public library but about an excellent state library that made just such a mistake. For years, this library had juggled a full range of services to libraries throughout the state while at the same time doing an excellent job of serving state and local governments. Residents frequently found their way to the library, and reference and local history collections were in constant use. At any time of the day, stack areas and reading rooms were full of people, and it was clear that more space was needed. However, the library was located right in the center of town in one of the most congested neighborhoods. If it were going to expand, it would have to move. A search began for a suitable property.

Unfortunately, it happened that another state agency had recently vacated a building situated on a large piece of property several miles away. Why not renovate and expand this building? At first the state librarian demurred. However, the financial advantages appeared to be overwhelming. With the funds available for the project, the library could have more space. It could add new departments and provide new services. Ultimately, the project was approved.

Today, the library sits in the midst of a vast, empty parking lot. Its reading rooms are empty. Staff from state and county offices no longer stop by to look up information for their reports. Genealogists and history buffs find the library too far from town to make a special trip. In fact, most local residents have not yet found the library because it is so far from the beaten path. State decision makers used to pass the library on their way to work. Now, they scarcely remember that it exists. Librarians have worked hard to rustle up business and have to some extent succeeded by increasing telephone and e-mail inquiries. They regularly fax pages of the reference works that were once in such high demand. However, these remote services do not begin to equal the activity that once kept the library so busy.

Instead of moving forward, this library has spent a great deal of money and devoted many, many hours of labor to moving backward, to actually reducing its impact on its community. After the move, it now serves a smaller percentage of both state employees and local residents; it has become all but invisible.

The Library Exterior

Let's get back to our public library tour, for we are nearing our goal. As we approach by car, we may fail to see the sign in front of the building. It's small in size with lettering that has faded over the years. Infrequently pruned shrubbery almost obscures it. This means that we must navigate across several traffic lanes and one-way streets to get ourselves turned around and approach it once again.

Now where do we *park?* Although some libraries boast ample parking space, others have decided it is a luxury they cannot afford. After all, a parking lot takes up quite a chunk of real estate. It may have been sacrificed the last time the "landlocked" library was expanded. Automobiles were not in common use when the old Carnegies were built, so a parking lot was an afterthought, tucked into whatever small space was available.

From an architectural point of view, the library building is much more interesting than the bookstore. Libraries are often strikingly impressive buildings. They tend to become local landmarks, and architects enjoy the opportunity to let loose their creative imaginations. The problem is that although every

Figure 2-1 Although bookstores are often built like warehouses, this Barnes & Noble is actually a converted power plant.

element of bookstore design was devised to support the bookstore's function—in other words, to control costs and sell books—library architecture may have little to do with library function.

Funding for a local landmark can be relatively generous. Residents are proud of their libraries and want them to make a statement about the desirability of their community. On the other hand, library operating budgets are always limited and rarely adequate to cover the staff and other resources needed to keep such high-maintenance structures in good shape. This means that these imposing buildings may quickly develop a "down-at-the-heel" look. What looks impressive at first glance may appear unkempt and out-of-date as we get closer.

Entering the Library

Well, we've been standing out here in the cold admiring the architecture for too long. Let's go inside. Remember that when we entered the bookstore, that first look encompassed some very attractive book displays and professional signage. Our first view of a library may be a security checkpoint or 3-M book-detection system. Yes, bookstores use the same systems to protect their merchandise from theft. *However,* they are much less in evidence because those striking displays perform dual functions. In addition to luring customers into the store, they also serve as barriers, leading customers through the "in" door and away from the exit. Most bookstore customers are only aware of the security system as they are leaving when they pass through the tape detector.

Some library entrances are even less appealing. In libraries built during the 1960s and 1970s, visitors may enter what is little more than a cinder-block stairwell. It may provide access not only to the library but also to restrooms and possibly to the library's meeting room. When you get right down to it, nothing is as ugly as cinder block. Patrons must then endure not one but two off-putting vistas since the security system still lies in wait.

The library meeting room, however, provides a valuable community service that a bookstore would have little interest in. Because the mission of the library is to serve the community, it does not consider a large space completely devoid of library materials to be wasted. Bookstore space is valued according to its ability to increase profits. A room that simply sits there and waits for the next community group to hold a meeting or the local orchestra to conduct a practice session would not be consistent with the bookstore's goal.

Once past the security system, the customer's experience depends on whether this is a large or small library. Generally, in smaller ones, the circulation desk serves as a starting point at which arriving customers are welcomed. The circulation desk is the command center or "action central" from which most library services are dispensed. When patrons come in, the desk is their first stop. They almost always pause to pass the time of day with their neighbor, whether volunteer or staff member. The news of the day is exchanged, and the book or video being returned is critiqued. Over time, staff in smaller libraries become fonts of information. They know what's going on in their community (juicy gossip included) and the tastes of their patrons. It is not unusual for them to put a book aside for Mrs. Jones, who's a recent widow and in need of escape reading, or search *Books in Print* to see if there just might be another volume in the series that a young customer has become enthralled with. If a library user is out of work, sympathetic staff may not only suggest a book on résumé writing but also provide both the computer and the word processing know-how to get the job done.

In larger libraries, customers probably find themselves in a lobby area dominated by a mammoth circulation desk. However, the circulation desk is really for the benefit of *exiting* patrons, checking *out* their materials. There is usually no one to welcome arriving patrons. New or infrequent visitors invariably stand baffled and perplexed, trying to get their bearings.

The design of the circulation desk may further discourage interaction. While the bookstore checkout desk is waist high, the library's desk tends to be roughly chest high and more nearly resembles that of a bank. The bank counter is high for a reason. There is a great deal of money on the staff side, and for the sake of security, customers must be kept firmly in their place. Why must we be so off-putting in the library? Do we imagine that customers are going to leap over the desk and begin checking out their own books? Are they likely to abscond with that pile of returned videos?

If there is a line at the desk, most people hesitate to ask for help. If they do ask a question, the circulation clerk is frequently unable to assist them. Although small libraries encourage cross-training, the circulation staff in larger libraries almost never leave the desk. This means that their concept of what lies beyond the entry area is often hazy. They may point vaguely in the direction of a reference or information desk, but since neither the desk nor the sign pointing to its location is visible from the entry area, the vague directions are of little help.

Visiting the Stacks

Let us move on, however, past the lobby with its display case of dusty fossil rocks, past the harvest gold and avocado green seating area, into the stacks proper.

Unlike the bookstore, which makes the books the focus of attention, libraries hide their books and media in long narrow rows where the light is often too dim for customers to read the titles. When you get right down to it, the way we display our collections differs little from the old days of closed stacks that were accessible only to the library staff. In fact, many older libraries simply removed the staff-only signs and left the stacks precisely as they were. Bookstores of the past had a similar look of dusty, moldering tomes in long, dark aisles, but they learned it discouraged sales. Libraries, however, have not gotten the message.

Let's stop here and pull out a few volumes. We'll take them to a table and look at them under the light. Notice how dirty they are. Would we really want to display these books? They certainly don't look like the enticing volumes on view in the bookstore. Actually, they look more like objects that fell underfoot during a cattle stampede. Covers are dog-eared, and Mylar jackets have become so dingy that it is no longer possible to read much of the jacket information, even in the brightest light.

When we arrive at the video collection, we find that they are in even worse shape. To prolong their useful lives, most libraries remove videos from their colorful cardboard boxes and place them inside study plastic cases. Part of the original box is often tucked inside and displayed through the front cover. Good idea? Definitely. That way the customer can read the title, cast, plot summary, and reviews. Or can they? After inspecting the videos in a number of libraries, I can attest to the fact that many libraries indiscriminately obscure this information with their date-due slips, stickers, and labels. No effort is made to see that key information remains readable. Even the title is obscured by "Be kind, rewind" stickers. The cardboard packaging in which most videos arrive is extremely colorful and appealing. Naturally! It is intended to sell the product. Why is it, therefore, that librarians consistently waste this free advertising? If we want customers to use the library more often and check out more materials, why do we fail to take advantage of the natural marketing materials we have at our disposal in the form of book jackets and video containers?

Let's back up, however, and take a look at those computer books we passed a few moments ago. Here's one on Windows 3.1, another manual on DOS, and yet others that introduce the reader to dBASE and WordStar. Notice a pattern? These are certainly not titles you see in your local bookstore. Clearly, no librarian has weeded this collection in years. Of course, the budget is tight, but if these titles don't circulate, why allow them to take up space? The shelves are stuffed so tight that it's difficult to remove a volume. If a staff member did some serious culling of obsolete materials, there might be room to display the more popular ones.

The Joyful Children's Library

Ah, at last! Here we are in the children's department. Notice the difference. We're surrounded by bright colors and attractive displays. We're surrounded by people too, since children and their parents are among the library's most devoted customers. Books, tapes, and videos are all within easy reach of small hands. Their delightful covers, complete with charming drawings of dragons, elves, and children, can readily be seen from a distance. It seems brighter here too, and the low shelving and wide aisles make it easy to identify materials, even on the bottom shelf.

Of course, bulletin boards featuring Arthur and Harry Potter are not appropriate for adult services, but don't grown-ups deserve an equally inviting atmosphere? Don't they have just as much right as children to an enjoyable encounter with reading? Although both children and bookstores have discovered that simply being around books can be a delightful, sensory experience, librarians seem determined to hide their light under a bushel.

Bright displays and eye-catching bulletin boards may be totally absent in academic libraries. Many years working in colleges have made me wonder how librarians picture the average college freshman. The academic experience should awaken students to the joy of learning, yet the academic library often convinces them that world must be deadly dull. Do librarians imagine that freshmen are color-blind, that they are such dedicated scholars that they don't notice the dreary environment in which they must complete their assignments? Although public libraries usually make some effort toward creating a pleasant atmosphere, college and university libraries sometimes appear to be trying to make a visit to the library as boring as possible. Atmosphere alone will not solve all the problems of today's academic libraries, but it can have a very significant impact on use.

Meeting Customer Needs

Let's get back to our public library tour, however, and save the academic library for another day. We're here at an especially good time because story hour is scheduled to begin in a few minutes. Look over there at that sad little girl. Her mother has just been told that she failed to preregister her child for this popular event, and so little Susie will not be able to enjoy the crafts or hear the exciting tale that will soon mesmerize the other children.

This is a good example of the difference between libraries and modern bookstores. One can readily understand that the children's librarian wants to limit participation to what she considers a manageable group. She is an educator and seeks to provide a positive learning experience under the best possible conditions. Yet Susie and her mother will probably leave empty-handed with a negative or even hostile attitude toward the library. Borders, on the other hand, would see them as lost customers. To deliberately lose potential sales would be foolish, and so they would probably find a way to squeeze Susie into the group. After all, Susie's mom will be at leisure to browse the best sellers for half an hour or listen to selected tracks of featured CDs. With all that time on her hands, she will probably buy something. Pleasing both mother and daughter thus becomes an important priority. If the event were really popular, the manager might even pull a staff person from other duties and create another story group.

Behind the Scenes

Since we're here, it would be impolite not to say hello to the library director, so we'll head for the library's administrative offices. Let's take a look at the staff work areas on our way. Ouch! What a mess! If the public areas of the library are dreary, the workrooms and offices are infinitely worse. It looks as if every old typewriter the library has ever owned, every damaged artwork, and every ream of yellowing tractor-feed paper have been stuffed in here.

Some time ago, I was visiting with colleagues at a rather famous and highly regarded library. I would almost call this a model library because of its outstanding collection and its innovative services. Librarians employed at this library are an elite corps, rightly admired throughout the library profession. But the library building is an older one, and as you enter through the front door, the smell of dust immediately assails your nostrils. Public areas of the library are dreary, the furnishings being a mixed bag of worn but still elegant oak tables standing side by side with particleboard and Formica. Staff areas are downright appalling. You could almost be in a bombed-out city. Boxes are piled everywhere. Walls that haven't been painted in years are covered with torn scraps of paper, coffee-stained flyers announcing events that took place five years ago, and brittle Scotch tape. Dented and much-abused yellow oak desks are squeezed in between Wal-Mart computer tables. Cables are strung like clothesline, and you cannot walk across the room without navigating an obstacle course of obsolete equipment, teetering stacks of magazines, and vintage desk chairs.

If I were impolite enough to comment on the mess, I would probably be told that there is not enough money to purchase new furniture because the collection must come first. To some extent, this may be true. However, I tend to think there are other reasons as well. I think as a profession, we may actually take pride in a down-at-the-heel look. In academic libraries, we may be saying, in effect, we think only of higher knowledge, not frivolous materialism. In public libraries, we may be trying to prove that we are honorable conservators of public funds.

The problem with these sentiments is that they are *not* in tune with those of our customers. Though a grungy library work space may make a librarian feel more noble or more like an academic, it's an instant turnoff for the majority of the people who use the library. For the most part, our customers are not scholars who labor in dusty ivory towers; they are college students, working parents, ten-year-olds, and retirees, all of whom are influenced by mass culture. The media daily describe exactly what success looks like in material terms. It is made clear to them that the absence of these material objects is a clear indication of the absence of success.

Once bookstores too had a similar, pokey image. They were supposed to be musty, crowded places where books were piled to the ceiling and true scholars could commune with their muses and revel in moldy tomes. In fact, for me, the perfect bookstore was always the one so appealingly depicted in Christopher Morley's "The Haunted Bookshop." Unfortunately, most of those bookstores are out of business today. Although it may be painful to face the fact, most people would rather browse through their books while savoring cappuccinos in a bright, shiny Borders. Bookstore owners have discovered that although the old image was charming, it really didn't help to sell books to a large and diverse customer base. We as librarians must face the same sad fact.

Taking Our Leave

Oops, there's the intercom. The library will be closing in fifteen minutes. Although the bookstore down the street will be open well into the evening, library hours are limited. We'd better check out these books and be on our way. But look at the crowd around the circ desk! Where is the line? There doesn't seem to be one. People are just crowding up to that mammoth desk and vying with one another for service. Maybe that's why the desk is so high. Maybe the library staff think all those people will mob them or storm the citadel.

As we discovered in the last chapter, in most bookstores there is a clearly delineated path to the checkout desk. Stanchions or theater ropes separate customers making purchases from those still browsing. Books and other materials have been artfully arranged along the path to make the wait less arduous and, of course, to increase the possibility of one last impulse purchase. The orderly line is easier for the bookstore clerk to deal with too since there is not an unruly crowd clamoring for his or her attention.

Well, we were not trampled to death, and our materials have been checked out. I can't read the date that's stamped on my book. It looks as if the library hasn't purchased a new date-due stamp for decades, but I'm certainly not willing to force my way through that mob again. By the way, I noticed a feature film I'd like to watch but decided against borrowing it. The last video I borrowed from the library was so worn that it got tangled in my VCR. The one before that was so old that my TV screen showed little more than fuzzy silhouettes and horizontal lines.

Notice that it's now dark outside. Although the bookstore parking lot was ablaze with lights, the library lot is almost pitch dark. Changing the bulbs on those tall lampposts requires a hoist that the library doesn't own. The custodian rented one last year, but he is waiting until a few more bulbs burn out to make another rental worthwhile.

Although the library seemed busy, especially with so many people being herded out of the building at one of the busiest times, the number of customers did not begin to compare with the bookstore. Even though many of the customers were checking out the same materials available in the bookstore for twenty, thirty, or forty dollars, the average community resident seems to prefer the bookstore.

Accepting this reality is difficult. We probably chose the library profession because we believed that libraries had something very precious to give to society. In library school, this philosophy of library service was expanded. We came to understand that people can live richer, more fulfilling lives when they are fully informed. As reference librarians, we discovered how the right information at the right time can solve so many of life's problems. Isn't this what libraries are about? Why should libraries lower themselves to compete with crass commercial establishments?

To be there when needed, the library *must become a lifelong habit.* Only the customer who checks out travel books or mystery novels month after month will turn naturally to the library for information. When regular library customers need medical information, they will remember the reference shelf on which the prescription drug encyclopedia resides. When regular library customers have problems at work, the images of the popular psychology or business skills titles on the "New Book" rack may come to mind.

However, when a mother scarcely knows where the library is located, it will not occur to her to investigate dyslexia at the library to understand her child's problem. This is true not only of public libraries but of all types. The college freshman, who is all but unaware of the library until the night before a paper is due, will find little help. It is only after many less-stressful expeditions through the library that students become aware of its resources and how they are organized.

Thus, libraries must become *habit-forming*. For this to occur, the library must attract patrons in the same way bookstores have developed sophisticated strategies to attract customers. Although we will not forget our own history, we will accept the fact that bookstore chains may be better in tune with the pulse of life in the twenty-first century. In the following chapters we will consider ways in which the bookstore model can be adapted to the library's needs without abandoning any of the ideals that brought us to the library profession.

RESOURCES

Pinder, J. A. "Change to Survive." *Public Libraries* 41 (November/December 2002): 305.

Raymond, J. "Librarians Have Little to Fear from Bookstores." *Library Journal* 123 (September 15, 1998): 41–42.

Sannwald, W. W. "Espresso and Ambiance: What Public Libraries Can Learn from Bookstores." *Library Administration & Management* 12 (fall 1998): 200–211.

Sullivan, M. "One Happy Library User." *Public Libraries* 40 (September/October 2001): 264.

chapter 3

Focusing on the Bottom Line

One of the questions that often confounds librarians is why people don't make better use of libraries. After all, they're not only *free* but they provide an extraordinary range of materials, from scholarly research tomes to pulp fiction. Not only do they try to meet the needs of every age group, from toddlers to seniors, but they have worthy goals like creating an information-literate society. Libraries somehow manage to juggle all these roles without forgetting the paperback romance rack or the Harry Potter reader. Where else can people possibly find such great bargains all in one place?

The Bookstore's Single Objective

Bookstores too may wonder why they aren't reaching more potential customers. However, simply wondering does nothing to increase corporate profits. Knowing which segments of the population are buying books is information of enormous importance for the bookstore's profitability, hence its bottom line. If you were a fly on the wall at meetings of boards of directors, department heads, and even lowly clerks, you would hear much the same thought expressed in a variety of ways: how can we make more money? Although this is not an especially noble aspiration, it is clear and to the point. Sure, the bookstore's executives want to support community goals and otherwise make the world a better place, but they never lose sight of their one paramount objective—the bottom line.

Librarians, in contrast, have *lots* of goals and objectives, most of which are highly idealistic. The mission statements of libraries are full of such high ideals, and we as librarians have every right to be proud of our profession. Libraries, however, are at a serious disadvantage when compared to bookstores. We have no simple road map that takes us directly to our one paramount goal. Although high-minded and noble, our ideals can send us in an almost infinite number of different directions. There's little in our mission statements to tie us down to earth and force us to work toward a common goal.

Over the years, I've felt terribly frustrated by the variety of different goals that seem to coexist in the same library. Rarely has a profession held such high standards that seem to lead nowhere. When I was still a wet-behind-the-ears young librarian, I wondered why books were purchased that never reached the shelves until the information they contained was out-of-date. It seemed to me that elaborate procedures were developed to deal with contingencies that never occurred. While patrons left the library empty-handed, extra steps were added to the cataloging process just in case some day some user might want to know whether a particular volume could be considered a Festschrift or contained a foreword.

Yet libraries have long been staffed by well-educated, highly motivated people. Why didn't their combined labor and expertise add up to a more rewarding library experience for their customers? Even to a rank beginner like myself, it seemed as if my colleagues were headed in very different directions. When goals and objectives were in conflict, how did one determine which should take precedence? This was the question that even senior librarians seemed unable to answer.

In Search of a Bottom Line for the Library

Although the bookstore's monetary bottom line isn't usually relevant for a nonprofit organization like a library, the *concept* of a bottom line is a good one. What is the one single value that should always come first? When different library priorities are in conflict, wouldn't it be desirable to have one simple, easily defined measure of success against which to compare disparate views? After years of trying, I have not been able to reduce the concept of a library bottom line to a single word or a single phrase. It is clear that the bottom line must be a measure of library effectiveness. It must be an objective measure, and that means it probably should be quantitative rather than qualitative. Otherwise, there would be no agreement about success or failure. After trying out different measures of success, I've concluded that there is probably none better than the total number of people who use some service provided by the library. The comparison of this figure with the total population served by the library provides a pretty good indication of the library's effectiveness.

Most library administrators are less than happy with their usage statistics. Many report that circulation has dropped sharply in recent years. For the library to prosper, it must be recognized as important by decision makers in the community. That means that either these decision makers have had personal experience with the library themselves or the message has been brought to them by others who regularly use library services. It is, therefore, not enough to be able to proclaim that "X" number of people have checked out a book or attended a library program during the past year. We must know whether this number represents the community. In other words, we must compare this figure with the number of people who have not used the library. Our funding, and hence our survival, depends not on raw numbers but on the likelihood that any given individual in our community is familiar with the library and will support its needs.

How can we as librarians know when we are reaching these decision makers? How can we know when we are making the kind of impact on our communities that we would like to make? One answer lies in making better use of the information available to us. It is for this reason that collecting better statistical information is important. However, what kind of information should we be collecting? Bookstores too collect a lot of statistical information but with a clear end in mind. The bookstore wants to know how much money is coming in through the sale of books and other merchandise and how much is going out in operating expenses. To evaluate its success, the bookstore need only subtract its expenses from its sales receipts. Of course, there's a little more to it than that, but the fact remains: the bookstore has a clear bottom line, and success or failure is readily apparent.

The Diversity of Library Services

Libraries, however, provide a much wider variety of services than bookstores. They include traditional ones like lending books as well as providing journals, newspapers, government documents, and reference materials for in-house use. In recent years we have broadened our lending role to include CDs, DVDs, and books on tape. One of our most recent and most popular services is providing Internet access. Although technology has become vastly more important to a modern definition of libraries, we continue to provide information, answer reference questions, and simply make space available for reading and study.

Once we get beyond those basic services, the range widens, and no two libraries are exactly alike. Some provide facilities for literacy and job training. Individual study rooms allow small groups to meet, study, and receive tutoring services. Most libraries house local history collections, and many provide support to local businesses. Libraries also house meeting rooms, serve as music venues, and provide space for art exhibits. In some communities, the library is the only safe and neutral space where people from different walks of life with different agendas can meet and talk. When we consult library literature, we find still other examples of libraries supporting lifelong-learning projects, sponsoring political candidate forums, maintaining websites that promote citizenship, and facilitating basic adult education.

If we tally all the numbers from all these different activities, we will probably end up with a truly astronomical number. Yet the statistics don't tell us very much. I would never advocate abandoning such record keeping, because our numbers look very impressive on our annual reports and included in our funding requests. However, they tell us little about our impact on our community as a whole. Once people make contact with a library, they gradually become regulars. They avail themselves of more of its services and participate in more of its programs. As we all know, one family, all by itself, can tote up several hundred ticks in our annual statistical tallies. When we simply add together our attendance figures, we are counting the same people over and over and over.

One of the reasons that libraries have no clear single objective is that they are so responsive. They are rooted in their communities and are the center of many local cultural activities. They have even taken on the responsibility of providing "things" and services that don't, at first sight, seem to have much to do with the library's traditional role. For example, it was logical that libraries would provide computerized databases since they were already subscribing to periodicals in paper. Later, Internet access was added because it has become such an important conduit for the transfer of information in the modern world.

Libraries have found that local residents need computers for other purposes, however, and so provide a wide variety of computer software programs like word processors, spread sheets, and graphics programs. Children have always been an important focus for libraries. As they became involved in activities that promoted reading, libraries further broadened their activities to include programs like "Books for Babies," story hours for toddlers, special programs for preschoolers, and enticing summer reading competitions for reluctant readers. As different groups have emerged and demonstrated their special needs, libraries have responded, providing large-print books and computer workshops especially for seniors and purchasing gay and lesbian literature as well as information about alternative lifestyles.

Do you begin to see why it is so difficult for libraries to establish a bottom line? Of course, other organizations have a variety of programs, and modern corporate conglomerates juggle dozens of different businesses under one management umbrella. In the profit sector, however, there is always the dollars-and-cents answer. How do we find an equivalent in the nonprofit sphere? We respond, of course, that we want to do a good job. We want to know that we are successful at each of these varied endeavors, but how? Which are the numbers that can guide rather than confuse us?

The Value of Library Statistics

Let's first take a look at the information the library currently collects. Most school, public, and academic libraries complete some sort of annual statistical report for either the state or the federal government. Such reports include questions like how many reference or interlibrary loan transactions the library handled during a given period of time. Much of the statistical information generated by such reports is both flawed and of limited usefulness. For example, it's very difficult to really keep track of reference transactions. All too often, reference librarians suddenly realize that they haven't been keeping track and quickly make half a dozen ticks on the tally sheet. If they feel just a little concerned that the number is not large enough or does not show them in a favorable light, then they might add a few more. It's true that sampling reference activity from time to time is helpful in scheduling personnel, but does the information gleaned tell you very much about the library or its impact on the community? Probably not.

What about information that is not collected manually? Library automation programs can print out a variety of different reports. For example, they can produce tables showing circulation of materials to different types of users. If the library has thought carefully about usage and has input relevant patron categories, such a report can provide useful information. The library can, with confidence, discover what percentage of books are circulated to children or to college students or to residents outside the city limits. Reports can also be generated showing circulation figures for different types of materials. If popular psychology books are circulating briskly, selectors have reason to purchase more of them. If circulation is low, then funds are better spent on other materials.

Although this kind of information is useful, it does not provide the kind of clear guidance that a bookstore gets from its bottom line. Although computer stats are more accurate and therefore provide more useful information, circulation totals do not tell the real story. In general, automation systems do a better job of telling you about your collection than they do about your customers. How, for example, does the number of items circulated translate into the number of customers who use the library? Where do those customers live? Are they representative of the larger population?

Is it possible for your automation system to tell you not only how many items were checked out but also how many customers checked out materials? Many systems do not include this as a standard or "canned" report but may be able to produce this magic number in the form of a customized report. If you can get this information out of your automation system, you will find it much more useful than raw circulation data. One customer may have checked out only one item during the last year, but another, who is working on an advanced degree or addicted to romance paperbacks, has checked out fifty. Is one customer any more important than the other?

By a series of happenstances, I have been involved in implementing several new library automation systems in the last few years. Each, whether a small system like Follett or a massively complex one like Unicorn or Horizon, has some provision for generating reports. When they first arrived on the market, I viewed the infant library automation systems with enthusiasm. Maintaining manual statistics is an onerous job, and as we've seen, the results are nearly always flawed. Since computers are so adept at manipulating data, I reasoned, we would now have access to sophisticated statistical analyses and so learn much about the library. Well, it's true that we now have mountains of data, but do the automation systems generate real information that can be used as a basis for decision making? Not very often.

It's true that the basic stats are easier to calculate and more accurate—the number of items checked out, the total number of cardholders, and so forth. Take a good look, however, at the "canned" reports that your system can generate. Would you ever dream of running most of them? Looking at the seemingly endless list of report templates available in my current automation system, I can't imagine why anyone ever wasted his or her time creating them. Probably, I reason, they were created by computer programmers who knew nothing about libraries. They saw that the data was available and determined to make use of it. Then, on further consideration, I wondered if this wasn't yet another indication of our overall confusion. Since we really don't know how to evaluate our success, we develop ways to measure everything, hoping that it will all add up to a blinding insight.

Equating the Bottom Line with Customer Satisfaction

Later we will be comparing Amazon.com's online catalog to a library OPAC. Our catalogs consist of MARC records created according to the exacting cataloging rules for which librarians, not computer programmers, are responsible. Librarians were only peripherally involved in the development of Amazon's enhanced catalog. If you've ever searched the Amazon catalog, you've found a wealth of useful information. Most of the information included in a library's MARC record, however, is of no interest at all to the customer and of almost no interest to the library staff. Hardly anyone really cares how tall a book is or how many pages are included in the front matter. Yet most of the record is devoted to just such trivia, of interest mainly to the rare book market.

The Amazon catalog exists for the purpose of selling books and other materials. To do this effectively online, corporate executives have concluded that the more they can tell customers about the books, the better. However, they don't mean how many pages are in the preface. In fact, if you look at a typical Amazon web page, you'll see only a very small section given over to bibliographic data. Most of the page consists of book reviews, opinions of other readers, sample pages from the book, audio clips from the CD, rankings that indicate popularity, and suggestions for other books and media that customers might enjoy. All this information is provided with the goal of bringing the customer closer to an affirmative decision.

Does the information in a MARC record assist customers in deciding whether this is a book or video they might want to check out? Not really. True, there are a few clues hidden in the record that the cognoscenti may be able to interpret, but that clearly is not the main focus of the record. While the Amazon catalog is fully integrated into the store's goals, the MARC record seems like an intellectual exercise that librarians have developed to test their skills.

If the library's bottom line is serving our customers' needs, how does the MARC record, which has occupied the entire work lives of countless librarians, relate to it? Certainly you could make a case for some of the record fields. However, if we were to see the catalog as Amazon does, our OPACs would be directed not at librarians but at customers. What are they looking for? Viewed from this perspective, it's hard to make a case for the time and expertise that have been put into it. In fact, you could make a much better case for substituting jacket blurbs and tables of contents for many of the more esoteric fields. This would require not expertise but merely an inexpensive scanner.

Measuring the Library's Success

Considering the number of detours the library profession has taken on the road to customer service, how can we find the right road? As with an auto trip, it is not really possible until we have clearly identified our destination. Even though we lack the bookstore's bottom line, we can surely identify a single objective toward which all libraries should progress as quickly as possible. Street numbers or addresses make it easier to find specific locations, so let's give our destination a number. Let's say that our goal is participation by half of our community in some library activity in the next twelve months. The following is a very brief, very incomplete set of directions for arriving at your destination:

Determine your library's service population. If yours is a city library, then this would be the number of city residents. If yours is a university library, then total the number of students, faculty, and staff.

Create a report in your automation system that will tell you the number of individuals in your service area who have checked out some item in the library collection in the last twelve months. Be sure you work out a way to exclude customers who are not included in this service population. Most systems can do this, but you must designate a field in the patron record for residents or nonresidents, students or nonstudents. If this is not possible, you might sample customers some morning at the circulation desk, asking each if he or she lives inside the city limits, attends your university, and so forth. Let's say that three-quarters of those you sample are included in your service population. If your sample is a sizable one, you can, with some trepidation, assume that the same percentage applies to checkouts. The point is to compare apples with apples.

Determine how you will count other services. There is usually too much data to count manually, and it is difficult to adapt your automation system for this purpose. Therefore, it is important to develop reliable sampling procedures. First, work out a way to identify the people attending library-sponsored events. They might sign their names on a sheet or fill out cards when they arrive. Sample the names to determine the percentage of program attendees who are new to the library and have not used any other service during the past year. It is only the number of new people who can be counted toward your community participation goal.

Consider how you will calculate Internet users who are not already included in circulation and program attendance counts. You might choose to use the sampling technique above, or you might actually adapt your automation system to include Internet use. Many libraries have some way of checking out a card or other object that entitles a customer to use a computer. The item is bar-coded so that computer users can be included in the circulation report. Remember that it is more important to know how many residents use your computers than to simply know the number of times the computers were used. Of course, some of your users don't have library cards, but they are often travelers. If locals don't have a library card, they can be encouraged to apply for one.

Consider other services the library provides. How can you identify customers who are not already counted? Remember that you needn't go on counting them month after month. What you need is a good representative sample. Since this will probably mean collecting the names of the people who use these services, be sure that you explain what you're doing and why you're doing it. Otherwise, customers could view your sudden interest as an invasion of their privacy.

Verify your findings. No matter how careful you are in gathering statistics, errors are inevitable. One way of verifying your findings is to sample a group attending an activity that has nothing to do with the library. For example, you or another staff member might volunteer to sell tickets for the Rotary spaghetti dinner at a table set up at the local shopping mall. The point is that neither the event nor the place is in any way connected with the library. While you're making change, ask ticket buyers to complete a brief questionnaire—just a question or two. You might ask when they last visited the library or whether they've visited the library during the past year. Extrapolate the results of this sample to the library's service population. In other words, if the library serves 12,000 people and one-third of your spaghetti-craving respondents visited the library during the past year, then you might conclude that about 4,000 residents are library users. How does this compare with the statistics you have been collecting within the library?

Collecting Only Useful Information

Does it sound as if this is going to be a lot of work? You're right. It will be. However, remember that our libraries are already in gear to collect vast amounts of data that we include each year in our annual reports. Much of that data is of absolutely no value, so we might want to consider substituting more relevant numbers. Now that we have identified our destination, we shouldn't have to waste our time with these many dead ends, but parent institutions as well as state and local governments may have other ideas. Take a good look at every piece of data you're collecting. Ask who needs it and how much work is required to get it. If you are collecting any statistical information that is not being used in decision making, is not especially helpful for public relations, and is not required by some other agency, then you should probably stop collecting it.

Remember that there's no point in using valuable staff time unless you have a clearly identified destination. That means when you get there, you stop. You don't need to see the same results over and over. You gather statistical information to help you make decisions about your community, and, of course, it is helpful to see whether library use has increased since last year or last decade. However, as one looks at the pages and pages of figures that most libraries collect, one has to wonder whether they will ever make the slightest use of them.

Once you have a clear picture of the segments of the community your library is serving, you will want to find ways to reach and attract those segments that are not being fully served. To do so, it will be necessary to take a good look at the library experience itself and the way customers perceive the library and its staff. It's time, therefore, to move on to the subject of customer service.

RESOURCES

Baker, S. K. "The Knotty Problem of Priorities and Relationship: A Response to the Top Issues." *College & Research Libraries News* 63 (December 2002): 789.

Hoffman, H. H. "Contents or Container? Priorities for the Online Catalog." *Public Libraries* 39 (May/June 2000): 132–33.

Hunter, K. A. "Setting Journal Priorities by Listening to Customers." *Journal of Library Administration* 28 (1999): 91–103.

Lippitt, M. "Balancing Priorities." *Executive Excellence* 19 (December 2002): 9.

Veal, R. E. "Understanding the Characteristics, Concerns, and Priorities of Adult Learners to Enhance Library Services to Them." *Reference Librarian* 69/70 (2000): 113–18.

chapter 4

Valuing Customer Service

In the preceding chapters, we have compared a typical bookstore to a library. In this chapter, we will return to our tour, concentrating on personal interactions between staff and customers.

Superficially, at least, staffing patterns are similar. The library's circulation desk might be compared with the bookstore's checkout desk. Unless they are quite small, both operations also have one or more information or reference desks. Also, scattered through the building are computerized catalogs or databases to provide additional assistance to customers.

Checkout Desk versus Circulation Desk

Although floor plans differ, both the bookstore and the library customer usually encounter the checkout or circulation desk first. Working at either desk can be stressful with lines of impatient people, but some differences are immediately obvious. First, the bookstore desk staff are as knowledgeable about the store's inventory as other staff. Bookstore clerks often impress the customer as "book people," literate and comfortable with both books and customers. Unless they are busy, they usually answer most basic questions themselves, referring more complicated questions to their information desk. (Of course, there are always some duds, but with few exceptions, they are pleasant and polite to customers.)

It is difficult to predict what one will encounter at a library circulation desk. The size of the library is an important variable here. In a small library, there really is no such thing as a circulation staff. Most library staff members do a variety of different jobs depending on the immediate need, and most have a broad knowledge of the library and its collections. In a larger library, however, a separate staff usually spend all or most of their time behind the large desk. Even staff work areas and offices are located behind the desk, so no one need venture into the public areas of the library.

Despite the fact that circulation clerks in larger libraries come into contact with more patrons than other library staff members, circulation is often seen as the job requiring the fewest qualifications, including "people skills." In fact, it is not uncommon to see library pages or work-study students staffing some circulation desks. One rarely has the impression that library circulation clerks are "book people" or, for that matter, "people people." It may be that familiarity with the world of books and ideas simply has no place in the job descriptions set by state, county, or municipal governments with which the library is affiliated.

Circulation training in larger libraries is often minimal, concentrating on computer routines. With few exceptions, library circulation staff compare unfavorably with the clerks staffing a bookstore checkout desk. Customer service training is usually limited or completely lacking. It may be that because the library's bottom line is so fuzzy, circulation staff are not trained to "sell" the library or its materials and services. In fact, they probably know less about the library and what it has to offer than many staff members who never deal with the public.

Overdue Fines

One thing that often sets the library apart from the bookstore and alters the customer's experience at a library circulation desk is the "overdue fine." Of course, bookstore customers must pay for their purchases, but in the case of the library, it is not the money that is the focus of the experience; it is the sense of shame inflicted on the library customer. Over time, library staff have added an eleventh commandment to the established ten: "Thou shalt return thy books on time." It is not an exaggeration to say that some circulation desk staff look on customers with late books as sinners. They talk about them in the staff lounge and during staff meetings, and when they encounter them face-to-face, their disapproval is readily evident.

In general, the library is rarely discussed in the mass media. Yet if a television comedian mentions the subject in a sketch or monologue, you can bet that the joke has something to do with overdue books and their attendant fines. The reason a joke about draconian punishments for overdue books resonates with audiences is that they have at one time or another been made to feel like convicted felons. Adults remember that sinking feeling when, as children, they were informed that they owed the library what seemed like an astronomical amount of money. Often, they responded by avoiding the library because they didn't have the money and didn't wish to confess their transgression to their parents. That sense of dread experienced as children doesn't automatically disappear when we become adults. Circulation staff rekindle it when a message pops up on the computer screen that a book is overdue or a fifty-cent fine is unpaid.

The jury is still out on the subject of overdue fines. Some articles in the literature make it clear through a series of chart's and graphs that overdue fines are not cost-effective, that more time and money are put into collecting fines than are ever returned. Others say that if there were no overdue fines, many more items would never come back, and so this cost must be taken into consideration. I personally lean toward eliminating fines because it is so difficult to collect a fine and be friendly and welcoming at the same time. It is almost impossible, even for pros, to enlist a library supporter when they must say something like "It's so nice to see you again, but you can't take this book out until you pay your fine." Unfortunately, too many circulation staffers are not customer service pros, and they don't even try to soften the blow.

If you decide that fines are necessary, then do provide extra training for the circulation staff. Make it clear that there is nothing immoral about forgetting to return a book on time. We all do it. (In fact, library staff are notorious for keeping books past their due dates, but they are either exempt from fines or able to renew their own materials.) Emphasize to the staff that winning friends for the library is an important part of their jobs.

Those same people who failed to notice the overdue book in their car trunk for six weeks are going to vote for or against the bond issue. Some of them may even sit on the city council or belong to a civic group considering a donation to the building expansion fund. Keep this in mind the next time the subject of overdue fines comes up at the library board meeting.

Comparing Small and Large Libraries

Let's take a look at two very different libraries. Right off, I should tell you that I'm prejudiced. It seems to me the first of these libraries *works*—in other words, it effectively serves the needs of its users. The second, though its budget runs to many millions of dollars a year, doesn't work. That's because it fails to provide adequate customer service. Of course, it's true that a large library has a multitude of problems that a small library needn't endure. Although the small library's very survival is daily threatened, its simplicity of operation and natural integration with its community affords it some innate advantages. Nevertheless, though the director of the research library would probably spurn any advice from so lowly a source, he or she would be wise to heed its example.

The first library we'll consider is located in rural Wyoming. Serving a population of only about 600 residents, it is a stand-alone library, too small to be a full-fledged branch of the county library system. Its tiny budget comes mainly from donations and bits and pieces of federal programs. Use of a small building is provided by the village. The librarian does not hold an MLS. For her, the library is a labor of love, as it is for her small army of volunteers. Sometimes there is funding for the librarian's salary, sometimes not.

Nevertheless, the library chugs along, serving the entire community very effectively. Whether you encounter the librarian or one of the volunteers at the small circulation desk, you will be well served. They know many of the books, videocassettes, and audio programs as dear friends, since they were the ones who cataloged and processed them. Maybe they even borrowed them for a quick read or viewing before they reached the public shelves. Not only do they know the collection but they also know the tastes and preferences of many of those 600 souls. Interlibrary loans are booming, but two requests for a title represent a mandate from the community. The library will purchase the item if the budget can be stretched that far.

Please don't think I believe all libraries should be like this one or that library staff should receive insufficient and undependable compensation. Funding for library salaries is rarely adequate and not a problem to be taken lightly. Nevertheless, this small population receives excellent customer service. The success of the library is attested to by attendance and circulation figures that, proportionally, would be the envy of larger libraries. In fact, the library community was delighted to learn that the librarian was voted Citizen of the Year.

The Stressed-Out Research Library

The second library that I'd like to consider is a university research giant of national standing with a multimillion-volume collection. Although branch libraries are scattered across the campus, the central library finds itself serving not only a large portion of the university's faculty and graduate students but more and more undergraduates as well. This latter development is the result of budget cuts in the once-exemplary undergraduate library.

When one enters the vast, multistoried central library, only security guards and other library users are visible. The large and imposing open space appears to be empty of staff until one looks past the line of users waiting impatiently to check out books. Behind a circulation counter that could easily accommodate a dozen or more clerks, two student workers attempt to cope with the always-lengthy queues.

The Information Desk

If one continues past the circulation area and on into the catalog room, one will at last encounter the information desk. A few years ago, the information desk was moved from the front lobby and consolidated with the catalog-assistance desk to cut costs. That budget cut, however, was followed by another that further diminished the role of the information desk. Now it may not be staffed at all, since its operation depends entirely on volunteers. These are usually library staff members and library science graduate students who offer to take an occasional shift. On weekends, there is unlikely to be anyone occupying the "catbird seat" beneath the large sign that reads Information.

The information-desk volunteers attend a brief training workshop at which they are taught to handle directional and very basic reference questions. Unfortunately, shifts are infrequent (usually a few hours a month), and much of the knowledge acquired is soon forgotten. Since the desk is located near the catalog area, users assume that the information-desk attendant can answer their questions concerning the OPAC, the infrequently used card catalog, and the weighty historical and international catalogs. Because of the size of the collection, the numerous branches, and the space shortage that has resulted in tucking books into any available cranny, questions are frequent and complex. Many are simply beyond the skills of the volunteers.

Although users are occasionally referred to the reference librarian, such referrals are rarely acted upon. This would mean finding one's way to the reference room and waiting a considerable length of time until a librarian is free. Instead, users are more likely to make a guess at the meaning of the hieroglyphics on the OPAC screen, a guess that is often incorrect and sends them off on a wild-goose chase.

Catalog queries are not the only difficult questions addressed to the information volunteer. Many users find their way to the desk because it appears to be the only source of assistance. Volunteers do the best they can, even summoning several friends who happen to be passing and conferring with them at length. Nevertheless, the volunteer is often unable to answer questions definitively.

Vast, Empty Stacks

When users enter the elevator and progress to the remote regions that house the library's seemingly endless book stacks, they leave library public services entirely behind. One often has the sense of venturing into uncharted territory without the help of a native guide. On each floor, users find empty desks once occupied by a librarian or a paraprofessional (or expected to be occupied when the library building was planned), but these positions have largely been eliminated or staff members have been reassigned to other duties. The desks remain, often accommodating OPAC terminals, library handouts, or a few ready-reference titles.

The offices around the periphery of these public areas are still occupied, but their inhabitants are not really expected to assist library users. Of course, students sometimes knock timidly on office doors, but displaced university faculty and librarians with other responsibilities are under little obligation to assist drop-ins. Experienced graduate students pass on tips to new arrivals about the "nice ones" who will go out of their way to help a student. Such service, however, is viewed as above and beyond the call of duty. Most questions are addressed to the undergraduate shelvers, some of whom become remarkably knowledgeable about the library's collection.

Much of the acreage that constitutes the library stacks is totally barren of staff, even of student assistants. Rumors circulate about ghosts and exhibitionists who wander at will. Like other large and cavernous libraries, this one has its own urban legends, like the tale of the body that lay undiscovered for weeks. Telephones are all but invisible, and few provisions have been made to deal with questions or emergencies.

Reference Assistance

So where are the reference librarians? Unlike a number of academic libraries, this one continues to maintain a reference room presided over by reference librarians or at least some facsimile. The use of the plural here may be misleading, since the number of librarians who staff the reference desk and spend a large part of their time assisting users has declined sharply. This too is because of budget cuts, the belief that the information desk reduces the demand for reference services, and, to some extent, the many articles in library literature heralding the death of reference. Although these articles are often quick to point out that what is meant is traditional reference focused on print resources, library administrators have interpreted these articles as permission to reduce the size of the reference staff.

Having failed to find the information sought in the maze of stack levels, a user may return to the main floor, belatedly seeking out the reference room. Behind another large desk, built to accommodate a raft of librarians, sits one bona fide reference librarian and one conscript from another library department. Unlike the information desk volunteers, most library professionals are required to take a turn at the reference desk each month. They work their shifts with varying degrees of enthusiasm.

The reference desk is situated amid banks of computers that provide access to FirstSearch, ProQuest, Lexis, and other online resources. Since loading printer paper has been declared a nonprofessional task, a separate electronic information lab, presided over by a student worker, accommodates the users who wish to search these same databases and print out their searches.

Excepting the assistance described above, the reference librarian and the ersatz reference librarian handle nearly all the questions of all the patrons in need of assistance in this vast library. Much of their time, however, is really spent dispensing technical instructions on the appropriate buttons to click for each online service. Occasionally, one overhears the librarian discussing the content of a student's research or sophisticated search strategies, but a glance at the line waiting at the reference desk usually brings such discussions to a hasty conclusion.

Some distance away, students search the same databases in the electronic information lab. The student assistant presiding over the lab also dispenses technical instructions on the appropriate buttons to click. The chief difference between the job of the professional librarian and that of the student worker seems to be the student's additional tasks of holding on to student IDs and loading paper into the bank of ancient printers.

The reference room is set apart from the rest of the library by doors and corridors. Reference librarians appear to be on an invisible leash, confined almost entirely to these precincts. Large libraries have differing policies concerning the reference librarians' exact duties, but in practice they are unable to go very far afield. A venture into the library's more remote stack areas might take ten minutes or so, more time than can be devoted to a single student when a queue of impatient users is shuffling about the reference desk. Instead, librarians present patrons with maps on which they inscribe cryptic comments and give complicated instructions about mezzanines not listed among the elevator buttons, Dewey storage backwaters, minimum-cataloging stacks, and distribution shelves. A one-sentence explanation of the Library of Congress classification or a printed handout showing the LC alphabet concludes the interview. The possibility of a lengthier consultation may be mentioned, but it usually comes to nothing. By the time an appointment is available, this assignment will be history.

Close observation reveals that reference queries are usually handled in two steps. First, students encounter the ersatz reference librarian, who encourages them to pour out their questions and who may accompany them to their computer terminals. The questions, more often than not, are beyond the expertise of one who spends no more than a few days each month on reference duty, so many students must await the services of the stage-two, bona fide reference librarian. The stage-one librarian, therefore, maintains a sort of holding tank intended not to answer queries but to make users feel that their needs are being attended to. The work-study student in the Electronic Resources Lab could probably do a better job of answering routine computer questions because unlike the ersatz reference librarian, he or she is permanently assigned to the area.

The original idea of accurately delineating professional, paraprofessional, and clerical roles was an excellent one. At considerably lower cost to the library, students and staff may successfully take on many responsibilities once performed by professionals. With appropriate training, they might actually do a better job than the harried reference librarian. The information desk was one outgrowth of this well-considered movement. Although it has improved the quality of service in some libraries, the information desk has signaled the departure of library staff, both professional and paraprofessional, from the library public service staff in others.

Comparing Customer Satisfaction

Let's take a moment to compare the two libraries. What's that I hear from the director of the research library? They're not comparable? They occupy entirely different library universes? *Not so!* Any two libraries can be compared if we simply focus on our rough equivalent of the bottom line. Does the library meet the needs of its service population? When customers leave the library, do they feel satisfied that they achieved their goals and enjoyed pleasant, positive interaction with the library staff?

Again I hear the anguished voice of the university library director. If he or she has a bottom line, it's the collection. Research libraries have an obligation to the university, to the nation, and to the world to safeguard the scholarly output of the academic community. Valuing customer service is all well and good, but academic and research libraries have loftier goals.

There is no question that the custodial role of academic and research libraries is important, but why? Isn't the function of the collection to serve the research needs of the university community and, to a lesser extent, the needs of other scholars? Day after day, students and faculty fail to identify and locate the materials they need for their research. If no one can find them, how does the presence of books growing brittle, tapes disintegrating in their cabinets, and computer data becoming increasingly unreadable contribute to the mission of the library? Of course, libraries have an obligation to preserve information for posterity, but what are they doing for their customers in the here and now?

When you get right down to it, the research library is doing a disservice not only to today's users but to posterity as well. Purchasing and preserving large collections of materials requires a lot of money, and budgets are determined by higher-echelon university administrators. These decision makers quickly come to share the opinion of students and faculty. They too find the experience of visiting the library an unpleasant one. They too are turned off by its down-at-the-heel look, its inattentive circulation staff, its bewildered information volunteer, and its empty, cavernous stacks.

In that other corner of the library universe, our small public library serves the local mayor, who is a regular library customer. Her children attend story hour, and she depends on the library for both information and recreation. Like everyone else in the community, she tells the librarian if something fails to please her, but for the most part, the library is a place she enjoys visiting. When she hears of some available funding, the library is high on her list of worthy beneficiaries.

Can the same be said for the university's president or other high-level administrators? Few have ever entered the library. If they need information on enrollment trends or federal grants, they delegate the task to a staff member. The library is definitely not a place where they want to spend their time. More up-to-date, accurate information could help them do their jobs better, but why endure such an ordeal? If you were the university president and you viewed a visit to the library as an ordeal, would you lose sleep over its inadequate budget?

When library administrators bemoan low staff salaries, they might remember that bookstore wages are even lower. Bookstores are, in fact, rather notorious for poor pay scales, and this is a feature that no library would wish to imitate. Nevertheless, bookstore personnel are, for the most part, intelligent, well read, and friendly. Whatever their natural limitations, they have had customer service training that has made it perfectly clear that their first obligation is to serve their customers.

The Responsive Public Service Staff

Writing this book has provided many opportunities for busman's holidays. It has given me a wonderful excuse to visit libraries on vacations, on weekend excursions, and on the way to conferences. My conviction that circulation in most larger libraries is a "throwaway" position filled by the library's least skilled staff members has been confirmed again and again. Cataloging is an intricate task with so many specific rules and so many opportunities for error that we wouldn't think of hiring a neophyte. But what can you do wrong in circulation? If books are correctly dated and overdue notices sent promptly, what more can you ask?

My answer is that we can and should ask a great deal. In fact, maybe we should exert more care in hiring circ staff than any other positions. They should be our best and brightest. If the public think only of circulation staff when they judge the library, then the staff must project precisely the positive, customer-friendly image we are seeking. Not just anybody can do this, and even those with natural talent require training to consistently project a knowledgeable, enthusiastic image. It costs us little to focus on service; nothing we do will make as big a difference in achieving our library's mission.

Let's return for a moment to the title of this book, *Creating the Customer-Driven Library.* Is it possible for libraries not only to emulate the bookstore's customer service emphasis but to provide even better service? Why not? The bookstore's staff may be well trained, but most are not really committed to the bookstore's mission. In fact, though mission statements are standard in corporate America, customer service is not the bookstore's real mission; it is merely a means to an end.

Librarians, by contrast, have deliberately and at considerable expense educated themselves to work in libraries. We make do with poor salaries and inadequate working conditions because we really believe in what we are doing. We truly want to serve our customers. Isn't it possible that we can provide better service because we can bring more of ourselves to the job? Of course, as was pointed out during the discussion of the circulation staff above, librarians are often not the ones who work directly with customers. Yet most people who are attracted to libraries share these same values.

When you hire new staff members, do you ask questions that will give applicants an opportunity to express their enthusiasm? Of course, it's important that they be good with computers and even more important that they have excellent communication skills. But do you find out whether they really care about libraries? *The ideal staff member is someone who enjoys books and people in roughly equal measure.* The perfect staff member doesn't imagine Nirvana as an endless fount of enticing books but as an endless expanse of satisfied readers curled up enjoying the library's treasures.

The Library's Not-So-Secret Weapon

Think for a minute about the corporation-owned bookstore model. A chain may own several hundred stores. At corporate headquarters, professional staff earn high salaries devising the decor, designing the displays, planning the promotions, and selecting the materials. At the bookstore in Wichita or Syracuse or Pasadena, lower-paid staff then implement these professionally wrought plans.

Most major decisions are made at the corporate level. Although ideas from local staff may be solicited, they may have very little freedom to adapt their store to community needs. Although local bookstore staff may be individually very talented, they are not often permitted to deviate very far from the corporate template.

Libraries, on the other hand, are highly individual. In fact, probably no two libraries are exactly alike. Of course, librarians are a close community, and we share ideas freely. The number of library workshops and conferences attests to that. However, we are also individualists, and our libraries are fertile ground for our talents. At one point, I had an opportunity to listen to a presentation by the children's staff of my own library. Of course, I was aware that they are a talented group. Hadn't I laughed till my sides felt like splitting at their riotously funny children's theater presentations? I was, nevertheless, astounded at the creativity of their presentation. Each staff member has put his or her own personal stamp on the library's children's programming. Although they borrow freely from professional publications and from their peers in other libraries, their program is extraordinarily innovative and imaginative.

Then I thought about all those other libraries like ours that are not reinventing the wheel but striking out into new territory. That is where libraries differ from bookstores. They are not cookie-cutter copies of one another, nor are they meant to be. Instead, they can pool the creative talents of their staffs to reach out in new directions. Is it possible for libraries, on the one hand, to effectively train all staff members to rival the bookstore's high standards of customer service but, on the other hand, encourage them to bring their own uniquely individual talents to their work? If this goal can really be achieved, then we'll have the best of both worlds.

RESOURCES

Bartle, L. R. "Designing an Active Academic Reference Service Point." *Reference & User Services Quarterly* 38 (summer 1999): 395–401.

Cassidy, A. "No Invisible Librarians Allowed: Visiting Your Library as a Patron." *PNLA Quarterly* 66 (summer 2002): 5–6.

Christianson, M. "The Irate Patron Is Right: Try Putting Yourself in a Student's Shoes." *College & Research Libraries News* 62 (February 2001): 189–91.

Sager, D. J. "Learning from Our Mistakes." *Public Libraries* 40 (July/August 2001): 207–11.

Van Fleet, C., et al. "Mr. Green's Axiom: Customer Service or Just Plain Good Service?" *Reference & User Services Quarterly* 42 (fall 2002): 6, 8.

chapter 5

Identifying Customer Needs

Anyone taking a good look at the contemporary library will notice immediately how rapidly it is changing. Libraries have done an amazing job of transforming themselves from their old identity as "guardian of the books" into places where everyone, young, old, and in-between, can find computer programs, large-print books, DVDs, videos, mass-market paperbacks, books on tape, and music CDs. There are so many different formats for almost every subject that library patrons—with a little help—can usually find exactly what they want.

Even small academic libraries now make available an assortment of research tools once found only in large research libraries, and public libraries provide research support that would have astounded librarians just a few years ago. In short, the materials most libraries make available are pretty representative of the culture and technology of our time. They are right in tune with our twenty-first-century interests and values.

Unfortunately, however, this cannot be said for the library's services. We cannot feel so confident about our success at keeping up with changing lifestyles. When, for example, are we usually open to the public? Although most men and women work a five-day week, the library continues to be open primarily during regular business hours. Most libraries are closed Sundays, open limited hours Saturdays, and lock their doors early on Fridays.

Changing Neighborhoods, Changing Lifestyles

Why is this a problem? Perhaps it would help if I give some examples drawn from real libraries. Let's start with a large city library, the main branch in a sizable system. It's a beautiful library, an architectural masterpiece. You will find this imposing, marble landmark in the midst of skyscrapers, high-rise apartments, office buildings, and downtown decay.

However, it is obvious that this is a library that has seen better days. As suburban branches prospered, the central library lost ground, and economy measures were initiated. One of these economies was closing the library on Mondays. The original thinking was that by remaining open only five days a week, substantial savings could be achieved on staffing and other operating expenses. Since Saturdays were popular with the public and Mondays were somewhat lighter in patron traffic, it was decided to close on Mondays.

This meant that the library was open two days a week from 10:00 a.m. until 6:00 p.m., Fridays and Saturdays until 5:00 p.m., and later on Wednesdays until 8:00 p.m. Even though this library has done an excellent job of stocking the new media and making available as many of the newest best sellers as its budget will permit, it often resembles a morgue. Only during the lunch hour and after school does it come alive.

Yet some other urban libraries have truly become the center of their communities. Like bookstores, they have adjusted their hours to attract the commuters who work in the city and live in the suburbs. They wouldn't dream of closing on a weekday because that's when they get much of their business, and they stay open through both the morning and evening rush hour to allow patrons to stop by on their way to and from work.

Successful urban libraries have carefully analyzed their demographics. They have looked at pedestrian traffic and transportation patterns as well as distances from schools, senior centers, and other places where people gather. Library programs are developed not at random but after careful study of the needs of people living and working nearby. Then the libraries pinpoint their advertising to attract their target populations just as a Borders or a Barnes & Noble would do.

Balancing Staff and Customer Needs

Let's return, however, to our not-so-successful urban library example. The decision to close on Mondays was made to save money and allow the library to focus on other needed services and materials. Has this happened? No! Very little money has actually been saved. That's because, in the end, many library staff members continue to work on Mondays. The Monday through Friday workweek is so engrained that staff insist on working the same hours (after several budget cuts, most remaining staff tend to be senior, full-time employees who exercise considerable clout). Even some public service staff members have successfully made the argument that they need "down" time to get their work done. This means that many library employees work more or less the same schedule they always have Monday through Friday. The Saturday crew is mainly composed of part-timers, junior staff, and security guards, supplemented by a few disgruntled supervisors.

If you were to suggest such a schedule to the manager of a chain bookstore, you would probably be laughed out of his or her office. With few exceptions, bookstore staff are scheduled only when the bookstore is open and are there to service customers whatever hours and whichever days of the week the bookstore is open. (Once a year they may close for inventory.) In general, bookstore staff arrive a few minutes before opening and rarely leave more than half an hour after the store closes to the public. Many bookstore staff are part-timers scheduled only during peak hours.

Let's take a quick look at the hours of a typical suburban branch library. They're more in tune with the needs of local residents, but there is still a "reality gap." For example, the Hours sign on the front door states that the library will open at 10:00 a.m., but staff arrive for work at 8:00 or 8:30 a.m. Why is this? The answer you are likely to receive is that the staff need to get the library ready for the public. They have jobs to do that cannot be done when the library is open.

Hmmmm. Is this true? Let's cross the street to that college library just past those impressive gates and check their hours. Their sign states that they open at 8:00 a.m. because that's when classes begin. College and university libraries are usually expected to be open any time classes are in session. Isn't it interesting that both college and public library staff arrive for work at just about the same time? Why doesn't the college staff need time to do their work while the library is closed? I'm sure that if you asked, they'd tell you that it would be convenient to have some extra time, but somehow they manage.

I'm afraid there's no getting around it. Most library staff prefer to work normal business hours, and the library schedule is built around their demands. But most of the library's patrons are at work during those same hours, and so they are unable to take advantage of the library's services. Bookstore chains know this. They know that much of their business is done during the evenings, and so they remain open until ten or eleven at night. They know that weekends are their busiest times and so are open for business on both Saturday evening and Sunday.

Is there some reason why people want to go to a bookstore on a Saturday evening but are content with more limited library hours? That requires another "hmmmm." Take a good look at your library hours and your library staff schedule. Isn't it true that the schedule is based more on staff preferences than any analysis of public needs? How has this been allowed to happen? Could it be that deep down we share a belief that the public doesn't really know what it wants or needs, that librarians can make such decisions without reference to public preferences?

Does the Librarian Really Know Best?

During the nineteenth century, librarians chose books to uplift their communities, and, to some extent, they were successful. They chose books to help immigrants learn English and become good Americans. They chose books that demonstrated positive values like thrift and sportsmanship. They selected primarily "good" literature and high-minded philosophical tomes.

Much later, about mid-twentieth century, I remember being unable to get my beloved Nancy Drew books at the library because, as the librarian told me, they were not good literature. While well-written, "elevating" children's books sat on the library shelves gathering dust, my friends and I developed our own lending libraries, begging our parents for book money and circulating Nancy Drew, Cherry Ames, and Judy Bolton among ourselves. I've never ceased to resent such high-handedness on the part of public libraries. I send a mental "I told you so" to that authoritarian librarian of the past each time another article praises Nancy Drew as one of the few positive role models for young girls of that period.

There's certainly nothing wrong with having high ideals and desiring to make the world a better place. Many of us become librarians because we think we can make a difference. Our professional organizations go to court to defend the First Amendment, and we believe that a discerning, information-literate populace can create a more humane society. This sense of mission, however, should never cause us to close our ears to the voices of our users. We do not and never will know our users better than they know themselves. To be effective, we must bring people into the library, and to do that, we must mold the library to their preferences, not the other way around. (For the record, edification is not high on many people's reading lists. They read what they want to read. If they can't find it in your library, then you give them no choice but the bookstore down the street.)

In the "good old days," married women often stayed at home during the day. They ran their households and tended their children. Kindergarten and preschool programs are a fairly recent innovation, so children usually remained at home with Mother until they began first grade. A visit to the library once or twice a week was good therapy for both Mother and her children. Mother enjoyed the opportunity to get out of the house, and her children looked forward to their library visits as well. Life was simpler since children were not chauffeured to five different lessons, in addition to soccer and cheerleader practice. They had time to play with friends and enjoy the library's children's collection. That meant that the library was a busy place on weekdays.

How have so many librarians failed to notice that times have changed? Women are no longer able to come and go during the day because they now work at full-time jobs. Young children are likely to be in day care, and as they get older, after-school activities occupy an increasingly large share of their time. By default, evenings and weekends have become the only time when many busy people can visit the library. Again, how can it be that libraries, which have so successfully navigated other societal transitions, have failed to notice this development?

Listening to Our Customers

The old days, when librarians dictated what their patrons would read, are long gone. Libraries still seek out the best of popular culture, but they no longer ram their opinions down anyone's throat. Nevertheless, we continue to think we know what people need and when they need it. Maybe the reason is that we do not have any clear evidence of these preferences to use in making decisions. For example, we have willingly expanded our definition of a library to encompass a wide variety of media, probably because we can see the result in our circulation figures, one of the only statistics that resembles the bookstore's bottom line. Our circulation figures tell us clearly what our customers want and what they don't want.

When we have clear, objective information, libraries can and do respond. The problem is, how do we obtain such information about other customer needs? In theory, the answer is fairly easy. We can make better use of information we currently collect and identify ways of obtaining the missing pieces. In practice, we may find it more difficult.

Anticipating Busy Times

So let's begin with the information we already have on hand and consider how it can be used more effectively. Remember earlier in this book when we were touring a typical public library? We were dismayed to discover little Susie in tears because she was excluded from the children's story hour. Story hour attendance is one of those aspects of library operation about which we have plenty of information. We have many years of anecdotal experience as well as solid attendance figures. We can anticipate roughly how many children will arrive for most programs. Given a goodly margin for error, we can even predict attendance variations in summer and winter or during holiday seasons.

Of course, there are always surprises, but we should rarely be surprised at the number of participants in our regular program. Why is it then that knowing "X" number of children will show up, we don't prepare for them? The children and their parents are our customers. There are few libraries that can't schedule an additional volunteer to help keep order or another children's staff member who can split the group in two. All this can be planned ahead of time so that it doesn't create undue hardship for the library.

Fine-Tuning the Library Schedule

How do we make use of our gate counts? Many libraries have an automatic people counter, usually included with their security system. Those that don't have security systems often have inexpensive, wall-mounted counters. The usual practice is to take the count, divide it by two if the system doesn't do it automatically (since everyone who enters eventually exits, causing the counter to blip twice), and record the resulting number at the end of the day. We usually do this pretty regularly because it makes a very large number for our annual reports.

Some libraries even record hourly totals of customers in the library. Yet few do anything useful with the information. This is a shame because these numbers can tell us a great deal about our library customers. Here's a simple exercise that will yield a profile of their habits:

1. Determine your average hourly attendance. Start with what you consider a pretty average month. Average means different things for different types of libraries, but don't choose the holiday season or, in the case of a college library, the month when research papers are due.
2. Calculate the number of hours the library was open during that month and then divide monthly attendance by number of hours. This will be your magic number (if you don't entirely trust this number, you might want to do the same calculation for another month. Your magic number would then be the average of the two).

3. Now pull out some of those hourly tabulations if you have them. If not, start now to keep more precise records of attendance. You can assume that the library was pretty busy if the hourly count is above the magic number and on the quiet side if the count is below it.
4. Start looking for patterns. Librarians are fond of saying that they just can't tell when they're going to be busy. Suddenly one day, the whole town swoops down on the library. Or for some unknown reason, sometimes it seems as if everyone is boycotting the library. This is occasionally true, but usage patterns exist nonetheless.
5. Do you consistently find low numbers in the morning and higher numbers later in the day, or is it the reverse? Does the library seem to clear out at midday and come back to life when school lets out? Can you spot different patterns on different days of the week? Once you begin to see these patterns, what can you do with the information? How do these ups and downs correspond to established staffing patterns?
6. Take a good look at the hour before closing. (In truth, this isn't really a normal hour because you probably begin encouraging patrons to leave the library fifteen minutes or so before closing. Some libraries even announce that the library will be closing in half an hour.) If, therefore, attendance during this hour hovers above, let's say, 70 percent of your average hourly rate, then maybe you're closing too early. The higher your attendance figure, the more evidence you have that your community needs later hours or more hours.

Since the library budget is probably stretched tight, where will you find the money to extend your hours? Look at the rest of the day. How quickly does the library get in gear in the morning? Again, assume that the first hour you're open is not quite normal. Unless you have a crowd waiting at the door, it usually takes from fifteen minutes to half an hour for things to get going. If, however, nothing much ever happens during that first hour, and attendance hovers well below 50 percent of the average, consider opening and closing an hour later.

Attendance figures alone will probably not provide enough information to make your decision. Consider surveying patrons about why they choose to visit the library at certain hours. Would they find it very inconvenient if they were forced to come an hour later? Is it possible that patrons aren't aware when you're open? If this is the case, you may need to advertise your hours more widely.

The most difficult usage pattern to work with is the one that shows a slump in the middle of the day. Patrons may come early and stay late but they don't take full advantage of the hours in-between. This causes problems because it is during those in-between hours that you probably have the best staff coverage. The staff members who open in the morning are still on board, and the evening staff have arrived.

A large bookstore wouldn't consider this a problem. Since most of their staff is part-time, managers simply schedule them as needed. Library boards and administrators are generally more humane. Since staff want full-time jobs with benefits, we try our best to oblige. This may mean, however, that we're wasting our salary budgets and failing to staff the library during peak periods.

Full Service versus Expanded Hours

Let's look at another example of a real library, in this case, a suburban branch that opens at 10:00 a.m. and closes at 6:00 p.m. four nights a week with a long day on Wednesday and a short one on Saturday. Each day, the library experiences a busy period for an hour or two after opening. Then business slows to a yawn until school lets out. Most library usage occurs in the later part of the day. The hour between 5:00 and 6:00 p.m. is one of the busiest since commuters often stop by on their way home from work.

When local residents petitioned for later hours, the library director demonstrated convincingly that there were no funds available for this purpose. Then a cantankerous board member demanded to know why staff couldn't simply be scheduled more sparingly. The library director replied that this would interfere with the quality of library service. If hours were increased, the library would not be able to provide reference service or staff the interlibrary loan desk during those extended hours. Did most people really use these premium services, the board member asked? Well, no, the library director responded—but they should.

If patrons were to use the library in the way librarians think they should, they would consult with the reference librarian frequently, search the catalogs of other libraries, request interlibrary loans, and generally make regular use of the library's more sophisticated services. Do they do this? Not really. Generally, patrons are satisfied if they can just visit the library when it's convenient. Most of the time, they simply want to check their e-mail or borrow popular books and videos. College students may need a little more assistance, but they are usually content with a place to study, some computers with Internet access, and the opportunity to check out materials. These activities require very little staff assistance, and if the library permits do-it-yourself checkout, patrons may have almost no interaction with staff. Thus, if the library is providing nothing more than a safe, pleasant environment and the most basic services, it is satisfying the majority of its patrons. Although as librarians we would not be comfortable administering a library that provided only these services, there are times when getting back to basics is best for our patrons.

If we were to be completely honest, the library director in our example was thinking more of staff well-being than patron satisfaction. This is understandable. Librarians certainly do not want to emulate the bookstore that hires part-time staff at little more than minimum wage and provides no benefits or job security. Although library staff are not well paid, most at least enjoy secure, convenient full-time jobs in a pleasant work environment.

Many highly qualified people, however, are looking for part-time jobs that provide benefits, especially health insurance. Although such benefits increase staffing costs in one sense, they may actually improve service and reduce costs in the long term. Libraries that provide health care, vacation, and sick leave to part-time staff report that they have many more applicants for vacancies and more flexibility in scheduling. However, unless library directors are to hire mainly part-timers, the only other way most of them can really extend hours is to split staff workdays to conform to busy periods. In other words, some staff members may have a break of several hours during the middle of the day. In some libraries, this is considered cruel and inhuman punishment; in others, such scheduling is simply a matter of course. If split shifts are confined to one day out of five, many staff members find that having a weekday afternoon available for shopping and other personal business is a perk, not a burden.

Let's get back to the library director above who is so passionately defending the library's hours to his board. He argues that extended hours would mean second-class services. It would not be possible to provide all services during all hours. It is interesting that this should concern him. If you were to visit his library on any Saturday, you would probably find little professional assistance available. In fact, despite the crowd on this busiest day of the week, the library staff is at low ebb, and any kind of useful assistance is hard to come by. In other words, we're back to the same cyclical argument.

The Responsive Library

Let me tell you about a completely different kind of library. It is neither an urban landmark nor a suburban branch. Once again, it is a very small, minimally funded rural library that exists on a wish and a prayer. Let's compare its hours to those of the central, metropolitan library in the example above. Do you remember that the city library closed Mondays? The small library is open six days a week, sometimes with paid staff, sometimes without. Do you recall that the city library closed most weeknights at 6:00 p.m.? The village library is able to remain open later for schoolchildren and working people because it closes during the midday lull. From noon until school lets out, the doors remain locked unless a local organization needs the tiny meeting room. Actually, such uses are frequent because the library is truly the center of the community.

The library both gets and gives, receiving small amounts of money from the village budget, the General Education Diploma (GED) program, and the "Lights On" program for children from low-income families, while providing a wide spectrum of library services in return. As in most public libraries, the story hour here is always a big success. In fact, it regularly attracts almost the same number of children as does the city library with its million-plus population. If most of the village's children want to hear a story and create a felt and Popsicle-stick masterpiece on Saturday morning, is there some reason why city children don't want to do the same?

It is easy to get out the word about children's programs in a small community. News of upcoming events spreads through the village in hours. Energetic marketing is needed to communicate information about the city library's program. With some effort, though, it would be possible to triple or quadruple participation in the urban children's program. Is this really a goal? Definitely! What could be more important than inspiring a new generation of library users?

If you were to ask the director of the city library about her hopes and dreams for the library, a more central role in the community and higher usage figures would undoubtedly be at the top of her list. Yet, again and again, opportunities are missed because users' needs are not really considered.

The Pulse of the Community

Even with these "extras," the village library is clearly not modeled on a large, modern bookstore. It doesn't have an espresso café, and its signs are all hand-lettered. Nor does it boast professional displays although its many volunteers keep it looking bright and appealing. The way in which it most resembles the bookstore is its clear focus on the bottom line, but instead of dollars, it is *customers* who are important to the library. Because this community's library staff and patrons are also friends and neighbors, the smaller library responds instantly to the pulse of the community. It is often larger, better-funded libraries that somehow lose track of this vital connection as their decision makers become increasingly more distant from their customers.

Although both large bookstore chains and large libraries may share this problem of detachment from their customers, bookstores are at an even greater disadvantage. In fact, the offices of the bookstore executives who make major policy decisions may be thousands of miles from any particular bookstore. One would think that the library director, whose office is usually housed in the main library building, would be more in touch with the pulse of the library's community. Unfortunately, this may not be true.

In the case of the library director, distance is not measured in miles. It is more a virtual or psychological distance. The library director may have no contact whatsoever with library customers because his or her day is filled with so many other pressing problems. Every hour is spent with bureaucrats, college administrators, library boards, or with mountains of paperwork. Budget planning, budget defending, and budget cutting occupy considerable time. In addition, the director is often preoccupied with personnel problems, accounting irregularities, and government rules and regulations.

Since many libraries are poorly funded, the library director may also have to serve as human resources director and chief financial officer. Other organizations of comparable size are more likely to hire professionals for these functions. The salary scales of large libraries, however, may be so low that the library fails to attract qualified applicants. Instead, apprentice bookkeepers and administrative assistants are hired for routine tasks, leaving the more demanding responsibilities to the director.

There is a tradition in libraries that we hire two kinds of staff: professional librarians, who earn higher salaries, and nonprofessional or paraprofessional staff, who are paid on a lower scale. Computer personnel are so obviously needed and so scarce that most larger libraries have accepted the necessity of creating a special category and more attractive pay scale for them. Yet libraries still may not understand that other professionals are needed as well. As a result, the library director ends up wearing all these hats.

In the midst of their multitudinous duties, library directors may give little thought to what is happening in the public areas of the library. In fact, they occasionally distance themselves from public services out of personal preference. Some time ago, I was talking with a library director who was at war with her board. She was feeling somewhat overwhelmed and wanted the freedom to work on Sundays in solitary contentment while the library was closed. This way she could concentrate with no one to bother her. She could write her reports and organize her time with no outside interference. She wondered why the board couldn't see that she would be more productive working Sunday than working Friday, when the library was full of people and the staff were pestering her with problems.

Somehow it had not dawned upon her that those people and those problems *were her job.* Of course, we could all write a better report or construct a more precise budget in a peaceful setting, but should we really be allowed to barricade our doors and ignore other library activities? Wouldn't we be thinking only of ourselves? Satisfying our compulsion for precision and order? Wouldn't such a schedule further reduce contact with the library staff, who are in a much better position to know what's going on? Even with the most convenient of schedules, isn't it hard enough for director and staff to communicate with one another without raising yet another barrier?

Learning about the Community

The successful bookstore chain does not simply rely on sales figures and feedback from store managers. It conducts a wide variety of studies to determine the needs of the local community. It pays marketing firms astronomical sums to study demographics, conduct focus groups, and create surveys and questionnaires. These extensive efforts are aimed at determining who customers are and what they want. Although the costs of this kind of professional marketing research are high, they are more than repaid by the increased revenue that results.

Libraries, naturally, do not have the "big bucks" to hire Madison Avenue marketing experts. Yet the basics of marketing research are not difficult to grasp. Existing library staff can be taught to conduct simple but effective studies. They can use the same tools—focus groups, surveys, questionnaires, and demographic research—to fine-tune library services to more successfully respond to community needs. Although it would be even better if both library staff and library director could interact with every user the way the village librarian does, marketing research, though second best, is still a very effective substitute.

Although the routine statistical information libraries collect can tell us a great deal about who is using our services and what materials they are checking out, it is much more difficult to identify people in our community who are not using the library—the "noncustomers." Although marketing professionals working for bookstores do a better job of discovering who these noncustomers are, they do not have the same responsibility a library has to serve the entire community. Their concern is merely to identify the market segments that buy books, CDs, and other bookstore merchandise. Libraries, on the other hand, are abandoning their mission if they fail to serve a variety of economic segments and age groups.

Reaching Younger Customers

Consider how well your library serves your community's young adult population. Most public libraries have young adult collections, and, of course, high school libraries are aimed specifically at this population. Yet, in general, we haven't been very successful with reaching out and serving teens. Although computers have invigorated many programs, statistics indicate that few teenagers use a library unless a school assignment forces them to enter our portals.

This brings up another issue of concern to libraries versus bookstores. Unlike bookstore staff, librarians have a lot of freedom in the materials they select. They read reviews, peruse publishers' ads, and consider their own library users and then use their best judgment. All things considered, they usually do a pretty good job. We have to admit, however, that unlike bookstore employees, the library staff have gotten older and grayer in recent years. High school and college career counselors, influenced by such publications as the *Occupational Outlook Handbook,* have counseled students away from library science careers. There is an underlying assumption, whether right or wrong, that the bricks-and-mortar library will not survive the computer age. Not only library professionals but also paraprofessional staff tend to be in the over-fifty age group. Is this a problem? Well, yes and no.

Most people tend to instinctively understand the needs and concerns of others like themselves. Even with the best intentions in the world, they have difficulty identifying with people they see as different. Few groups are as different from one another as middle-aged library staff and teenagers. Think about the last time you had to buy a gift for a son, granddaughter, niece, or nephew in this age group. You probably had absolutely no idea what to buy unless presented with a wish list. Although soliciting wish lists from your young adult users is a great idea, it still doesn't really solve the problem.

Marketing research has to take the place of those personal wish lists. There is considerable information available on the tastes of teenagers in the national media, but you can conduct your own local research as well. For example, market researchers often create focus groups consisting of representative members of the target audience they wish to reach. Similarly, some libraries have been successful in recruiting a "teen advisory board" to assist the library. This strategy has the advantage of adding the opinions of "real live" teenagers to the selection process. Bear in mind, however, that these are probably young people who are already involved in the library, who are interested in books and reading, and who identify with the library's mission. See if you can expand the library's horizons a little further, and try to identify young adults who are not already involved with the library and its programs.

Reaching Other Groups

Young adults, of course, are not the only group with unique needs that we in the library profession do not fully understand. Take a quick look at your library staff. With few exceptions, they are probably white, middle class, educated, female, and over fifty. Now look at your library users. There is somewhat more diversity here, but if you exclude children and their parent chauffeurs, the remainder are likely to be white, middle class, educated, female, and over fifty. This tends to be the group most naturally attracted to libraries.

Yet the library has much to offer other groups as well. Most book selectors consciously try to choose materials that will appeal to a variety of different tastes. However, they stop there. Somehow it is assumed that young men, African American women, and Native American children all know that the library has much to offer them. How are they supposed to find out if they scarcely know of the library's existence? Much of the population in many communities either knows nothing about libraries or imagines that they are still mired in the nineteenth century, dispensing only uplifting books and unfriendly shushes.

Since bookstores are so good at getting the word out to the customers who will buy their merchandise, they have much to teach us. Our goals may be different, but those same proven techniques will work for us just as they work for the bookstore. We too can adapt our image to a changing society and then spread the news that libraries are alive and well and raring to take on the twenty-first century.

RESOURCES

Calvert, P. J. "International Variations in Measuring Customer Expectations." *Library Trends* 49 (spring 2001): 732–57.

Cuesta, Y. J., et al. "Getting Ready to Market the Library to Culturally Diverse Communities." *Alki* 18 (March 2002): 6–9.

Gavier, M. J., et al. "Enhancing and Promoting Library Services to Attract Diverse Populations." *Colorado Libraries* 27 (winter 2001): 12–15.

Hahn, S. E., et al. "Assessing Customer Demands: Making Changes That Count." *Library Administration & Management* 16 (winter 2002): 16–23.

Quinn, B. A. "Adapting Service Quality Concepts to Academic Libraries." *Journal of Academic Librarianship* 23 (September 1997): 359–69.

Robertson, G. "Seniors: What They Want and What They Get in Canada's Public Libraries." *Feliciter* 47 (2001): 304–6.

Tesdell, K. "Evaluating Public Library Service—the Mystery Shopper Approach." *Public Libraries* 39 (May/June 2000): 145.

chapter 6

When the System Crashes: Using Technology to Enhance Not Defeat the Library

All but the smallest libraries now provide computers for their customers. Staff members have computers on their desks and use them to perform most routine tasks, and nearly all of us would agree that the computer catalog leaves the old-fashioned card catalog in the dust. In many ways, computers have rescued libraries from the budget blues of the past few years. They have made it possible to operate moderately efficient libraries that provide more services to customers with reduced staff. We must admit that although we have become dependent on computers, we are not always their masters. We have bought the latest hardware and software without fully understanding what it will take to keep our systems operating. We accept poor performance and bad data because we really don't know what else to do.

The Beleaguered Customer

Last year, my student friend needed some books from her local community college library. (To protect the innocent, let's call her Susan.) When Susan arrived at the library, she found Out of Order signs taped to all the computer monitors. The system was down, she was told. It should be up and running in a few hours. In the meantime, she could browse the shelves (the OPAC catalog was, naturally, unavailable), and the clerk could check out books manually. Because the titles she needed were scattered throughout the library, browsing was ineffective. In the end, Susan found only one of the references she needed and took it to the circulation desk. The clerk produced a scrap of paper on which she scribbled Susan's student number and the book's bar-code number. She promised the system would be available when Susan returned.

It turned out that several days passed before Susan found time to visit the library again. The first things she saw when she entered were the same Out of Order signs on the computer monitors. Yes, the system was still down. It was expected to return to life at any moment. A computer technician was working on it, but his first priority was the college accounting system, which was also misbehaving.

Susan's term paper was due in two weeks. What could she do? The student assistant at the circ desk turned her over to the reference librarian, who promptly produced the weighty volumes of the Library of Congress Classification. "Let's see. If we had books on that subject, where would they be?" Armed with a call number for a hypothetical book, Susan again tackled the stacks. The call number did produce a book but not an especially useful one. However, she'd be late for class if she didn't hurry.

At the checkout desk, the student worker again scribbled some numbers on a slip of paper and tossed it into a large trash container. Susan was horrified. "Oh no, I'm not throwing it away. That's where we're putting the checkout slips until the system comes up." The basket, Susan noted, was nearly full.

By now a little gun-shy, Susan gave the library several days before she returned. But the term-paper situation was becoming desperate, so there was no way to avoid another library visit. In addition to periodicals, her instructor had specified a minimum of ten book-length sources. Susan now had two. Again the paper-covered monitors greeted her as she walked in. Today, though, every inch of the circulation desk was covered with shoe boxes. The circ supervisor, who had become all too familiar, told her that after filling three trash baskets with checkout slips, they had decided to try to organize them. The problem, of course, was that all they had were numbers. The library had requested a list of students and ID numbers from the registrar's office, but there was no way to know which book connected with which bar code. All that information was in the terminally ill automation system.

"Maybe you could use the Internet," the reference librarian suggested. "If you can find the books you need in some other library, then you could check the same call number here, and voilà!" Well, *voilà* was not quite the word Susan would have used. Fortunately, it happened to be Saturday because she ended up spending the entire day in the library. The World Wide Web certainly yielded a wealth of library catalogs and potential references. After Susan jotted down a number of titles and call numbers, the reference librarian rather tardily explained that many were not Library of Congress numbers. Too late, she remembered the weighty volumes the reference librarian had produced during her last visit.

Her next list of call numbers produced some useful sources. Yes, the system worked, but all Susan's effort produced something less than a book an hour. Finally, Susan banged the last book down on her study carrel. This was not *voilà!* This was ridiculous!

Susan stormed out of the library vowing never to come back. However, the term paper still loomed ominously. She cut her classes on Monday and drove sixty miles to the state university's large research library. After several hours of wandering lost in an endless maze of book stacks with only bored work-study students to direct her (the books were on the seventh level and the reference librarian on the first), she vowed never to enter another library.

Susan kept her promise. She managed to complete her assignments, accessing the World Wide Web from the comfort of home. She knew the sources she was using were less reliable than those in the library. She deliberately chose topics she knew she could find in the limited full-text magazine database accessible from the library's website. Of course, access to the database went down in midsemester, so her research options were further reduced. Fortunately, most of her instructors had had their own run-ins with the library, so they tended to avoid assignments that required library research.

Unfortunately, this is a true story. The system in question was unavailable for a grand total of four months. It occasionally revived for a day or two, but each time, the signs were soon taped back in place. That first month was apparently spent waiting for the college technician to investigate the problem. Since the library occupied a lowly position in the community college firmament, several other jobs came first. When the technician was finally able to devote his attention to the library system, he found that the "800" technical-assistance phone number, provided by the automation vendor, yielded only voice-mail messages and interminable waits on hold. Weeks were devoted to playing phone tag with the vendor's staff. In the end, it was finally determined that the library's system was incompatible with the new operating system the college had recently installed. No one had told the library the college was considering changing its operating system. No one had ever consulted the library director about compatibility.

So what was to be done? The library automation system, costing many thousands of dollars, could not run on the central college computer. No, there was no money in the budget for a new library system, and, of course, the college was not going to abandon the new operating system. In the end, an unsatisfactory compromise was reached. After a few more weeks, the library was back in business with a not-very-satisfactory PC-based system. Even though the new system was eventually up and running, data were never fully transferred from one system to the other. Once the system was essentially functional, the technician never had quite enough time to solve what he considered "minor" problems.

When the Bookstore's System Crashes

Now, let's bid farewell to the community college library and find a bookstore that is also experiencing a systems crisis. At first, it looks as if things are in even more of a tizzy here than at the library. Everything has come to a halt. The computerized cash registers are silent. Customers are milling around. Clerks are wringing their hands. The manager will not allow any sales to take place because the bookstore depends on the computer system for accountability. While the library continued to limp along without its computers, the bookstore does not even pretend to function. The computer has become absolutely essential to modern commerce.

Suddenly, the cash registers spring to life. Computer monitors throughout the store announce that the system is once again in working order. A total of fifty-two minutes have elapsed since the system went down. Of course, every crisis is not resolved this quickly, but the system never stays down for days on end, let alone months.

It's that old bottom line again. If the computer system is down, the store cannot make money. Remember the library's trash baskets full of checkout slips? Can you imagine such a thing happening in a bookstore? Each of those slips would represent dollars, and dollars are never treated in such a cavalier fashion. Speaking of dollars, it cost money to bring the bookstore's system up so quickly. Either the bookstore had its own resident technicians or paid an exorbitant bill for an emergency house call from a local computer business. The library, in contrast, was wed to the community college's central computer. It had no funds of its own to repair or replace the system. In addition, the library's technical demands had a lower priority than other campus departments similarly dependent on technology.

"It's not the library's fault," the library staff insist. It's the college that should be blamed. Public libraries similarly lay the blame on their city and county administrators, school libraries on the principal's office. What they seem to forget is that they got themselves into these messes with their eyes wide open. I don't mean that the library's low profile in many organizations is entirely its own fault. Removed as it is from the eye of the storm (recruiting students, pacifying taxpayers, etc.), it is understandable that the library is often ignored. Few librarians, however, make a concerted effort to enhance the image of the library. Few make sure that decision makers know how important the library is, what a vital role it can play in the organization's overall mission. In addition, administrators often know so little about the way libraries function that they fail to understand the havoc that will result from a computer system failure.

Dependence on Technology

Modern libraries depend as much on technology as bookstores. True, librarians may be more willing to risk their "merchandise" in the absence of verifiable records than the bookstore manager. But, essentially, the two automation systems are similar. They tell staff and customers what books are on hand, and they ring up or check out customers' selections. Almost all record keeping is done on the computer. All data needed to run the operation efficiently are stored in the computer. Once that commitment is made, the health of the system is absolutely central to their effectiveness.

When the community college's automation system was chosen, the library director was already a veteran of college politics. She knew where the library stood in the college hierarchy, and she had already experienced long delays when the library needed equipment or repairs waited on the administrative back burner. With this insider knowledge, why did she risk dependence on the college's already overworked technical staff? Why did she commit all the library's records without any assurance that they would be safe and available when needed? The answer is probably that she felt powerless to pilot her library through the computer age. This is a feeling that many of us are experiencing, but if we want our libraries to prosper, we must rise above it.

What does a bookstore do when their system is terminally ill? Large chains usually have a centrally located technical staff trained to deal with just such emergencies, but small, independently owned bookstores experience the same problems as libraries. However, it's that old bottom line again. If they can't sell books and maintain adequate financial records, a computer crash is an emergency and must be treated as such. In the community college library above, the computer system's demise was every bit as serious. Students and faculty were unable to obtain the materials they needed, but the library remained open. Because everyone continued to go through the motions, the situation was never viewed as the serious crisis it really was.

Public libraries must usually rely on their own staffs. In one sense, this is an advantage since they are not at the mercy of an organization with different priorities. But they have a different set of problems. Since their salaries are not high enough to attract experienced computer programmers and technicians, they rely on technically sophisticated young amateurs. Some time back, I had what you might call an epiphany experience—a moment of enlightenment when I saw clearly what was happening in my library and probably libraries all over the country as well.

My son had a great website, and he was terrific at video games. These were apparently the qualifications that convinced his boss that he could install a computer system for her three small coffee shops. Soon he amazed me with impressive jargon about point of sale, accounts receivable, and inventory modules. I was feeling understandable motherly pride until I asked how he was handling backups. Backups? Umm . . . well . . . he'd get to those soon.

The system being installed was created by another young man, hired to write code for a sister business establishment in a nearby city. My son complained that the system crashed frequently, and he had discovered several blatant errors. The store owner freely confessed to ignorance in all computer matters. She had purchased the system after being assured by a colleague that it worked fine. Besides she was not prepared to spend the extra money a more reliable one would cost.

At my own workplace, we had spent the past year looking for a computer manager who would be responsible for several hundred computers. The salary we were offering certainly looked good to me. It compared very favorably with other salaries in our library, but everyone we interviewed reminded me of my son. Most were in their early twenties, having only recently graduated from video games. Most could wax poetic over java script and CGI. I was too embarrassed to mention backups to computer professionals, but deep down I had the feeling their reaction would be a collective "Umm . . ."

Why is it, I wondered, that other libraries managed to find technicians and programmers but we couldn't? When I began comparing notes with friends and colleagues in those libraries, however, I discovered that they were no better off. In fact, in the public and academic libraries I investigated, entry-level technicians were in charge. It was they who decided which programs would be installed, which requests would be honored, and whose computers would be upgraded. Not only small operations but also larger libraries with multimillion-dollar budgets depended on their expertise.

Most nonprofit organizations are in the same boat. In 1999 we worried about the frightening consequences of the Y2K problem. What worries me now is the thought of the hospital computer servers maintained by those same technicians who can create cool web pages. Have they really been fully trained to maintain those life-support systems?

Hiring Technical Staff

Don't get me wrong. I have nothing against attractive web pages. What concerns me is the absence of credentialing or an apprentice system for computer jobs. The need for information workers has grown so rapidly in recent years that the pool of qualified job applicants cannot meet demands. To remain competitive, most organizations must computerize their operations. Since both hardware and software are usually available at an affordable cost, libraries are pressured to initiate major automation projects. Like my son's boss, librarians may freely admit to ignorance in computer matters, but they daily contract for other sophisticated skills. Why should computer expertise be any different?

When library managers hire new personnel, they start off by evaluating résumés. They look for related job experience and course work that would prepare the applicant for the current opening. They verify employment and may even request college transcripts and evidence of certification. The résumés a supervisor receives from technical applicants usually defy such evaluation methods. Most computer skills are self-taught, since the field is changing too rapidly for the academic world to keep up. Courses taken five years ago may be almost useless in today's high-tech environment. Yet this isn't the only reason why most of the applicants lack formal credentials. As most of us have realized, it's a seller's market.

The computer industry has always been the preserve of the young. The stories of kids gathered around a flickering cathode-ray tube, eating pizza, and founding multibillion-dollar empires are legion. Nearly everyone knows about Steve Jobs and Steve Wozniac creating the Apple computer in their garage. Even more have heard the tale of Bill Gates, the Harvard dropout who wrote DOS and gave birth to Microsoft almost overnight. Bright young minds will continue to be the fertile soil in which new discoveries germinate. It takes time and many mistakes, however, to acquire good judgment.

As libraries purchase ever more computers and create increasingly sophisticated in-house networks, they find that such installations require a specialized technical staff. Unfortunately, every business enterprise, every government agency, every educational institution—in short, every modern organization—has arrived at the same conclusion. Again and again, libraries find themselves forced to hire young, inexperienced technicians with little or no experience. The library becomes their training ground and the library's computers their guinea pigs.

Managing Technical Staff

Since the technicians we hire often lack any formal training or qualifications as professionals, we might better look on them as talented amateurs. We will need to face the fact that our libraries are providing the experience, which will very shortly enable these young people to advance to much more lucrative positions. Often, after even a few months of library experience, they can move on to jobs boasting salaries that would make a librarian salivate. The library's increasing dependence on computers means increasing dependence on these inexperienced, entry-level staff members.

Traditionally, library staff members gain power and responsibility as they move up the ladder, acquiring increasing experience and expertise in library functions. Your technical staff probably do not fit this pattern, yet they wield extraordinary power. Their competence and their choice of priorities can determine whether the library is able to serve its customers.

Despite their importance to the library, your new technicians are not unlike other young adults in their first real jobs and must develop the basic work habits that will make them successful staff members. They must become familiar with library policies concerning absences, tardiness, telephone and personal computer use, and the many other standards of behavior the library staff are expected to meet. Customer service is of considerably less interest to them than tinkering with the computer system. What they consider a cool technical accomplishment may throw library services into a tailspin. Until they have achieved some understanding of library functions and library goals, they need close supervision and mentoring.

After some less-than-pleasant experiences, I have discovered that policies that seem obvious to more experienced library staff may have to be explicitly spelled out to newer staff. For example, it is not acceptable to run a personal business on the library's time and with the library's computer equipment. Neither is it acceptable to solicit business from library patrons. Fellow librarians report that it is not uncommon for technicians to maintain computer repair businesses while at work and to draw their customers from the ranks of the library's users.

Unfortunately, the librarians and other supervisors who should be monitoring their work and work habits often have little idea what they're doing. It is not uncommon for fledgling technicians to take advantage of the situation by deliberately obfuscating their work with technical jargon. Supervisors must remain firmly in charge of technical functions and must have a clear idea of what changes are being made to the library's hardware and software.

Planning for Continuity

Operating systems and software almost inevitably require some adjustments or customization to function effectively in the library's environment. Whether your library network runs on a lowly PC or a large, powerful computer, there is an all but irresistible temptation to create or modify a program just for your library. Custom settings and even programming may be needed to enable one program to communicate with another.

On the other hand, the technicians who make those modifications are probably not long-term employees. The lives of most young people are in flux as they investigate different educational goals and career paths; young technicians are in such high demand that they change jobs frequently. This means that next year or even next month, someone else will be hired who must quickly become familiar with your system, including all those changes and adjustments developed by previous staff.

From my own experience, I've concluded that many young technicians are allergic to writing out any documentation of their changes. They tinker with the library's system just as they do their own personal computers. The supervisor should make it an ironclad rule that every adjustment to the library's network be accompanied by written documentation. Of course, your technicians possess technical expertise that their library supervisors lack. Even so, any supervisor is fully capable of insisting that technical staff regularly report and document their activities in understandable written English. If, after repeated failures, you discover that a technician is not sufficiently verbal to do this, ask another staff member to work with him or her to produce the required documentation. This way, the library will be richer by a second person who is aware of the changes.

Be sure that every change in hardware and software settings is described in clear, nontechnical prose. You might want to include more general information like the kind of routine maintenance that's needed to be sure your data remain accurate. What problems have been encountered, and how have they been fixed or worked around? Program bugs can constitute dangerous shoals, and documentation should include tips for avoiding them. Librarians are uniquely talented when it comes to organizing information. The documents related to your computer network and its components constitute some of the most important information in your library. Use your professional skills to ensure its safety and ready accessibility.

Be extremely cautious when a technician tells you that he or she can save you money by writing a software program. If a commercial program is available that performs the desired function, it will almost inevitably be cheaper and more reliable. Homemade or custom programs lack the flexibility of their commercial equivalents. They are usually written for a specific situation and do not adapt easily to changing needs. Since a library never stands still, your technology needs are changing constantly. You've invested a lot of time, energy, and frazzled nerves in a program, and you want to get your money's worth out of it.

Uniting Technical and Traditional Staff

When a new library program is being chosen or some other hardware or software purchase is being considered, involve as many library staff members in the process as possible. Be sure that your technicians are not working in a vacuum. Ask staff members to test individual modules or routines and make suggestions for improvements. If possible, staff members should test the complete program under a variety of circumstances.

This leads into what I call the "clash of cultures," or the vast chasm that exists between the traditional library staff and the "techies." The most effective way to send your technicians in search of other jobs is to isolate them, to make them feel unappreciated and uninvolved with other staff members. Go out of your way to fully integrate technicians with other library staff. Put them on party committees; invite them to meetings. Even more important, find ways for them to see the library from the *customer's perspective.* Help them to understand that bringing down the system for maintenance while the library is full of patrons is not OK. Satisfying customer needs is as much their responsibility as it is any other staff member's.

Some time ago, I had occasion to visit a nearby library to attend a meeting. While I was there, I thought I would do a bit of research. I found the OPAC easily and was relieved to discover it was part of a larger, newer library automation system. The search screen was extremely user-friendly, and few customers would have difficulty with a basic search. After entering the appropriate keywords, however, I got a long list of hits that had absolutely nothing to do with my search.

Maybe I was doing something wrong. I tried again with different words. Then I tried "Advanced Search" with the same oddly assorted hits. My colleague the library director was passing by so I enlisted her help. She repeated my searches with the same peculiar result. Hmmm, maybe she had forgotten a step. After all, she rarely had the opportunity to work directly with the public. The reference librarian was summoned and soon after that, the cataloger. Both had exactly the same experience. Eventually, half a dozen librarians, some of whom were attending the meeting, were clustered around the OPAC.

A month or two later, I happened to be talking with the library director and asked if they'd ever discovered the problem with my search. She looked embarrassed. It wasn't my search that was at fault, she replied. It was the entire catalog module. While the staff side of the automation system had been functioning flawlessly, no one had noticed that a major error had been made when setting up the public catalog. It had been up and running for more than six months, and throughout that period, customers were getting the same meaningless responses when they did certain keyword searches.

Why hadn't the staff noticed? The director was unsure. Yes, a few customers complained, but staff assumed that their users simply didn't know how to search properly (shades of those nineteenth-century librarians who knew better than their patrons). The reference librarian usually searched by subject and experienced no difficulty. No one on the staff apparently ever tried to imagine how a customer used the OPAC catalog. Each had access to a personal computer and a program module that worked fine for him or her. They simply assumed it must work the same way for the patron. How often do we assume our customers view the library the same way we do? We neglect signage because we can find our way around. We assume everyone knows that we have specialized equipment for the visually impaired because we know we have it.

Computers are tools that can help to achieve the library's goals. Similarly, technical support staff maintain those computers for the purpose of achieving the library's goals. Other library staff members serve as mediators between computers and customers to enable them to make full use of the library's resources, thus achieving the library's goals. When library staff lose track of these relationships, they damage and may even destroy the libraries they serve. Yet when these relationships are central to their perception of their work, computerization enhances and supports library services. As we move deeper into the twenty-first century, maintaining control over our computers will be one of the most important challenges that will confront us. If we succeed, we may dominate the information age. If we fail, libraries will be found only in history books.

RESOURCES

Breeding, M. "Defending Your Library Network." *Information Today* 18 (September 2001): 46–47.

Brennan, C., et al. "Murphy Was a Librarian: A Case Study in How Not to Handle a Systems Crash." *Computers in Libraries* 22 (March 2002): 10–12, 72.

Cook, C., et al. "Users' Perceptions of Library Service Quality: A LibQUAL+ Qualitative Study." *Library Trends* 49 (spring 2001): 548–84.

Ferguson, A. W. "Back Talk—Cataloging: Integrating Web Resources into OPACs." *Against the Grain* 14 (April 2002): 85, 86.

Hamilton, D. "Stop the Miracles." *School Libraries in Canada* 20 (2000): 40.

Hughes, J. E. "Access, Access, Access! The New OPAC Mantra." *American Libraries* 32 (May 2001): 62–64.

Ross, T. M. "Eleven Steps toward Decreasing Computer System Downtime." *Journal of Information and Image Management* 18 (June 1985): 13–15.

Theimer, S. "When a 21st Century User Meets a 20th Century OPAC: How Word Choice Impacts Search Success." *PNLA Quarterly* 66 (spring 2002): 11–12, 23–24.

chapter 7

One Library, One Goal: Establishing Clear Priorities

Like libraries, bookstores are organized into a number of different departments and divisions, each with its own staff and department head. Again, just like a library, some of these departments have no direct contact with customers. Unlike a library, however, all departments share one goal—to sell more merchandise. To stay in business and remain successful, every employee must, in some way, contribute to this goal. When budget cuts must be made, a competent bookstore manager considers what cost savings can be achieved without negatively impacting sales.

Conflicting Library Goals

More years ago than I care to admit, I was a very junior reference librarian in a large academic library. As the new person in the department, it became my lot to track down new books that had somehow failed to appear on the library shelves. Under most circumstances, this would not have been an especially onerous task, but it became my own personal nightmare. The problem was that it meant playing unwilling mediator between the head of acquisitions and the chief cataloger, who were not speaking to one another. A typical trip into the bowels of the library might go something like this:

"Don't blame us. We sent that book to cataloging three months ago. You know how they are. Can't do anything right. Did you ever take a look at the backlog in the dungeon?" Unfortunately, I knew the dungeon all too well. It was the dark, moldy basement where many of my missing books seemed to end up. The walls were damp, the ceiling low. I could barely see the shelves by the light of the suspended 40-watt lightbulbs.

This classic response from the acquisitions department would be to send me to cataloging, where all the blame would be heaped on acquisitions. Over the course of many trips to this underworld, I realized that these departments lived in a world completely of their own making, with no connection to the library activity going on above them. Each department had high standards from which they could not deviate no matter how desperately a patron might need or want a particular volume. A "rush" request simply meant shaving off a day or two from the process.

In those days before OCLC and RLIN, catalogers were dependent on their own efforts or on the Library of Congress. Unfortunately, LC cataloging was rarely good enough for the professional catalogers, and the exquisite procedures developed by the acquisitions department ranked just below the Bible or the Constitution in importance of adherence. Rebellious young radical that I was, I wondered why a catalog card (no computers back then) had to be a work of art. I wondered why the cataloging department spent untold hours editing call numbers and arguing over obtuse rules as if a decimal point or two could mean the end of civilization, as we knew it. Upstairs, angry patrons were unloading their frustrations on reference librarians, while down below, catalogers were seeking earthly perfection.

To add insult to injury, reference librarians and patrons rarely understood why a book was assigned a particular call number or subject heading. The logical universe of the catalogers completely eluded us all. Yet even the director of this large research library lacked the fortitude to put a stop to these antics. True, he sent out frequent memos about productivity, but even he was not quite sure what really happened in the catacombs or why.

Integrating Library Priorities

Those days, thank heavens, are gone forever. No library today can afford to turn up its figurative nose at an OCLC record. Computers and budget cuts have caused libraries to abandon many of those cherished procedures. Despite such progress, however, libraries have never managed to focus on one single objective. Try to imagine a bookstore in which a sizable proportion of the staff has established goals and priorities that have absolutely nothing to do with selling books. Then imagine that the achievement of those goals could actually result in selling fewer books. It doesn't take much imagination to predict the wrath that would come down on the heads of those staff members.

The example above was an extreme case. Nowadays, most tasks have been streamlined, and most serve a useful function. Yet there continues to be a problem with priorities. Take, for instance, library classification, which still eludes library users. In a bookstore, books are shelved by the author's last name within broad subject groupings. Each of these groups is usually designated by a large sign on the shelves. This is a far-from-perfect solution, and it's true that books are frequently misshelved. Nevertheless, most customers manage to find books without assistance.

In libraries, books are usually assigned call numbers based on the Dewey decimal or Library of Congress classification. Many thousands of hours have gone into developing these classifications, and some sections are constantly being revised. Since so much effort by so many highly trained professionals has gone into library classification, one would think that it would be easier to find books in a library than in a bookstore. Not really!

Our Customer-Unfriendly Classifications

By coincidence, I recently discovered a series of books at Borders the same day they were received by my own library. These books, all about Native American tribes, were all shelved at Borders beneath the same large sign. Where, I wondered, would a library shelve them? Checking the Library of Congress Cataloging in Publication (CIP) data in each book, I discovered that some were classified in the social sciences (Dewey 300s), while others were widely dispersed throughout American history (Dewey 970s). Checking OCLC, I found several more call numbers for each title. Finally, looking in my own library catalog, I discovered that similar books about Native Americans were scattered throughout the library. Although we owned several general titles about the culture of the Navajo, for example, they were shelved aisles apart. This is partly because both Dewey and the Library of Congress have several times revised their classification tables to reflect the social and political spirit of the times.

As public librarians well know, children are fascinated by Native Americans, and school assignments on the topic are among the most popular. Yet, in many libraries, there is absolutely no way children can browse one section of the library and find what they're looking for. Should we abandon cataloging and classification altogether and arrange our collections like bookstores? Definitely not! The world of information has exploded in recent years, and organizing information and making sense of it is a job that surely needs doing. The chaos of the World Wide Web shouts for organization. As librarians with highly relevant academic training and experience, we are better equipped to bring order to the chaos than any other group. The problem is that sometimes in the process we have failed to focus on our users and their needs.

Customers Come before Theory

Naturally, there is no one logical way to organize library materials. The needs of a small public library will be very different from those of a research giant. An abbreviated call number may be more than adequate in a small collection, while the research library may require every decimal an unabridged set of classification schedules can provide. What is needed is *consistency.* Even more damaging to our libraries is our failure to consider the skills and habits of our users. Why can't we just ask ourselves how they will look for library materials?

The answer to this question lies in our heritage from the nineteenth century. The period was marked by both the development of the modern library and the creation of a variety of classification systems. Central to early classification efforts was a belief that there is a structure out there in the realm of ideas that today we might call the information universe. Everything fits together. Each piece of knowledge interlocks with others somewhat like a jigsaw puzzle. In both biology and chemistry, classification efforts of the same period (for example, taxonomic classification and the periodic table) were integrally related to scientific advancement. Although Melvil Dewey took a more pragmatic approach, library classification had and continues to have some of that same sense of mission, a belief that there is a correct order that it is somehow important to understand.

When the computerized database and the World Wide Web made their appearance, hardly anyone turned to libraries for assistance. Even though our classifications continue to be updated on a regular basis, professional organizations and Web developers started from scratch, developing thesauri that better met their needs. When the enormously successful Yahoo! was developing its own subject classification, Srinija Srinivasan, the head of the Cataloging Division at Yahoo! participated in an ALA panel discussion. She explained that Yahoo! had chosen to "re-invent the wheel" because traditional classification had not kept up with the times.[1]

Automation and the MARC Record

It is not acceptable for any library staff member to have a goal that takes precedence over the paramount objective of serving customer needs. This axiom must be extended to include vendors and bibliographic utility networks that provide services to libraries.

The latter part of the twentieth century saw the development of large online networks that made it possible for catalogers to exchange cataloging data. Records were transferred from one database to another, providing a golden opportunity to adapt library cataloging to the modern world.

These online utilities represented a revolutionary advance, greatly reducing the need for original cataloging and making it possible for a smaller staff to catalog more books in considerably less time. In theory, the staff hours once used to painstakingly type and file each card could be redirected. This should also have freed up library resources to be focused on the needs of users. Although it is true that technical services staffs are smaller than in the past, benefits to users have been limited. In fact, the needs of users have sometimes suffered, as when the high cost of subscribing to bibliographic utilities has resulted in cutbacks in collection development and public services.

OCLC and the other utilities, through their vast cataloging networks, have come to exercise enormous influence on library practices and policies. True, they are cooperative in the sense that cataloging records are provided by libraries all over the world. However, they have established standards in the interest of uniformity that often seem to have no direct relationship to library goals and priorities. They have in a sense served as policemen insisting upon consistent but highly complex cataloging practices that facilitate the exchange of records among libraries.

Amazon's Catalog

Since we are comparing libraries with bookstores, it might be helpful to compare OCLC's WorldCat to the catalog of the virtual bookstore, Amazon.com. Steve Coffman, of the Los Angeles Public Library, in his article "Building Earth's Largest Library" is highly critical of the way libraries have approached automation.[2] In his stinging criticism, he advocates adopting Amazon's approach to a variety of the library functions. Among his recommendations is the adoption of an "enhanced catalog" similar to Amazon's. He writes that the online bookstore "has managed to duplicate much of the experience of examining a book by fleshing out those bare-bones catalog records with all kinds of information and content. Many of the titles on the Amazon site have at least a picture of the book jacket, cover blurb, full text of reviews from professional reviewing media, customer reviews, author interviews, table of contents, and selected pages of text.

While that may not equate to the same experience as actually holding the book in your hand, it can come pretty close. In some cases—full text of reviews, for example—Amazon actually provides more information on the title than you could find in the typical bookstore."[3]

Compare this description of an Amazon catalog record with the typical OCLC record. According to Coffman, "The fact of the matter is that your basic catalog record—whether BIP or AACR2—is really an historical relic of a time when we had to fit everything we knew about a book on a 3 × 5 card. While this sort of bibliographic record might still work as a finding aid for books in physical collections where you can walk over to the shelf and examine them, our plain vanilla catalogs have proven woefully inadequate in helping people find and select books residing on shelves thousands of miles away—or even on the second floor."[4]

What would an enhanced catalog record mean in a library? Would it be so very difficult for a cataloger to scan a book jacket and include it as part of the catalog record?

Figure 7-1 *Chicago Manual of Style* Record from the Amazon Website (http://www.amazon.com)

Adding a scanner as an integral part of a cataloger's computer workstation would cost roughly eighty dollars. Jacket blurbs could also be scanned as well as selected paragraphs or pages of text.

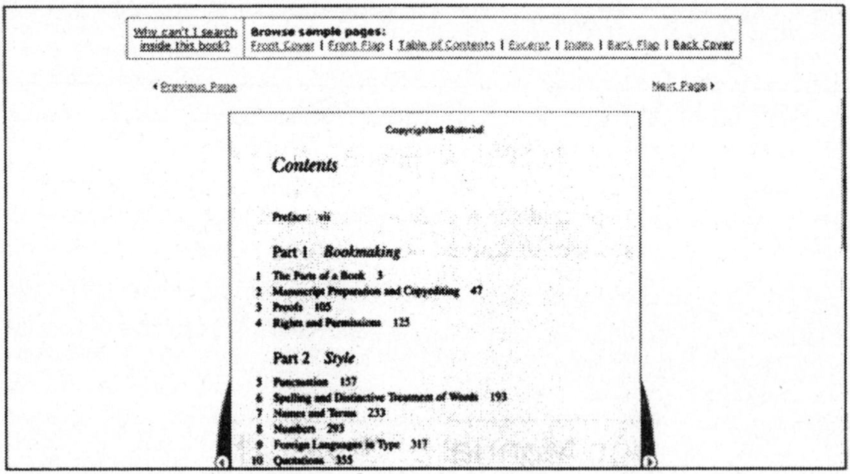

Figure 7-2 "Look Inside This Book" from the Amazon Website

Editorial Reviews

Amazon.com
What can we say? This weighty tome is the essential reference for all who work with words--writers, editors, proofreaders, indexers, copywriters, designers, publishers, and students. Discover who Ibid is, how to deftly avoid the split infinitive, and how to format your manuscripts to impress any professor or editor (no, putting it in a blue plastic folder is just not enough).

From Library Journal
The Chicago Manual of Style has long had a well-deserved reputation as the most important guide for preparing and editing book manuscripts for publication. However, is this 14th edition different enough from the 13th (LJ 11/1/82) to justify its purchase? The "thoroughly revised" and up-to-date chapter on edition: e.g., Cindex and MACREX replace KWIC as examples of automated indexing tools. The glossary of technical terms has dropped some terms but has also added many more: e.g., ASCII, comb... ▸ read more

Figure 7-3 Editorial Reviews from the Amazon Website

Customer Reviews

Avg. Customer Review: ★★★★☆

Number of Reviews: 24

Write an online review and share your thoughts with other customers.

5 of 5 people found the following review helpful:

★★★★★ **Fish Story,** October 24, 2002

Reviewer: chas dowd (seattle, wa) - See all my reviews

I have never fished, never even wetted a hook, but I just finished an entire book about shad fishing! Only John McPhee, finally hitting his stride again after two rather disappointing outings could do it.

His secret is telling a story through people, in this case through icthyologists, commercial shad fishermen, shad dart mavens, historians, and his own personal experience.

I particularly liked his interlude with the Bay of Fundy brush weir fisherman. As with many McPhee expositions, I felt that by the time I was done reading his chapter, I could have gone to the Bay of Fundy and built a brush weir myself.

And I can only hope that someday I will be able to write such direct yet luminous prose.

Figure 7-4 Customer Reviews from the Amazon Website

Once this became a normal step in the cataloging procedure, it would take little more than seconds. Other possible additions to the record might include reviews and author biographies.

Fortunately, software vendors like SIRSI and Horizon are beginning to include reviews and author biographies in their records for new and popular materials. They too understand that such information may be more useful in helping a user decide whether to read a particular book than its height in centimeters.

Amazon, however, does not stop at published reviews. It invites its customers to submit their own reviews, which are in turn rated by other customers. Reviews with the highest ratings are included on the main web page.

Admittedly, monitoring these reviews would be difficult for a library. Besides, Amazon can draw from the experiences of millions of readers. Published reviews, however, are easily scanned and controlled.

What Amazon is seeking to do with its customer reviews is to create a community of customers who are active participants, not passive observers. Active library users are no less desirable than active website participants. Library customers too want to feel that they make a difference, that their tastes and interests help guide the library in its choice of books and media. Libraries might, therefore, wish to emulate Amazon's "Customers who bought this book also bought" section.

Customers who bought this book also bought:

- The Elements of Style, Fourth Edition by William Strunk Jr., et al (Rate it)
- The Chicago Manual of Style by University of Chicago Press Staff (Rate it)
- The Copyeditor's Handbook: A Guide for Book Publishing and Corporate Communications : With Exercises and Answer Keys by Amy Einsohn (Rate it)
- The Associated Press Stylebook and Briefing on Media Law by Norm Goldstein (Editor), Associated Press (Rate it)
- Copyediting: A Practical Guide by Karen Judd (Rate it)

▸ **Explore Similar Items**: 19 in Books, 8 in DVD, and 3 in Music

Figure 7-5 "Customers who bought this book also bought" from the Amazon Website

Although it would be very helpful to include a similar section in the library OPAC record, Amazon maintains extensive records of their customers' purchases. Library circulation systems deliberately delete specific information on patron checkouts to protect their privacy. It should be possible, however, to remove identifying personal information while analyzing usage correlations.

In addition to providing a wealth of information that is absent from the average MARC record, Amazon includes standard bibliographic information as well as subject headings and keywords. However, Amazon clearly explains what you can do with this information. Take, for example, Amazon's "Look for similar books by subject" and "Search for books by subject" sections.

Most OPAC programs fail to make it clear that clicking on the hot-linked subject headings at the bottom of the record will produce more titles on that same subject. Amazon allows the customer to check as many subject headings as desired, but it is not usually possible to combine terms in an OPAC without switching to a search window.

Would library users prefer to view a bibliographic record that looked more like an Amazon web page than a library OPAC screen? Of course they would. So would the library's public service staff. They have never found the MARC record especially useful, and quietly, in their heart of hearts, they have wondered whether they are missing something. Year after year, they serve their patrons at the library's service desks, using the OPAC for little more than author, title, subject, and call number. To the old-timers it represents an improvement over the old card catalog. If the truth be known, public service staff sometimes believe catalogers live on another continent. Yet when they think heretical thoughts about the gospel according to MARC, even reference librarians feel strong twinges of guilt.

Look for similar books by subject:

Browse for books in:

- Subjects > Reference > Publishing & Books > Authorship
- Subjects > Reference > Words & Language > Reference
- Subjects > Reference > General

Search for books by subject:

- ☐ Authorship
- ☐ Composition & Creative Writing - General
- ☐ Editing
- ☐ Handbooks, manuals, etc
- ☐ Language
- ☐ Language Arts & Disciplines
- ☐ Printing
- ☐ Publishers and publishing
- ☐ Publishing Guides
- ☐ Reference
- ☐ Style manuals
- ☐ Writing Skills

Figure 7-6 "Look for similar books by subject" from the Amazon Website

Technology Requires Fundamental Changes

MARC records were developed during a period before scanners were in common use. In those early days of enormous mainframe computers, storage space was at a premium, so an elaborate system of codes was developed to minimize the amount of space needed to store information. Catalogers were accustomed to looking up the components of complex call numbers in lengthy tables, so the idea of coding other parts of the cataloging record seemed quite reasonable.

This kind of economy is no longer necessary. Even an inexpensive microcomputer can store hundreds of gigabytes of data. True, the Internet is slow at times, but Amazon's enhanced records can be accessed quickly enough to satisfy most users. There is really no reason why records cannot be larger and more meaningful. Scanning can allow the cataloger to add large amounts of useful information to a record without the necessity of dissecting, analyzing, and retyping it.

If library catalogers were open to the idea, publishers and software vendors might do much of the work for them. Quite a few publishers now routinely provide scanned cover art, tables of contents, pages of text, and selection guidance to Amazon. They could do the same for library utilities. It is in the publishers' interest to give library users as much information about their publications as possible. Catalogers would still be free to exclude material they considered too commercial for inclusion.

Just as an experiment, you might pull up a rather detailed MARC record from OCLC's WorldCat. Take a good look at the minutiae that is included. Most MARC fields are intended to provide a detailed physical description of a book or media package. For example, codes have been established to describe the physical medium on which a sound recording was made and include lacquer coating, cellulose nitrate, acetate tape with ferrous oxide, glass with lacquer, aluminum with lacquer, and paper with lacquer or ferrous oxide. These codes are, of course, very useful for preservation purposes. The public, however, wants to know not about the medium but about the music that has been recorded and the likelihood that they will wish to listen to it. Wouldn't a small "mpg" file attached to the record be of greater interest to library users than all those esoteric MARC fields combined?

In the case of a serial title, a cataloger spends untold hours determining whether the publication is bimonthly, semiweekly, daily, biweekly, semiannual, biennial, triennial, weekly, three times weekly, three times monthly, continuously updated, monthly, quarterly, semimonthly, three times yearly, normalized irregular, or completely irregular. A different code exists for each of these designations, but how often does even a scholar want this information? In truth, it is of use mainly for the library staff member gathering issues for binding and is probably obsolete six months after the record is created.

Very few fields in a cataloging record are devoted to describing the content of the media. Instead, they focus on the package. In this era when information is delivered in so many ways, it is true that a user needs to know what kind of equipment will be needed to make use of the material. However, so much of what one finds in a MARC record is really intended for a small in-group of professionals, not users.

Although it is no longer necessary to squeeze a few brief subject headings onto the bottom of a catalog card, one finds that subject headings are hardly more numerous or more descriptive of content than they were in the past. It's true that the MARC record itself has gotten longer now that catalogers are free of the restrictions of the catalog card, but few of these fields are of interest to users. One field that users really do appreciate is the table of contents. However, although users find a list of contents extremely useful when doing research or just deciding whether this would be an interesting read, it is rarely found in a MARC record. Why not scan it and provide a service to our customers without bogging down the cataloging operation?

Customer Service and the Library Staff

Coffman's article goes on at some length to extol Amazon's great customer service, which is programmed right into the website. Here I would part company with him. I agree that their website is very easy to navigate and has a great search engine. Books, often lost in a library's primitive OPAC, can be found easily using Amazon's powerful search engine. This, however, is only one aspect of customer service. A bookstore or library built of bricks and mortar has an enormous advantage over a website, no matter how user-friendly. They alone have the invaluable opportunity of bringing people together in a face-to-face dialogue. Computers can't smile or make eye contact. They just can't provide the warm human interaction that human beings seek.

Face-to-face dialogue, of course, is not always positive, especially when customers find themselves in the line of fire between library staff members. At the beginning of this chapter, I described a conflict between two technical service departments. In many libraries, however, there is no more ancient nor better fueled a battle than that between public and technical services. Knowing that they're playing with dynamite, many library administrators continue to tread carefully and try to steer clear of land mines. This cowardice, however, can do a great disservice to their libraries. A library is only as good as the service it offers its customers, and interdepartmental conflicts often result in unhappy, poorly served customers. A good library administrator must take a stand, and that stand must always be in support of library customers.

Translated into a real-life library operation, what does this mean? All tasks that involve direct interaction with the public must really and truly take priority. This does not mean that other library staff members are second-class citizens. A library caste system is the last thing we want to inflict on our long-suffering library staffs. It's the functions themselves, not the particular staff members who perform them. For example, almost anyone on the staff should be prepared to jump in when Mary Jones in circulation has the flu. This means that acquisitions or cataloging tasks may have to be placed on the back burner, and not only paraprofessional staff but professional librarians must be ready to step in. Cross-training is essential. If customer service is your top priority, it also means that the whole staff must be *sufficiently* personable that you don't cringe every time you must assign them to a service desk.

Unless you plan to keep the backroom staff in hermetically sealed capsules, they must be able to get along well with the public. It is not unknown for libraries to hire antisocial misfits who are magnificent at details but find it difficult to coexist peacefully with the human race. If these laborers in the vineyard have a hard time just getting along with their fellow staff members, let alone the public, they are clearly too much of a liability. Yes, of course, bookstores occasionally hire a social misfit, but bookstore personnel have been trained in customer service. It has been made clear to them that pleasing customers is essential if they are to be successful and if they are to remain gainfully employed. Customer service is nearly always a large component of evaluations. This is not always true in libraries.

It is interesting to take a look at the way library staffs tend to score on the Myers-Brigg Personality Inventory. The inventory has four different scales. On the introversion-extroversion scale, librarians as a whole lean toward the introvert end, with technical services staff somewhat further along the continuum. The term *introvert* as used on the test has little to do with whether someone is a party person. Instead, it's determined by whether they draw their strength from inside or outside themselves. Being the book people we are, the result is a foregone conclusion.

The test places at one pole people who respond primarily to sensory input. These are often our catalogers, who want things right. They notice details and expect their work to progress in a disciplined, methodical fashion. At the other end are the creative, intuitive types who are often our reference librarians. They can leap from philosophy to cryogenics in a single bound, but they can become very frustrated trying to cope with the intricate procedures their sensory colleagues devise.

This does not mean, however, that anyone on the library staff should be given license to defeat the library's customer service goals. Though it is true that a few antisocial job applicants may seek out libraries, thinking of them as caverns of silence where an angry "shush" can stifle all human interaction, we needn't welcome them to the fold. Your staff must work as a team, and such people are not team players. Even if they can churn out a credible volume of work, the havoc they wreak on your public image will ultimately interfere with the library's effectiveness.

Learning from Small Libraries

A few chapters back, I mentioned a tiny public library in a rural village. There are thousands of such very small, very effective libraries, and they're not just public libraries. You will find outstanding small libraries in law firms, branch campuses, and academic departments of large universities. The key to their success is their complete identification with their customers. Barriers between library staff and library users hardly exist. Because of their size they can be totally immersed in their environments, absorbing almost by osmosis the values and priorities of their customers.

As libraries get larger, they become more complex. Job descriptions become more specialized. Not only do staff members fail to interact with their customers but they scarcely know one another. The job of administering these libraries also grows more complex, and pressures increase. Almost every large library is stretched too far, and the result is a loss of control. Decision makers come to see their role as buying not only materials but also library staff. To stretch the staff budget, they find themselves calculating the lowest wage they can pay to get the specialized skills the library must have to function. An inevitable consequence is that public-service skills are undervalued.

The Research Library's Unique Challenge

Although any large library suffers from this malaise, large academic libraries seem to be particularly vulnerable. They are under the greatest pressure to purchase astronomically priced, highly specialized materials. They are also heavily dependent on student workers rather than regular staff because they are, by far, their cheapest source of labor. Since students are unskilled and work only a few hours a week, the jobs to which they can be assigned are limited. Circulation is viewed as an area that requires little expertise, so, inevitably, students end up replacing most other staff at the circulation desk.

Library automation has greatly simplified circulation functions, and library directors sometimes imagine the circ staff doing little more than scanning bar codes into the computer. As inflated salaries for computer personnel eat deeper and deeper into the budget, the circ staff may come to be seen merely as warm bodies. Students, being the ultimate warm bodies, are acceptable for this function. This is not a condemnation of student workers. The problem lies not with the students themselves but the way we choose to use them. Those same students often find jobs at local bookstores (I am not referring to university bookstores since many share the library's customer service problems), and they are all but indistinguishable from other employees. They may even be considered typical of the bookstore's supply of part-time staff.

On the one hand, academic libraries tend never to think of students as "real staff." They are never given thorough training, staff evaluations, or the focused attention that new, probationary staff members receive. Because they come and go with such frequency, it is often believed that training is wasted on them. *Yet we turn around and make them our chief contacts with our customers.* Few libraries are as complex and as difficult to use as the large academic research library, but there are few libraries where staff have such poor customer service skills.

Let's go behind the scenes and see what's really happening. The circulation supervisor is wringing her hands. Student assistants can't be trusted with real work. Any job you give them self-destructs on contact with their pudgy little fingers. All one can do is keep them out of harm's way.

How is it, you may ask, that a twenty-year-old adult who is intelligent enough to meet your institution's academic requirements, who is passing an advanced computer course, and who will in a year or two hold a professional position in the outside world paying twice your salary can't be trusted to do anything right? Illogical though this may sound, most academic librarians can dredge up plenty of hard evidence to prove their point. College students have had little job experience, and many absorb by osmosis their supervisor's view of their ability.

Next year or the year after, degree in hand, they will begin a "real" job. In the marketplace they are greeted with a whole new set of signals and expectations. Once again the signals are absorbed by osmosis. The new graduates become the employees their colleagues expect them to be or they are soon looking for another job. Simulating the conditions that prevail in the outside world is the key to developing competent, responsible student assistants. That's precisely what bookstores do because, of course, they really *are* part of that outside world.

Simulating Real-World Conditions

How do you duplicate the conditions actually found in the real-world work environment while taking into consideration all the requirements of the university's student work program? When you applied for your present job, you were interviewed by several people, and the job was explained in considerable detail. Yet prospective student workers are rarely actually interviewed: they are merely assigned. Then they are "trained," but more effort is probably expended teaching them how to fill out a time sheet than on what is expected on the job. Rarely are students ever asked about their majors or their hobbies or their artistic skills.

Students are individuals who bring unique talents to the library. Identifying, evaluating, and taking advantage of those talents can transform the library. A circulation supervisor was once blessed with the services of a pair of computer science majors, one of whom spoke Korean and the other an unintelligible (to her) Appalachian dialect. They could communicate only in computer jargon but somehow managed to fine-tune the circulation module and solve several major glitches that even the automation vendor had been unable to fix. Without close supervision, of course, this might have ended as a tale of disaster. The secret to achieving success was the realization that each staff member, no matter how junior, is *unique.* Each has some remarkable talents *if only* we will take the time to discover them.

When a bookstore conducts an interview, the manager makes sure that the applicant, whether student or old-timer, understands a job is not automatic. It depends upon the dovetailing of the store's needs and the applicant's talents. This may be a difficult idea to get across to your financial aid office, but the library should be able to function the same way.

Training Student Staff

Business and industry have learned that training is the most important factor in producing successful employees. Training should consist of a formal program with a well-defined body of knowledge to be mastered. Since customer service skills are essential to a successful library, they must be taught and later evaluated. During training, a student worker comes to share the goals of the library. It must be made crystal clear that public service is what the library is all about.

A probationary period should be part of the program. Just as a student must achieve certain goals to pass a course, he or she must do the same for a library job. Whether in a bookstore or a library, probation is a period during which the employee either learns the ropes or loses the job. It is important that expectations be spelled out in writing and certain staff members are designated as trainers. Students may be given a written list of competencies that must be mastered by the end of the probationary period. Training is then focused on achieving these competencies. Clear guidelines regarding work habits, lateness, substitutes, doing homework on duty, and so forth should all be included as part of training.

No matter how thorough their training, however, students must not form the bulk or core of the library's public service staff. With the limited hours available to them, they cannot possibly develop the expert skills and knowledge of the library's procedures that one can expect of a regular library staff member. Saving money on circulation by removing experienced professional and paraprofessional staff is probably the best way to destroy the library's credibility with its community.

Despite their problems, however, nearly all libraries, whether academic, public, or special, are blessed with some extraordinary library staff members. As I mentioned, this book has served as an excuse for a number of busman's holidays. Rarely have I met such personable and dedicated people. I recall an article in the *Wall Street Journal* a few years ago that listed the nicest to the nastiest people with whom to conduct business. Although I can't remember many of the rankings, I was thrilled to discover that librarians were near the very top. The article complimented us so profusely for our unfailing pleasantness that I felt a twinge of guilt for my occasional lapses. We sounded like such paragons of courtesy that even the Boy Scouts would take second place.

Although I feel a bit of doubt about the *Journal*'s survey methods when I encounter yet another twin of the unpleasant "Prunella McShush," we do have a lot going for us. Despite our problems, we have a lot of good material to work with. By consistently communicating the library's mission and goals to each new staff member, by mentoring them until they have internalized these values, and by creating a formal structure through which all this happens as a matter of course, we will continue to win popularity contests. Even better, we will win the respect and affection of our communities.

NOTES

1. S. Srinivasan, "How to Organize Internet Resources" (panel discussion, LITA Internet Resources Interest Group, American Library Association Midwinter Conference, San Antonio, TX, January 20, 1996).
2. S. Coffman, "Building Earth's Largest Library: Driving into the Future," *Searcher* 7 (March 1999): 36.
3. Ibid., 37.
4. Ibid., 34.

RESOURCES

Anderson, J. R. "Collection Development in the Electronic Environment: Shifting Priorities: A Conference Report." *Library Collections, Acquisitions, and Technical Services* 23 (winter 1999): 443–49.

Baker, S. K. "The Knotty Problem of Priorities and Relationship: A Response to the Top Issues." *College & Research Libraries News* 63 (December 2002): 789.

Freese, M. L. "Fostering Communication and Understanding at Hofstra University's Axinn Library." *PNLA Quarterly* 66 (spring 2002): 6–8, 23.

Griffiths, J.-M. "Deconstructing Earth's Largest Library." *Library Journal* 125 (August 2000): 44–47.

Hoffman, H. H. "Contents or Container? Priorities for the Online Catalog." *Public Libraries* 39 (May/June 2000): 132–33.

McClure, S. "The Use of a Survey to Establish Service Priorities in the Library of the National Museums of Scotland." *Library Review* 42 (1993): 23–34.

Rutledge, J., et al. "The Selection Decision: Defining Criteria and Establishing Priorities." *College & Research Libraries* 48 (March 1987): 123–31.

chapter 8

What's All This about Ambience?

Libraries, I'm sure we'd agree, never have enough money. Since we operate on very limited budgets, we tend to take a rather dim view of spending money for nonessentials. During hard times (and even sometimes pretty good times), we believe it is necessary to cut out the frills and focus on collection and basic services. It is not uncommon, therefore, that our libraries sometimes present a down-at-the-heel appearance that repels rather than invites. In fact, we may create an environment that is so lacking in attraction that it discourages all but those who must come to the library for a specific need.

Bookstore Decor

In general, bookstores are not expensive buildings. If you look closely, they are often little more than warehouses. However, they have made a science of appealing to their customers through their senses. A professional decorator has chosen the colors, textures, and finishes for the walls, carpet, signs, shelving units, and other furnishings specifically to create visual impact and lure customers into the store. Key to the bookstore's ambience is a sense of comfort and spaciousness. Books, in themselves aesthetically pleasing objects, are the focus of displays; oversize graphics direct customers to merchandise without creating clutter.

Large bookstore chains consider this money well spent, and as always, they are focused on the bottom line. They are willing to spend money only on goods and services that will deliver a return on their investment. It may be that because libraries have no bottom line, it does not occur to us that ambience or atmosphere should be part of the library experience. Yet to a populace whose attention is constantly being sought by visually stimulating attractions, the library may project all the signs of failure.

Responding to Customers' Sensory Needs

Marketing experts have found that the first impression a store or business makes on its customers is vital to its success. After that first impression, customers may remain in the store if their sensory needs continue to be met. The building, especially its interior, can be designed to enhance the image of the product or service by appealing to the eye, ear, and even nose of the customer. On the other hand, an unappealing environment can actually detract from or damage this image with the wrong sensory messages. Researchers have surveyed thousands of customers and found that they have six basic needs. All are impacted, to some degree, by the physical environment, and all of them are relevant to planning the library. However, some are more relevant to our kind of organization than others.

1. *Customers need to be informed.* They want to find help readily available that will enable them to find their way around and make good choices. This means their first impression of a library must not seem confusing. Service desks and good signage contribute to reducing confusion and reassuring customers that they are getting the most out of their visit. It's a good idea to place brochures, maps, and other materials that will orient customers to the library near the entrance. However, it is also essential to keep clutter to a minimum at this point. Other publications, like newsletters and flyers advertising upcoming events, should be placed near the exit, where customers will find them as they're leaving.

   When customers enter a store or library, traffic patterns should be obvious so as to contribute to their feeling of confidence. If, instead of a single aisle that takes them from the front to the back of the space, they must navigate around a maze of shelving and seating areas, that confidence will erode.

   Librarians should take comfort that marketing texts frequently list "being informed" as the first customer need. It is interesting that researchers have found that the quest for information is one of the main reasons why customers seek out a place of business. This is, of course, where a library can shine. We must remember, however, that simply surrounding customers with information-bearing objects is not the same thing as informing them.

2. *Customers need to be entertained.* They will return more often to a place of business if they enjoy the experience. If we combine these two needs, for information and entertainment, we can easily explain the popularity not only of libraries and bookstores but of theme parks like Disney's Epcot Center, where visitors enjoy entertaining encounters with science and technology.

   When it comes to defining the ambience of the library, both of these needs should be kept clearly in mind. The library should not appear boring. Customers should find things to do like previewing videos, listening to CDs, viewing art exhibits, or even working at jigsaw puzzles while they wait for a free Internet computer. The library's color

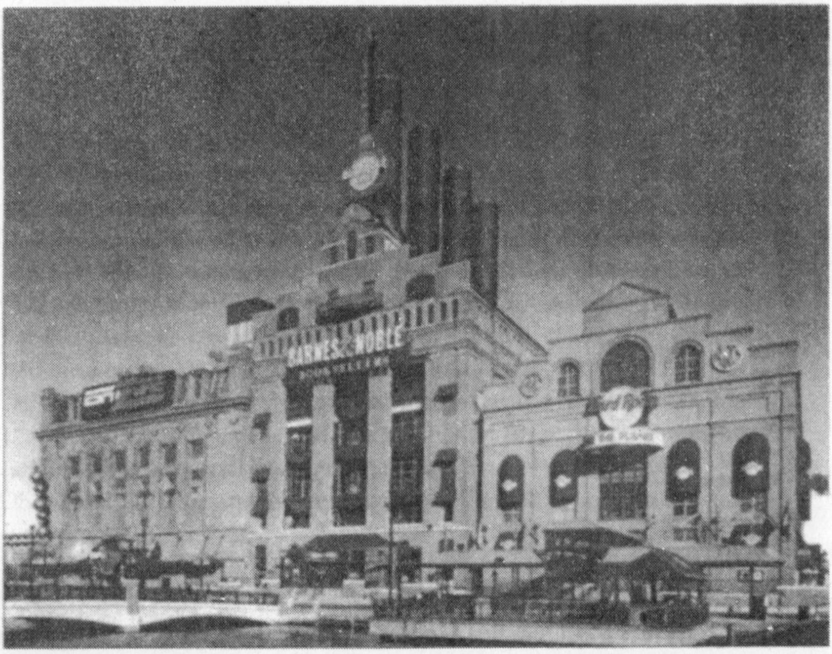

Figure 8-1 This bookstore invites customers to enjoy both the store and the enticing Baltimore waterfront.

scheme should be fun. Although reading areas should appear restful, the library should also stimulate the mind and awaken the imagination.

After being involved in several library building projects, I've become somewhat jaundiced about exciting buildings. It seems to me an architect's idea of excitement is a very wet, messy fountain located directly beneath a balcony. Experiences with little boys hurling books from just such a balcony have made me yearn for a plain, boring space that can be organized efficiently. However, this is not the way our customers view the library. There is much to be said for a library that makes them say "Wow" when they enter the front door. The San Francisco Public Library is a good example of a "wow" library, though it has been the subject of much criticism. Balancing excitement with functionality is difficult, but it should be an integral part of the library planning process.

3. *Customers need to get a good buy.* This customer need appears at first to be confined to the commercial realm. Consumers want to feel that they have made the right choices and gotten good value for their money. In the case of a library that circulates materials at no direct cost to customers, this need might be translated into satisfaction—the satisfaction one feels at discovering just the book, DVD, or CD one is looking for. If the library is laid out in such a way that popular items are buried among thousands of infrequently circulated materials, then the customer is unlikely to satisfy this need.
4. *Customers need fast service.* Although customers may spend hours reading and browsing in the library, when they're ready to leave, they want to go *now.* They become irritated if they must walk miles to a checkout desk, wait in the wrong line, or endure other customers pushing in front of them. The design of the library can facilitate service as well as distract and entertain customers while they are waiting. When we were taking our tour of the bookstore in the first chapter, we noticed that the store had created a clear path to the checkout desk, lined with appealing displays. The goal was not only to extract one last sale from departing customers but also to occupy their attention so they did not become bored or fretful—or change their minds.
5. *Customers need to feel safe.* A need that we don't often think about is safety. Customers want the library building to feel solid and permanent. They look for indications that the building is in good repair and being well cared for. Exhibiting the library's poverty by failing to replace worn

carpet and frayed upholstery will lose more customers than we imagine. Subconsciously, they will tend to expand their mental picture to include a dangerously out-of-date elevator. They may decide the piles of old newspapers and magazines are indicative of other fire hazards.

Be sure to update maps showing emergency exits, and laminate them so they won't become dog-eared. This makes it clear that the library staff has made provisions for emergencies and generally has matters under control. You're assuring customers that the library is looking out for their safety. Good lighting has a lot to do with customers' sense of safety. Check to make certain that the bulbs in "Exit" signs have not burned out. Search out dark stairwells and hallways, and install additional light fixtures if they are needed. Again, fresh paint, cleanliness, adequate lighting, and the absence of clutter all contribute to a sense of safety.

Be sure that parking lots and outside entrance areas are well lit. If the library should gain the reputation as a place where cars are broken into and customers are mugged, you can't expect to be very popular. Parents are especially concerned about their children and often look over the library and its surroundings carefully before allowing their children to spend time there. (Speaking of children, make sure children using restrooms are safe from lurking adult predators.)

6. *Customers need to feel special.* Our modern society specializes in "big." Modern merchandising is characterized by big stores and big businesses that cater to thousands of customers. Think of places like Wal-Mart, where masses of people swarm through the aisles. We human beings do not want to feel like part of a mob. We need to feel special. This means that we want the library to have a space just for us, a niche where we can read without people bumping into us. We want to be surrounded by pleasant sensory experiences and to feel that this is a place that is just right for us.

   Many libraries have an "institutional" feel that may be the result of decoration by committee. It also tends to result from the desire to choose walls, carpets, and furniture that will remain serviceable over a long period of time. Some librarians sabotage themselves when it comes to such things as color and carpeting. After living with harvest gold and avocado green for too many years, we say, "Never again!" We will have a beige library where no one will even notice the color—and they won't. Unfortunately, such reactionary decisions may backfire with library customers who want a homier, friendlier feel for "their" library.

Some studies of customer behavior have found that people begin to feel uncomfortable and perceive a space as unfriendly if they do not encounter anyone who directs or greets them within the first ten feet. This is one of the main reasons why large chains like Wal-Mart employ greeters. Although they serve a security function as well, they alleviate the negative impact of entering a vast, impersonal space. Placing the reference or information desk near the entrance is a way of achieving this goal. The circulation desk can serve this function also, but not if staff are too involved with exiting customers to notice those arriving.

Sometimes service desks actually discourage interaction with the public. Earlier I mentioned tall, massive circulation desks that look like fortresses, behind which staff can isolate themselves from their customers. Consider making the circ desk smaller and lower so that the staff members behind it don't look as if they're defending a besieged castle.

One library I visited had a rather large, unwelcoming lobby dating back to the 1970s cinder-block era. Staff placed a small information desk just inside the front door and staffed it with some especially outgoing senior volunteers who took great pleasure in getting out of the house and talking to people. Seniors were scheduled on the desk during most of the library's busy periods. Here, customers could pick up maps, brochures, and even applications to join the Friends of the Library group. In truth, the senior volunteers didn't know a whole lot about the library. What they actually spent their time doing was greeting visitors and walking them over to the reference librarian when they received a question. This meant that arriving customers chatted with an affable volunteer while they were led past several architectural barriers to the reference desk. Then they could be assisted in finding materials by a professional librarian. Some of these people had not known there was a reference librarian; others had imagined that the reference librarian answered only esoteric or academic inquiries. It came as a revelation to some of them that the librarian could actually suggest mystery novels as well as refer them to books on fly-fishing and stain removal. The library director swore that setting up the information desk was the smartest thing she'd ever done.

Increasing Public Service Presence

Sometimes it is not possible to place a service desk near the door and still effectively supervise more remote areas. Still, since personal attention from the library staff is an integral part of this feeling of being special, staff should be stationed near enough that customers needn't get lost searching through the library to find help. Resolving this conflict can be difficult. It may mean stationing additional staff members, who usually do their work behind a workroom door, in public areas. To do this effectively, all public service desks must be designed to allow staff to get their work done and *yet* respond quickly when customers need help.

In recent years, this balance has become more important because library staffs are getting smaller, and individuals must each wear several hats. *Multitasking* is the buzzword that describes these situations—and it's not easy. Staff members accustomed to being able to concentrate completely on their work far away from the madding crowd find it difficult to relocate to more public areas. It requires skill to keep an eye on public areas while at the same time performing acquisitions, serials, or other backroom tasks. Fortunately, computers have made the job much easier since software can be accessed from any computer on the library's local area network. Computers also reduce a lot of library jobs to routines that require less-than-total concentration. However, accuracy is no less important. It must be made clear that serving the public is a *real job,* and customers cannot be ignored. Naturally, we would all prefer to have more generous staffing. We wince when customers must say "excuse me" twice before getting attention. Yet it is far worse if they cannot find staff to assist them.

Spaces Where Customers Feel at Ease

Library buildings generally function most efficiently when they are designed as big, open spaces uninterrupted by walls. Such large spaces need high ceilings. Otherwise, customers and staff will have an uncomfortably claustrophobic feeling that the ceiling is coming down on their heads. But high ceilings can create a warehouse atmosphere that makes customers feel anything but special. We all like to feel that we are in our own personal space, and being out in the open increases our sense of vulnerability. It is possible, however, to lower the ceiling in smaller spaces like study and meeting rooms that need to be especially user-friendly. The ceiling can also be lowered in reading niches that are really part of the larger space. A lowered ceiling along the window wall can allow you to create comfortable seating areas where customers enjoy the sunlight. The space thus created above the dropped ceiling can be effectively used by the architect for running heating ducts or data cabling. It is also possible to create the impression of a lower ceiling by suspending lights, signs, or decorative elements to give the illusion of a smaller, more comfortable space. Just be careful that the result is not a forest of clutter.

The Importance of Color in Libraries

In earlier chapters, we have repeatedly made the point that the library's bottom line is attracting customers who will use the library's resources. Let's tour another library—this time your own. Picture customers arriving at the entrance to your library. What do they see as they enter the front door? That initial impact depends to a large degree on color. It takes a few minutes for customers to begin focusing on specific signs or displays. Their first impression is primarily one of space and color. Consider whether that impression is the one you want to present. Can you describe the color palette that greets the arriving customer or is it just a mishmash of discordant hues? In some libraries, one simply has a vague sense of "blah." To be more specific, it's an amalgam of dirty beige carpet; dingy, colorless walls; and dark book stacks.

If your library fits this description, you may be unsure of what should be done. Decorating a public space is a lot different from decorating a living room. Just where should you begin?

A friend of mine was once the volunteer librarian of a very small community library in Wisconsin. One day, she could stand the cold, unpleasant library no longer. Overwhelmed by a sudden inspiration, she went to the hardware store, purchased a few gallons of red-orange paint, and stayed up much of the night painting the library. When the library board discovered what she had done, they were horrified. Had she not been donating her professional services free of charge, she would probably have been fired on the spot. Then, week by week, the board became accustomed to the new environment. The expenditure of about twenty-five dollars totally transformed the library. True, it was sometimes a bit overwhelming, but the librarian noticed that customers came more often and stayed longer. Eventually, board members ceased to demand that the library be repainted, and there came to be a tacit understanding that having an orange library was not entirely a bad thing.

The Psychology of Color

Before proceeding with a library color overhaul, consider the effect that color has on you and others. Each major color produces a psychological effect on most people. Red has long been known to stimulate the appetite. Remember the red checkered tablecloth in your favorite Italian restaurant? Orange and yellow are seen as exciting. Studies have shown that they energize people. McDonalds' color scheme integrates appetizing red with the warmth and excitement of yellow—an inspired combination! Workplace studies have found that warm colors increase the pulse rate and reaction speed of employees. Conversely, pulse and respiration are slowed when people are surrounded by cooler colors like blue and green. Over time, the impact of these colors in the environment becomes less noticeable for staff in libraries, bookstores, and restaurants. However, for the customer who spends only an hour or so in the library, it can be quite significant.

Researchers who study the psychological impact of color tell us that it is important to match the color scheme to the activities taking place. Since we would like our customers to find the library a haven for reading and relaxation, it stands to reason that in some areas we want to create a soothing, restful environment. Cooler colors encourage long periods of concentration. Warmer colors, however, provide a sense of comfort and warmth, especially in northerly climes where customers want to escape from the elements and read in cozy comfort.

A positive correlation has also been found between introversion and cooler colors as well as between extroversion and warmer colors. Since librarians have been found to score toward the introversion end of the personality scale, they should be conscious that their preference for cooler colors may not be shared by their customers, most of whom score higher on the extroversion end of the scale. Color is, to a great extent, a matter of personal preference. When one person, whether decorator or library director, makes all the color decisions, the choices may cause a negative response from most of the library's customers.

Remember the story of Henry Ford, who decreed that customers could have any color automobile they liked as long as it was black? Well, in recent years, library customers have usually had any wall color they liked as long as it was white. I remember once visiting a county library in Ireland on a cold, wet, generally miserable day. With its white walls and large windows that all too forcefully brought the gray depressing day into the building, the library would not have attracted anyone. Walking back to my bed-and-breakfast, the rain began in earnest, so I ducked into a pub to dry off. Everything about the pub's color scheme seemed to be aimed at creating the impression of warmth and comfort. The wood paneling and rich, warm colors invited me to come in, find a cozy nook, and enjoy the local brew. Yet in Santa Fe, New Mexico, where I lived for many years, those same white walls are delightful. In the bright sunlight, they communicate a cool and restful ambience that is as inviting as the Irish library was depressing.

Color is important, not only to influence the psychological state of library customers but to provide a more physically comfortable library experience. Eye fatigue experienced by computer users can be reduced by minimizing the contrast in value between the computer screen and the walls and furniture around the computer work space. Soft colors of medium intensity on either side of the monitor are especially helpful in combating eye fatigue. The all-white library color scheme, which has been popular in recent years, increases glare and eye strain.

Color Choice Can Be Difficult

Many of us have had the experience of picking a wall color, a carpet sample, or an upholstery pattern, only to find that it looks like another color altogether when viewed in a "real-life" situation. Whether we are decorating our own homes or choosing for the library, we can't imagine what went wrong. That can't possibly be the color we chose. In truth, it is the same color, but perhaps the lighting is different from the lighting in the paint store. A paint shade can look entirely different lighted by fluorescent lamps than when viewed in natural sunlight. A wall in shadow seems to be yet another color. The color that really counts is the one that customers will see when they walk into the library. It is that color, seen under those lighting conditions, that will determine the success or failure of your color scheme.

Scale is another factor that affects the way colors look. We may have seen only a small swatch of fabric, but now it's covering an overstuffed sofa or used for floor to ceiling draperies. The once vibrant pattern of bright primary colors now looks gray or neutral because the colors cancel each other out when seen from a distance. When you are selecting colors, don't forget that most of your own personal experience has been acquired decorating your home. The size of the library reading room, when compared to your living room, is enormous. Colors look entirely different when viewed from a distance of a hundred feet or so. Patterns merge into a single solid color. Prints and patterns that look huge and garish in the home convey a totally different impression in a library.

Since most color and fabric swatches are very small, it is difficult to see them at a distance. If you were to prop them up and walk away, you probably couldn't even see the individual swatches, let alone determine their impact on the room. Instead, however, you might consider bringing fabrics from home and seeing how they look when viewed from far away and under library lights. You'll get a feeling for how large patterns merge into solid colors, and you'll see how the light you are accustomed to at home makes a fabric look entirely different from the way it appears in the library.

Decorators tend to create their color schemes around textiles. This is because there are literally thousands of possible paint colors to choose from but only a limited selection of fabrics that are sufficiently hard-wearing, reasonably priced, and aesthetically appealing to meet the library's requirements. Therefore, they will create swatch boards of fabrics for each space and then add coordinated paint colors. The customer is then presented with groupings of swatches and paint chips that will work harmoniously with one another. If you are working without a decorator, you can do exactly the same thing. If you are just freshening up your library, be sure to take these swatches and paint chips to different areas. Check, for example, how they look near a window. Check at different times of the day and when it's rainy as well as sunny.

If you are designing a new building or facing a major renovation during the course of which lighting fixtures will be replaced, your job is somewhat harder. It is possible to discuss lighting specifications with your architect and try to find another building that has a similar design. However, even though that building may have the same type of fixtures and lamps installed, every environment is different.

It is a good idea for you to take your samples on the road. Once you have the different color elements grouped together, you can take your swatch and paint boards with you as you do your shopping, visit other libraries, and generally go about your daily routine. Each environment will be lighted differently. You may discover that colors that worked well together in one light clash badly in another. Although some color change is inevitable, you will probably want to eliminate from consideration any colors that look completely different in different lights.

Instead of using these chameleon colors, experiment with related shades or tints of color. It is also possible that a different brand of paint reacts differently to the light environment. Selecting and discarding colors is a time-consuming process and best done by a professional, but professionals cost money. If your budget cannot be expanded to include an interior designer, then you or another member of your library staff can use the same techniques.

When professional decorators select colors, they show various samples to their customers to learn which colors create a positive response and which provoke a negative one. But the library is a space to which thousands of people will come. Each reacts somewhat differently to color. The response of any one individual may not be at all representative of the way most people react. Therefore, get a variety of opinions, asking both staff members and frequent customers to react to your color samples. Ask them to do it quickly and just give you their "gut" response.

Attacking Library Clutter

Over time, libraries acquire enormous piles of "stuff." It is both emotionally stressful and politically difficult to get rid of obsolete equipment and materials. How many of us have 16 mm projectors, 8-track tape recorders, or Beta videocassette players sitting unused? We purchase new computers but don't know what to do with the old ones. We know the collection is looking seedy, but weeding is time-consuming, and where will we put the books and media we withdraw?

In every library, there comes a time when librarians must ruthlessly reduce clutter. How many microfilm projectors do you really need? When was the last time you used those microcards? It may be painful, but they really have to go. Sure, someone may come along who needs just that book or filmstrip, but it's not worth storing it in the library. Thousands of such infrequently used titles add up to a library that most nearly resembles a down-at-the-heel thrift shop. If you are stacking boxes along the walls, get rid of them. If you have rooms of broken furniture waiting for someone to repair a leg or reupholster a seat, fix them or let them go. Put your discards into a yard sale, and if they don't find homes, take them to the dump. The process is a painful one, but there's no way a library can look inviting without plenty of open space.

Cleanliness May Indeed Be Next to Godliness

What makes a library inviting? A lot of answers come to mind. One might respond that an inviting space is light, bright, and comfortable. However, something that is so obvious that we sometimes fail to consider it is *cleanliness.* A library must be clean to be inviting. Yet grime is probably the most frequently encountered common denominator of failing libraries. If you were to tour a number of libraries, as I have, you would be surprised at how dirty they are. Although there are a surprising number of newer buildings that have already accumulated layers of grime, it is usually older buildings that are particularly vulnerable. Bookstores of the past, the small, cluttered ones that we remember from our youth, shared this problem and were often dustier and grimier than libraries. Modern chains, though, have approached custodial services as efficiently as they have dealt with all the other management issues that impact sales.

As a library ages, it becomes more difficult to clean. Gradually, layers of dirt accumulate that cannot be removed with normal measures. Custodians gradually come to assume that if it is going to look bad anyway, there's no point in continuing to put much effort into cleaning. Eventually, we end up with the kind of "antique" grime characteristic of so many of our libraries. Sometimes the problem is with an inept custodial staff, but more often it is one of attitude. The staff ceases to really look at their surroundings. They no longer see the library as a customer does.

Grime As the Customer Sees It

Our culture is one that stresses gleaming, hygienic cleanliness. Television and other media have drummed this ideal into our psyches, and we have come to expect our public spaces to be spic and span. As a society, we've become so obsessed with germs that people simply will not use a facility where they feel they cannot put their elbows on a table or use a restroom without encountering armies of microbes.

Because it has such a dramatic impact on public perceptions of the library and consequently library usage, cleanliness must become a top priority. For example, stains on the carpet must be cleaned immediately. They can't sit for days, weeks, or years. Restrooms must be inspected daily. But custodial service is an area where few librarians feel comfortable. With recent technological innovations in building maintenance, they're really not sure they know what's going on anymore.

Working with a Custodial Staff

Since librarians have little money to expend on cleaning and maintenance, their custodians are usually poorly paid and rarely receive adequate training. In the library organization, they have little status and may be nearly invisible to other staff members. Library directors usually have no training in custodial services, and so they feel ill-equipped to hire personnel, select supplies and equipment, assign duties, or develop a preventive maintenance program. Libraries, as I'm afraid I have repeated all too often, are financially stressed. Custodial services and building maintenance tend to be among the first budgets that are attacked when a budget cut is forced upon us. Yet if we are to create an inviting environment, which will attract customers, *we must find a way to get these functions under better control.* Here are a few suggestions that will help you achieve this goal:

- Become more involved in selecting and training custodians. Even if you outsource cleaning, you can still make a point of spending time with the people who do the cleaning.
- Evaluate the custodians or custodial service on a regular basis. Inform yourself about the tasks that should be performed each day as well as the ones that must be done weekly, monthly, or annually.
- Develop more-specific and to-the-point job instructions for custodians or include specific goals in contracts for custodial services.
- Take a good look at the custodial supplies and equipment that are being purchased. Don't allow large orders to be routinely placed without your knowledge.

- Meet with the custodians on a regular basis, every morning if possible. If you have a custodial team, get them together and ask questions. Find out how they spend their time and make sure you communicate the library's goals and priorities.
- Find out what is not being done. For example, custodial services contracts often have fine print excluding certain tasks. Your own custodians may have failed to tell you that there are lights they can't change because they don't have the right ladder or places they can't clean because they don't have a key.
- Become familiar with union contracts, labor laws, and other requirements that influence what custodians can and cannot do.

Many librarians report that they really don't know what their cleaning staff is doing much of the time. Ask your custodians to follow a daily cleaning schedule so you have an idea of which jobs are being done and when.

Timing is important to minimize inconvenience to customers. Arrange for restrooms to be cleaned before the public arrives. Schedule vacuuming and other noisy tasks when the library is closed or at low ebb. It's a good idea to develop a checklist of custodial tasks for yourself, and check regularly to be sure everything is getting done. You will need to be aware when things begin going downhill. If you wait until the problem is obvious to everyone, it may be too late. You may already have lost observant customers.

We often exclude our custodial staff from participation in library activities, so they may be unaware of our goals and even of the library's mission. Express interest in custodians' work, and let *them* give you a tour of the library so you can see it as they do. They will probably be delighted that someone is finally paying attention to them and are likely to tell you more than you ever wanted to know about blowing down the boiler or servicing the snowplow. However, this is all useful information. It will aid you in decision making and will give you a good sense for how long it takes to perform a job and what can reasonably be expected. Don't ever isolate the custodial staff. Include them as full members of the library staff, and consult them whenever they can contribute useful information to the decision-making process. Develop other ways to motivate staff, and distribute praise freely. Financial incentives aren't the only way to keep good custodial workers. Remember birthdays, reward extra effort, and make sure your custodians know how important they are to the success of the library.

Sometimes we forget that custodial tasks don't get done automatically and that staff become ill and take vacations just like everybody else. Make contingency plans for coverage if a custodian is ill, on vacation, or turns in his or her resignation. Be ready with a schedule of tasks that can be done when the weather is bad, when cleaning supplies fail to arrive, or when vandalism occurs.

Ask other library staff to become involved in keeping the library clean. Get them into the habit of noticing their surroundings. Ask them to report problems immediately. If they notice that custodians have done something especially well, encourage them to say thanks and to communicate informally with the custodial staff on a regular basis. Nevertheless, you will want to make sure the custodians don't have ten people telling them what to do. Assignments and criticism should be channeled through the supervisor. From their first day on the job, instill good work habits. Become more aware of promptness, attendance, quality of work, and morale among the staff.

Finally, it may sound too obvious to mention, but books mustn't smell. Most of us are aware that moldy books shouldn't be allowed to enter the library because mold is not only smelly and disgusting but it is also dangerous. However, we sometimes fail to notice that the library smells of damp and mildew. The problem may not have degenerated to the point that you have bona fide mold, but when customers enter, they sniff and turn up their noses. The library repels rather than invites. In general, the bookstore's stock does not stay on the shelves long enough to become moldy, and once a book leaves the premises, it does not return as it does in a library. Take precautions by never adding smelly books to the collection, no matter how desirable the titles, and stopping any leaks before they damage library materials.

Carpeting

Typically, libraries have chosen wall-to-wall carpeting for most areas because they find that it works well for book carts and wheelchairs, reduces accidents caused by slippery tile and loose rugs, and provides a soft surface for children to play and tumble. Unfortunately, carpeting tends to hold dirt and is much more difficult to clean than hard flooring. In visiting libraries around the country, I've found dirty carpets and large, ugly stains everywhere. More than any other single custodial problem, carpeting tends to make a library grimy and uninviting. The smell of dust pervades many libraries, and clouds of it billow up as patrons walk across the carpet.

It is difficult for a library to have the entire carpet shampooed on a regular basis. Steam extractors reduce drying time, but they are very expensive. The library is open so many hours a week that there is rarely an opportunity to allow enough time for freshly shampooed carpet to dry. There is a great deal, however, that can be done to keep the carpet in better condition between shampoos.

Try, for example, to keep dirt *outside* the building. Make sure that sidewalks and parking lots are clean: free of mud, leaves, oil, and tar. Most dirt comes into the library from outside on the soles of customers' shoes. If those shoes first encounter a clean sidewalk and then "walk-off" floor mats, much of the dirt will remain outside. Mats should have a healthy growth of pile to trap dirt and should be at least twenty feet long. They should be vacuumed daily. Winter is a particular problem since mats become wet and muddy. Vacuum them often with a wet-dry vacuum that sucks up water, and keep some spare mats on hand to allow wet ones time to dry out.

Much of the grime tramped into carpets could have been removed if they were vacuumed daily. When allowed to remain, dirt is pounded deeper and deeper into the fiber. Eventually, it takes a full-scale shampoo to remove it. Vacuum high-traffic areas like entrances, hallways, and service desk areas where people walk and congregate more often. If it is rainy or muddy when families arrive for story hour, then it is not too much to vacuum the traffic path into the children's department as well as the children's area itself twice in the same day.

You may want to consider investing in a pile lifter and using it weekly or monthly. It forces the yarns to stand up vertically so that vacuuming is more effective. Be sure that your vacuums are in good condition. Suction tends to decline as vacuums age, but regular maintenance will extend their useful lives. Be sure your custodial staff checks belts, beater bar and brush agitators, vacuum bags, and filters. Ask about when these tasks were performed, and emphasize that vacuum-cleaner maintenance is a regular part of the custodial routine.

Nothing, however, adds life to a carpet more than removing stains every day. Train staff to notice new stains so they don't sit for days or weeks getting harder and harder to treat. Establish a spot-removal program. Have supplies available throughout the building to make it easy to remove spots as soon as they appear. Staff sometimes think that custodial tasks are beneath their dignity. Make sure that when a custodian is unavailable, they know they are expected to deal with emergencies.

Another effective technique is shampooing smaller high-traffic areas rather than leaving them until the entire carpet can be cleaned. It is usually possible to cordon off and work around these areas if more time is needed for drying. Be sure you have a maintenance plan that specifies where and when cleaning equipment should be used. The library director or building manager should determine when the carpet is cleaned. It should not be a task that is decided upon at the whim of the custodian. Remember that most of the library's traffic is confined to the main floor. Fewer patrons usually find their way to other levels, and by the time they do, their shoes are free of most of the dirt they tracked in.

Therefore, your custodians should concentrate their efforts here, not apply the same effort to all areas.

All of these suggestions, however, will not eliminate the need to shampoo the entire carpet on a regular basis. Make sure that the custodial staff has the equipment to do this properly. Inexpensive, domestic-type carpet shampooers simply can't do the job. If you cannot afford the right equipment, then this should be a job for professionals.

Restrooms

Some years ago I facetiously promised to write a "Michelin Guide" to public restrooms in my town, rating them from zero to five stars. Restrooms are important to everyone. If a customer encounters a disgusting one, he or she will probably not voluntarily return to that store, restaurant, or library. If the library's restrooms always seem to have an unpleasant odor, there's a reason. Maybe the sanitary napkin bins are not emptied often enough. Maybe the floor drain needs a dose of antifreeze to isolate sewer gases. Never accept odor in a restroom as inevitable. Mold is also unacceptable in a bathroom, so don't assume that a library can't help but smelling damp and moldy. Mold destroys books and makes people sick. It must be battled, not endured.

Like our custodians, we tend to become accustomed to problems and then forget about them. Look at your library through new eyes. View it as your customers do. Ask staff from different branches to inspect one another's buildings. Whether the problem is ugly colors, chipping paint, stained carpeting, or dirty restrooms, looks really are important. If you can provide a library experience that truly appeals to the senses, both library use and customer satisfaction will skyrocket.

RESOURCES

Demas, S. G., et al. "Esprit de Place: Maintaining and Designing Library Buildings to Provide Transcendent Spaces." *American Libraries* 33 (April 2002): 65–68.

Harrington, D. "Six Trends in Library Design." *Library Journal Buyer's Guide* (December 2001): 12–14.

Peterman, H. "The Free Library of Philadelphia: The Library of the Past to the Library of the Future." *Journal of Youth Services in Libraries* 14 (winter 2001): 3–8.

Raymond, C. T. "The Library Administrator's Perspective." *Public Libraries* 39 (May/June 2000): 140.

Sager, D. J. "Interior Design Trends in Libraries." *Public Libraries* 39 (May/June 2000): 137–42.

Weiner, J., et al. "Creating Sustainable Libraries." *Library Journal Buyer's Guide* (December 2001): 8–10.

Welkie, J. "A Picture Is Worth a Thousand Words @ Plainfield-Guilford Township Public Library." *Indiana Libraries* 20 (2001): 31–33.

Woodward, J. "Countdown to a New Library: A Blueprint for Success." *American Libraries* 30 (April 1999): 44–47.

Zoeller, G. L. "The Equipment Distributor's Perspective." *Public Libraries* 39 (May/June 2000): 140–41.

chapter 9

The Art of Display

In recent years, the creation of retail displays has become a sophisticated specialty in the retail industry that libraries have generally ignored. For some time, however, experts have been conducting extensive research, discovering exactly what attracts customer attention, and then using this knowledge to create displays that best showcase their products. The profession that has emerged from this research is called "visual merchandising." Library patrons, who are daily enticed by the displays created by these highly trained pros, may find libraries boring by comparison. Yet the same techniques that attract customers to bookstores can be used to bring customers to the library and encourage them to return again and again. There is certainly nothing immoral or improper about adopting some of these proven techniques.

As has been pointed out in earlier chapters, however, libraries must shoulder responsibilities that bookstores needn't be concerned with. Since the library has a mission that goes beyond merely "selling" books and media, the library's own goals should be incorporated into its displays. Although, as blossoming bottom liners, we want our displays to increase attendance and circulation, some of our exhibits should support the library's other roles; in other words, they should educate and inform. Displays can be extremely effective teaching tools in all types of libraries. They provide opportunities for customers to easily and pleasantly assimilate information on a wide variety of topics.

Readers will find this chapter a little different from the others in that it will be somewhat more "hands-on." The reason is that it is not a topic that is commonly encountered in library literature. In fact, my own searches for "how-to" information for my own library were once very frustrating. It is not that visual merchandising is such a difficult or technically sophisticated specialty; librarians will have little difficulty learning the basic principles. However, articles do not even appear frequently in the business literature. For some time, I imagined that everyone in the whole world knew the secrets of creating eye-catching displays except me. More recently, however, the information has begun trickling down to librarians, usually through our sister profession of museum curatorship. Since it continues to be fairly difficult to find information about visual merchandising, and it is so central to the bookstore's success, I have decided it will be time well spent to go into the subject in some detail.

Arrangement of Materials

It has become axiomatic in libraries that books and other materials must be cataloged by subject and arranged on shelves in a logical order. One call number follows another, marching through the stacks, the order dictated by either the Dewey decimal or Library of Congress classification. For the most part, these systems have worked pretty well for us, and customers can, with practice, learn to find most of our materials. The problem is that each book becomes anonymous, squeezed in among thousands of others.

Bookstores want to call attention to their merchandise so that customers will make more purchases. We too want our customers to leave the library happily clutching several books and media programs. That way, they will probably bring them back in a few weeks and check out more materials. A cycle is thus established that eventually transforms an occasional customer into a devout library supporter.

Most of our customers do not arrive at the library with any special titles in mind. They want to look or browse around and find something that appeals to them. When books are stuffed on shelves, they are far from appealing. When videos and CDs, which are smaller than books, are likewise stuffed between dozens of other titles, they are all but invisible. It is certainly true that when customers have specific titles in mind or are researching a topic for a school or college assignment, they want to know where to look. It is not necessary, however, for every item in our collection to sit waiting in Dewey decimal order for students and researchers.

As librarians, we have a very good idea which types of materials are likely to be discovered through the catalog and then sought by call number. We can also anticipate which will be picked up on impulse. However, we may confuse our own experience of the collection with that of our customers. Library staff rarely browse; since they are nearly always searching for specific titles, they are usually much more aware of order or disorder than their patrons. It's hard to keep remembering that, at least in public libraries, this is not the way our customers usually approach the library.

Most public libraries now have a new book section. Even though loan periods for these titles are usually shorter than for other books in the collection, these titles circulate much more frequently. Once upon a time, my library received an unexpected, midyear budget cut. We were not able to purchase any more new books until the new fiscal year began. What were we going to do, we wondered? Everyone loved the new book section, and it quickly began to empty. To fill the rack, the staff began roaming through the stacks looking for appealing topics and attractive covers that did not look too worn. They sought out recent publications, but some were three or four years old. Each book was cleaned up if necessary, assigned a different loan period, and relabeled as a new book. Did customers feel cheated? No, most never even noticed. They continued to favor the "new book" rack even though they did occasionally complain that we didn't have the best sellers listed in the *New York Times.* Over the next few months, we saw only a slight decline in the number of "new books" circulated, and the average number of circulations remained several times that of other books in the collection.

This experience convinced me that customers check out books when they are readily visible, not necessarily when they are new. In addition, since the books were chosen by library staff members who knew a great deal about patron preferences, the library was providing what amounted to a readers' advisory service. Sometimes we forget how skilled the library staff becomes at anticipating customer needs. As librarians, we make use of this knowledge when we purchase materials, but then we make customers hunt for them.

Making Materials More Appealing

Customers also check out books and media that look clean and shiny. When we were taking the library tour earlier, the books and videos we came across were dirty and dog-eared. No one is attracted to grime. Most of us don't even want to touch those grungy jackets and containers. Of course, the titles that circulate frequently will start to look beaten up, but new jackets and cases will have them looking new again at very little cost. Once, when I volunteered in a very small library, we poor stepchildren were forced to accept discards from other libraries. It always amazed me that a book would arrive looking like it was ready for the trash bin. Yet when the old Mylar cover was removed, the original dust jacket was in pristine condition, perfectly protected by its polyvinyl armor. The same is true of videos housed in plastic cases and CDs in jewel cases. When you replace the packaging, you give the program a new lease on life.

Try an experiment in your own library. Spend some time in your stacks. Find books and media that haven't circulated in a while but still have their original dust jacket or cardboard packaging. Seek out items that you think might be interesting to your customers if only they knew of their existence. Don't choose anything that contains obsolete information; otherwise, ignore the date of publication. Discard the old packaging and place your choices in new vinyl jackets, cases, and boxes. Then set them up in the front of the library in a colorful display. Of course, actual circulation figures will depend on the specific items you chose, but average usage for these materials will probably be much higher than the average for the rest of the collection. One very creative tech services volunteer wraps wallpaper samples in Mylar covers when the original dust jackets are unavailable. He also finds photos of CDs and videos online, adjusts the size, and prints them out to substitute for missing cover art.

Once the materials you want to spotlight are looking their enticing best, the next question is how to display them. It does make a difference. Some displays attract far more attention than others. This is where the wisdom amassed by practitioners of visual merchandising becomes so important. Creating an effective display requires an understanding of the principles of color, design, lighting, and graphics. In addition, certain tools, props, and other materials will be needed.

Color

It is possible that color is the single most important component in any display. Creative use of color will greatly increase the number of customers who pause to look at a display, so don't simply use whatever you happen to have handy. In the last chapter, we discussed the importance of color in creating an inviting library environment. When incorporated into effective displays, color serves a similar function, but there are additional issues to be considered. Before delving too deeply into the subject, it might be helpful to start with some basic vocabulary. For example, where most laypeople would use the word *color*, professional designers refer to *hue*. Red, green, and blue are examples of hues.

Value, on the other hand, refers to the lightness or darkness of the hue. A lighter value is usually achieved by adding white to the hue, producing what is then known as a *tint.* Adding black to a hue darkens it and produces a variation known as a *shade.* As black and white are added, the hue remains unchanged. What does change is the value. Using different values of a hue in a display adds interest without introducing additional and possibly discordant or clashing colors.

Intensity is the term used for the saturation or purity of the hue. When we speak of the brightness or dullness of a color, what we really mean is its intensity. Bright colors have a lot of impact. However, it is sometimes desirable to lessen the impact of some elements in a display so that the library media become the focus of attention. Getting to know how different values and intensities of color create different impacts is an important aspect of a designer's training. Adding color to a display can make a greater difference in its impact than any other single step. To lessen the intensity of a hue, artists add gray to the pigment. Another solution is adding a complementary color on the opposite side of the color wheel.

Color Relationships

Speaking of the color wheel, it is a tool that is constantly employed by designers because it is so important in understanding the relationships of colors to one another. Color wheels are based on the three primary or basic colors from which all other colors are derived. When one primary color is mixed with another primary color, the result is called a secondary color. When two adjacent secondary colors are mixed together, the result is a tertiary color, and so on. Thus is produced a continuous transition of color, which provides the basis for nearly all color schemes. The following are the most frequently used color schemes:

Monochromatic. Color is limited to just one hue with varying values and intensities, often highlighted by black and white. The result tends to be elegant rather than exciting. Additional interest can be achieved with the use of different textures and patterns.

Analogous. The use of colors next to one another on the color wheel create an analogous scheme. This provides more freedom for the designer and unifies the display with a limited color palette.

Complementary. When colors that are opposite one another on the color wheel are used together, the result is a complementary scheme that can be extremely intense and exciting. As shoppers, we are all too familiar with the traditional Christmas color scheme of red and green. These complementary colors are used constantly by stores to attract customer attention. More subtle effects, however, can be achieved by varying the value and the intensity of the basic colors.

Split Complementary. This effect is achieved by using one basic color with two other colors located on either side of it on the color wheel.

Double Complementary. This is a good way of incorporating a lot of colors into a display. It is achieved by using two sets of colors directly opposite one another on the wheel. This means expanding the color pallet to four basic hues. For the apprentice designer, this is not the safest plan since so many colors can easily become confusing. It is possible, however, to choose one of the colors as the dominant one and use the others as accents.

Triad. In this case, the designer chooses three colors on the wheel that are equidistant from one another. Although this scheme does not offer as many pitfalls as the four-color scheme above, it can become too busy. Choosing one color to predominate is helpful. Another solution is using only one very bright color while toning down the intensity of the other two.

Neutral. Bright colors are not always needed to attract attention. For example, stark black and white can be extremely effective in calling attention to the library materials on display. The materials themselves may be multihued, or their jackets may also display a neutral palette. Black-and-white photos are especially effective in such a display, possibly with a bit of red for accent.

Getting Started

Apprentice library designers always wonder where to begin. How do they get started and how do they choose an effective color scheme? One solution is to take an especially alluring book jacket; it was created by a professional designer and incorporates all the basic elements of design. If you take your color scheme from the book jacket, it's hard to go wrong. Another possibility is using a fabric, since it has also been designed by a professional. It can become the backdrop for the display, and its colors can be used in other elements. Yet another possibility is to start with a painting or professionally produced poster.

Since color produces a mood, you might think about the mood you'd like the display to communicate to customers. Would you like the mood to be exciting, enticing them from across the reading room? Maybe you'd prefer to send a more peaceful message, encouraging them to relax. Blue, many people's favorite color, is cool and serene. To customers who have been rushing around town doing errands, emphasis on the color blue can lower the pulse rate and encourage them to slow down, take a deep breath, and maybe even sit down to read. On the other hand, blue is a cool color, sometimes even cold. You probably want to use it sparingly in winter when customers are shivering in boots and overcoats. In fact, we respond differently to colors in different seasons. In spring, we are attracted to green like bees to honey. Cheerful yellow, the color of sunshine, can be used summer and winter regardless of climate. Bright yellow against a dark background is always eye-catching.

The Display Designer's Toolbox

Although the library books and other materials will be the focus of nearly all your displays, it is not enough to simply pile them in interesting heaps. You will need a variety of different supplies and materials, depending on the type of display and where it is located.

Paint

When most designers start lining up the materials they will need for their projects, paint jars, tubes, and cans often make their appearance first. That is because paint is an extraordinarily useful and versatile medium that can be used for creating an infinite number of different effects. It can be marbleized, mottled, or striated, and, of course, it comes in an endless variety of colors. Latex-based paint is the usual choice for large areas, especially backdrops. It dries quickly and can be cleaned again and again with soap and water. It is easy to work with and can be applied with brushes, sponges, or rollers. Best of all, the painter can get cleaned up quickly and move on to other library tasks. Tempera paint is the usual choice for painting signs and graphics. Library designers usually avoid oil paint because of its odor and the difficulty of application.

One of the purposes for creating library displays is to give a space a new look. Even though new books and media programs are arriving daily, regular customers may become bored if everything seems to look about the same as it did the last time they visited. It is, therefore, important to create new looks built on new themes as often as possible. Nothing can achieve a quick change like paint. It can completely transform the impact of a space or a display. Since paint is so inexpensive, it should be an integral part of any display designer's tool kit.

Construction Materials

Most displays are constructed using some kind of board. Lightweight foam board is one of the designer's best friends; it is so light and easy to cut with an

X-Acto knife that it can be used to create almost any shape. Although it cannot support a lot of weight, it holds up well under all but the heaviest volumes. It is usually found in the form of paper-covered Styrofoam, such as Monsanto's Foam-Core, which can be found in most craft stores. Sintra, another variety, is heavier and more long lasting. Foam board can be sculpted, scored to create sharp sides and corners, stapled, painted, and glued. In general it can become almost any structure a library staff member can visualize. Since it has no sharp edges, it can be used to create castles and rocket ships in the children's department, Greek columns in the history section, or even a mini Taj Mahal in travel. It does have a tendency, however, to bend and fray at the edges, but if carefully handled, it can be used again and again.

For more solid construction of display bases, Masonite is a good choice. It comes in thicknesses from ⅛ inch to ½ inch and sizes up to 4 x 8 feet. It is more substantial than foam board and is a good choice for structures you plan to use again and again. Few surfaces lend themselves so well to paint, so you can go wild with scenic backgrounds. Hemasote, made of compressed cardboard, is also useful for small support structures and backdrops. Plywood is another good choice.

Fabric

Library designers get into the habit of haunting fabric shops looking for sales on remnants. A different fabric can completely change a display in a matter of minutes. There's no need to wait for it to dry, and it shapes easily, molding itself to any surface. You can scrunch it to fill in spaces or stretch it out to provide a smooth expanse of color. Some fabrics are almost artworks in themselves, incorporating all the principles of good design. You can staple it, tack it, nail into it, and still use it again and again.

Felt provides an especially good surface for displays. It can be stretched to serve as a backdrop to which photographs and other graphic elements can be attached. Small scraps of felt can be shaped into silhouettes as well as letters, numbers, and other design elements. Burlap is another good choice. Its coarse fiber and open weave make it almost indestructible.

Carpet

Few materials are as durable or as richly colored as carpeting. One very talented library staff member of my acquaintance has an arrangement with a local carpet store. The store has agreed to donate all the scraps of carpet that were once thrown in the trash. Each time the staff member stops by the store, she leaves with a large box of carpet pieces, many of which are not scraps at all but sizable lengths. Over the course of time, she has used the carpet like upholstery to cover boxes and boards of all sizes. Larger pieces are cut to the size of library tables and backdrops. In literally minutes, she can put together a display in much the same way a child puts together the pieces of a Lego set.

Paper

Since libraries generally spend very little money on display materials, paper is the most frequent choice. Seamless colored paper is available in widths up to fourteen feet although library and school suppliers don't normally stock paper wider than eight feet. Most children's departments keep several rolls on hand, and adult services will also find plenty of use for it as well. Nothing, of course, is easier to work with than paper; it can be cut to any shape or folded around any object. Since it is so light, anyone can install it, no matter how large the display.

The one problem with paper is that it really can't be reused very successfully. When a library staff has put a lot of work into a display, it is natural that they want to save it to be used again. For example, when seasonal displays are taken down, they are frequently put away to be used next Halloween or next Thanksgiving. However, they never look as good the second time around. Brightly colored paper fades quickly to dirty gray. Tears, tape, and staples are all-too-clearly visible. One good compromise is to use colored paper for background only, while creating other display elements with more durable materials. That way, the most time-consuming tasks won't have to be repeated, and a fresh paper background will take only minutes to install. Wallpaper is another good choice for backgrounds, but it is much more expensive than arts-and-crafts paper. Samples and partial rolls are sometimes available at an affordable price. Aluminum foil can provide glitz and glitter for small areas at a reasonable cost.

Other Materials

To the dedicated library designer, almost any material can be put to work as part of a library display. Other staff members may complain that library storage areas are starting to look like Fibber McGee's closet, stuffed with flea market treasures, yard sale bargains, and even prizes gleaned from dumpster-diving expeditions. Although every designer has his or her own favorites, here are a few materials that are especially well suited to library displays:

Ceramic and vinyl tile

Grass mats

Netting
Straw rugs
Rope
Pebbles and rocks
Hay
Sand

Props

A wide variety of objects not usually found in libraries can add interest to displays. They can help establish the theme that books and other media further develop. Found objects, thrift shop finds, and packaging materials of all kinds can all be worked into creative displays. Discarded crates are always in demand, and believe it or not, empty soda bottles, barrels, garden equipment, picture frames, and old photographs all have their place. For inspiration, think about the basic Dewey divisions. Crockery, pots and pans, and kitchen appliances all enhance a cookbook display. Tools and woodworking books go hand in hand. Costumes can find their way into almost any display, and musical instruments, even those that have seen better days, can be used to enhance a display of musical recordings.

Instead of paper or fabric, why not try screens, shutters, or window shades for your backdrop? Ladders and vases, as well as small chairs and tables, can be used to prop up library materials. When you get into the right frame of mind, the word *junk* ceases to have meaning. In fact, nearly everything that you might find at a yard sale can, in some way, be put to work in a library display.

Display Cases

When librarians think about displays, the first thing that pops into their heads is often the display case standing forlorn in the library lobby. When new libraries are built, these very expensive cases always seem to be included on the initial list of new furnishings. They are soon viewed as everyone's least favorite task. Stale, tired displays remain for years on end. The problem is that these locked glass cases are time-consuming, and they are not a good place to display books and other media. One certainly doesn't want to unlock the case each time an item is requested, and so they tend to be used for other things. Nevertheless, if your library owns a display case, there are some quite interesting things you can do to make it the focus of attention and contribute to the ambience of the library. Try not to make the display case a dreaded chore. There's probably someone on the staff who would view it as an opportunity to exercise creativity. If you have two such talented people, the project can become an even more enjoyable one.

Even though the library staff may not be too keen on filling the case, you probably have quite a large number of collectors among your customers who would view the case as an excellent opportunity to display their collections. Do you really want them? Well, of course, sometimes the objects are colorful and attention grabbing. Other collections are offensive or just downright boring. Library displays should be covered in your policy manual, with special reference to display cases. The policy should cover scheduling, guidelines for handling requests from external sources, responsibility, and security. The purpose for maintaining the cases should be stated as clearly as possible so that the library does not appear to play favorites. Involving local hobby groups is an excellent way to make more friends for the library, but do be sure that the library is not accepting more responsibility than you're comfortable with. That policy statement should probably state either that valuable items will not be displayed or the library is not responsible for loss.

One of the best uses of display cases is to promote library materials, services, and events. This may mean occasionally discouraging use of the cases by avid collectors. Take some time to think about how you can use a display case to market library materials, promote circulation, advertise library-sponsored events, and, of course, educate and inform the community. Consider setting up a display calendar roughly a year in advance. That way you can be sure the cases will be available to the library to advertise its own programs but can also be used to support community groups when not needed by the library.

Display Cases Require Commitment

Once you've made a commitment to maintaining display cases, solemnly promise yourself that displays will be changed on a regular basis. This means at least every six to eight weeks. Once committed to maintaining display cases, you do the library a disservice to let them get out-of-date. If this means a larger time commitment than you're comfortable with, it may be better to store your display cases or create permanent displays, possibly centered on the history of the library or community.

There are ways, however, to streamline the creation of new exhibits. Developing a basic formula can save a lot of time. In fact, a step-by-step written procedure can enable even the novice to put together a credible case. Once committed to maintaining one or more display cases, be sure you communicate that commitment to the staff member assigned to setting up the displays. Otherwise, the job becomes one that gets done only when extra time happens to be available. If you really don't think of your display cases as a reasonably high priority, store them. Don't allow them to exert a negative impact on your library's image.

Getting Ideas

Take a good look at what other libraries display. The World Wide Web will take you to thousands of libraries, and they frequently highlight their latest displays on their websites. You'll discover that they frequently make use of opportunities to celebrate book and library events; for example, an author's birthday can provide an excellent opportunity. Use the Web to get ideas for how other libraries use space and how they assemble colors and shapes, photos, and art objects to call attention to the theme.

Diverse elements can often be brought together into a coherent theme. Toys, for example, always attract attention, and there are so many different kinds that they can be used in almost any kind of display. Clothing too attracts attention, and unneeded costumes make excellent backgrounds. Local history is another theme that is always interesting as long as the objects displayed do not look grubby and colorless. There is something about miniatures that will always attract interest, and someone in the community undoubtedly collects them. Sometimes too, combining a collection with books about collecting can result in a fascinating case. Some creative staff in my own library put together a great display around the theme of "cabin fever." Model making, fly-tying, quilting, and several other popular hobby items were displayed with appropriate how-to books.

Museums

As you plan a display or exhibit, think about the way museums have changed in recent years. Remember how curators used to simply assemble a quantity of old "stuff" and put it all behind glass? In recent years, they have become very savvy about ways to attract new customers to their museums. The exhibits they now create are endlessly interesting. Color, striking type fonts, and dramatic lighting are all used to effectively call attention to the artifacts on display. Compared to the crowded cases of the past, there are fewer objects, and the sense of clutter is gone. Facsimiles of the original objects are often used instead of the real thing to allow visitors to handle them.

Libraries, however, have not always kept pace. Too often, the library's display case harkens back to the bad old days of boring and poorly lighted heaps of objects arranged any old way. How many times have you seen rocks or stamps or Civil War models all squeezed into a space that's much too small for them to be interestingly arranged? By the way, speaking of museums, most have far more artifacts than they can display, and they must maintain large storage areas to house all those items that are not quite important enough to be displayed. In fact, they have basements and attics that are crammed full of interesting objects serving no useful purpose. Curators are usually perfectly willing to lend less valuable items that can be coupled with library materials to create eye-catching displays. Old farming and garden implements herald the coming of spring, and antique clothing can be coupled with books on women's history. If the museum is willing to lend them, the objects probably have little monetary value, but they should be handled with care. Ask about how they should be displayed; for example, clothing probably needs to be stuffed with acid-free paper.

Lighting

There is not much point in creating an interesting display if it is poorly lit. No one will notice it, and your hard work will be wasted. The more expensive display cases come equipped with hidden lightbulbs or fluorescent tubes. However, if your case doesn't come with its own fixtures, you have several options. Installing small fluorescent tubes is your best bet, but it may require the services of an electrician. Battery-powered closet lights have become popular, and these can be attached with Velcro in inconspicuous places. Clear Christmas tree lights are another option since they don't have heavy power requirements and can be plugged into a small battery unit. Installing mirror tiles to the back of the case allows you to make better use of available light, and substituting glass for wooden shelves can also increase light.

Learn how to take photographs through the case without glare, and once a display is ready, take lots of them. If you use a digital camera, you can put the pictures on your website immediately and accompany the photos with information about the objects displayed as well as bibliographies on the subject. You might e-mail the photos to the local newspaper with a press release and then later reuse them in various library PR publications. Do keep track of the names and phone numbers of anyone who gave you advice or donated objects to the display. When you take down the exhibit, you won't want to spend hours trying to get the artifacts back to their owners.

When you run out of ideas, check *Chase's Calendar of Events.* If you haven't already browsed through this time-honored reference book, you'll be amazed at the holidays and celebrations it lists. You might be inclined to create a display around "The Pursuit of Happiness Week," for example. Birthdays of the famous or infamous provide other opportunities. If you're really hard up for ideas, you might celebrate "Baby Boomer's Recognition Day."

The American Library Association's website is another good source for ideas, and they're more in tune with the library's agenda. For example, a display built around Banned Book Week is both interesting and educational. ALA's Public Programs Office will also provide information about opportunities to schedule traveling exhibits.

Signage

Whatever type of exhibit you have created, customers must find it. If you have a suspended ceiling, consider hanging a large sign or banner above the display to both attract and direct customers. One idea I especially like is using a large piece of brightly colored felt stapled to a thin strip of lumber or dowel. Letters are cut out of contrasting felt and attached to the background felt in a way that makes them easy to remove later. The completed felt banner is hung from the ceiling with invisible fishing line.

Displaying library materials is an endlessly interesting topic and one of particular importance in making the library more enticing for our customers. For the most part, displays require more creativity than money, and this is where library staffs excel. Although your library lacks the budget for professional designers, you will probably find that your own staff can boast talent that would make a bookstore manager jealous. You just need to use it.

RESOURCES

Bolan, K., et al., "Makeover Madness: Tips for Revamping Your Young Adult Area." *Voice of Youth Advocates* 22 (December 1999): 322–23.

Brazer, S., et al. "Display Cases for Academic Libraries: Ten Tips for Display Case Persons." *College & Research Libraries News* 62 (October 2001): 904–8.

"Designing Spaces and Displays: Visual Merchandising Basics for Librarians: A Reading List." *Unabashed Librarian* (1994): 14.

Dutka, A., et al. "The Surprise Part of a Librarian's Life: Exhibition Design and Preparation Course." *College & Research Libraries News* 63 (January 2002): 19–22.

Litt, K. "Visual Merchandising of Books." *Unabashed Librarian* (1986): 3–5.

Rosen, J. "Millennium Merchandising." *Publishers Weekly* 248 (July 9, 2001): 18.

Sannwald, W. W. "Espresso and Ambiance: What Public Libraries Can Learn from Bookstores." *Library Administration & Management* 12 (fall 1998): 200–211.

chapter **10**

Finding Their Way: The Importance of Signage

Unlike bookstores, libraries spend thousands of hours cataloging and classifying their materials. While bookstores organize books only into general categories, libraries identify and describe the subject matter of each item, selecting for it a precise location in the information universe. Then, for some unknown reason, they often neglect to share this information with their customers. Effective signage and logical arrangement often make it easier to find materials in a bookstore than in a library that annually spends a sizable portion of its budget on cataloging.

The Library's Signage

Look around your neighborhood. Notice that graphically effective signage has become big business, a multibillion-dollar industry, in fact. Because library budgets are always stretched, however, librarians have tended to ignore recent developments. Signage continues to be a function that libraries leave not only to amateurs but to staff who have no interest in design or signage principles. In fact, the only time many libraries spend money for signs is when they construct a new building. Thereafter, professional signs become quickly outdated and are soon supplemented by dozens of homemade, dog-eared scraps of cardboard and construction paper that bear no resemblance to one another. Even worse, signs consistently tell patrons what they don't want to know. For example, the sign reading Biography is positioned to catch the attention of patrons leaving the area, not those arriving.

As library collections grow and building additions are delayed, the library becomes more and more crowded. The once logical arrangement gives way to the practice of stuffing materials anywhere space can be found. As we all know, shifting large parts of the collection while retaining a logical arrangement is highly labor-intensive. What we tend to do instead is shift a little here and a little there, postponing a major reorganization project until the last possible moment. The carefully devised classification leaps from floor to floor with no rhyme or reason.

Basics of Good Signage

Think about the signs in large chain bookstores. You might even want to picture the signs in your local supermarket. If they have been well designed, they guide you to the items you're seeking and contribute to the overall impression of color-coordinated, eye-catching decor. If a knowledgeable professional designer has been involved, you will first follow large, overhead signs to the general area and then find your way among smaller and smaller signs until you have arrived at the shelf or bin that may have your book or CD. Again, if the signage system has been well designed, you will have no sense of clutter. The signs will get you where you want to go without overwhelming you with information. You will not encounter a sign showing the location for Cambodian history when you enter the front door. Yet think about libraries. How often do you first encounter a chart with the entire Dewey decimal system? To make matters worse, the charts are often purchased from library vendors and include no indication of where books are actually shelved. Thus, you are immediately overwhelmed with choices before you are ready to deal with them. I sometimes feel that librarians are wonderful at assembling quantities of information for their customers; the problem is that our customers are not always able to deal with the avalanche of options we provide for them.

Signs are an absolutely essential ingredient in your library's success formula. They are one of the most important means of communication between the library and its users, and nothing is more important than communication. The effectiveness of the library depends on its ability to tell the public what it is all about, to publicize its mission, to encourage the use of its materials, and, most of all, to make sure users have a positive, productive experience.

Hmmm, I think I hear someone out there snickering. You're asking, "Why should we bother with signs? Nobody reads them." While it is true that many signs are ineffective and rarely read, library users do seek out signs when they are trying to find their way around the library. They will read your signs if they are clear, understandable, and meet their immediate need for information. Since we are daily bombarded with advertisements, unwanted flyers, and intrusive placards, we require cues to focus our attention. Signs become merely clutter when they are small, disorganized, and differentiated only by random designs and color selections. They are just a kind of visual noise that customers will move among and between without actually seeing. In our contemporary society, where we are battered constantly by thousands of images competing for our attention, we simply cannot assume that customers will notice the 8 ½ x 11 inch sign we tape to the end of a stack range.

Comparing Bookstore and Library Signs

Take another look at the bookstore's signs. They share a common look that allows customers to associate the shape, color, and design with help when and where they need it. It is important to the bookstore that customers find their way to materials that they may purchase. If they wander too long without finding anything they want, they will eventually tire and leave. Bookstore marketing philosophy does, of course, encourage customers to become sidetracked by enticing

Figure 10-1 The Newsstand sign at this Barnes & Noble can be seen from across the store.

displays, but if they are looking for something specific, they must find it quickly before they become frustrated. If customers are tired, angry, or annoyed, they will not react positively to merchandise displays. They will not be swayed by advertising. If they are teetering on the brink of a decision, their bad mood will send them out the door empty-handed.

Libraries don't want customers leaving empty-handed either. If they don't find anything that interests or excites them on this visit, they may not come back. If the signs they encounter fail to meet their information need, in other words, information that results in getting them to materials of interest, then their perception of the library will be altered.

The Right Signs in the Right Location

Imagine a customer entering through the front door of the library. He stands there briefly looking around. What now? Maybe he is merely killing time before an appointment with his accountant. He is looking for current magazines that will help him pleasantly wile away half an hour, so he needs to know that they are straight ahead and to the right. Here's a woman who has come to use the Internet, but the computers can't be seen because they are hidden behind the reference area. Even if yours is a small library, don't assume that these customers will be able to find their way without assistance. Small libraries are often the most confusing of all because space is limited and so we hide resources in unexpected nooks and crannies. As you imagine this scene, your first thought is probably to tack up a sign pointing to the correct location. The problem, however, is that you will have many different customers looking for equally diverse library materials. How can you anticipate all their needs and yet avoid creating a sign jungle?

Libraries are not the only organizations that frustrate their customers with poor signage. Haven't you visited a government agency or business where signs are plastered everywhere, some professionally produced but most homemade and dog-eared? They're a mess. They communicate a message to visitors that says this office or department is not very efficient, well organized, or up-to-date. Besides that, such signs are ineffective; there are so many that they are ignored.

Again, you may argue that signs aren't really necessary anyway. Just take all those dog-eared signs down. Customers, you say, ask directions to the restrooms when professionally produced signs are in plain sight. It's quite true that some people are more likely to ask a question than read a sign because of differences in their information-seeking behavior. Although library users are probably more tuned-in to written messages than others, many may respond best to the spoken word. In addition, color blindness, spatial perception, and many other factors all influence the effectiveness of signage. An information desk just inside the library entrance would serve these people better. They could stop and chat for a moment, feel a sense of welcome and well-being, and ask their questions to a real live human being. If you provide such a desk, that's great. However, once out of sight of the information desk, your customer will probably need additional guidance. There is really no substitute for good signage, and even taking all the problems above into consideration, there is ample evidence that users are more likely to have successful library experiences if good, well-designed signs help them find their way.

The Signage System

How can you provide enough signage to allow your users to find their way around the library without cluttering up your small space? How do you design signs that harmonize with the decor yet stand out sufficiently to be noticed? Which areas will your users find on their own without difficulty, and which will require several signs at different points? The answer to these questions lies in developing an effective signage system. In all probability, what you have in your library is not a signage system, unless the building was completed last week, but just a lot of signs. What we are talking about is a systematic approach to signage that allows you to communicate information more effectively to your users. Here are some characteristics of a good signage system:

- A signage system includes all signs in the library, not just certain types of signs. This means that even utilitarian and emergency signs are part of it.
- Signs are designed and placed only after a careful analysis of your user needs.
- The system includes enough signs to meet your customers' needs but not so many as to confuse or overwhelm them.
- Layout, color, and other design elements are all part of the system. They are not random decisions.

Good signage, however, requires careful planning. Signs serving a specific function, for example, those designating ranges of call numbers, are similar in color and design. Users gradually learn to look for that type of sign when they have similar information needs. Signage terminology must be carefully thought out. This means that one sign does not identify the Circulation Desk while another points out the location of the Checkout Desk. Neither should there be one sign pointing to Audiocassettes and another to Books on Tape. Many libraries may begin with well-designed signs, but they quickly become out-of-date. Signs should be easily moved or replaced as changes occur and collections grow. They should also be made of durable materials so that they don't quickly become dog-eared. If you're making your own, be sure they're printed or painted on a rigid, durable surface and laminated. If your signs are professionally produced, information about the vendor, style, colors, and materials must be retained and kept on file so that new signs will be compatible with existing ones. Unusual custom colors should be avoided because it will probably be impossible to match them in the future.

Responding to Customer Needs

Signs are, in part, designed to reduce the number of simple directional questions asked at service desks. Therefore, consider what questions customers really ask. Signs can also make users aware of the full range of library services. Thus, good signs should be visible throughout the library. Too often, a library begins a signage project, succeeds in providing more signs than any customer would need in a single area, and then everyone involved in the project loses interest. Just as terminology used on signs should be consistent, so should graphic elements. Signs should make use of symbols and terminology that customers have become accustomed to in other public spaces like airports and hospitals.

Consider placing building directories in lobby areas and near stairs and elevators. Professionally produced directories can be exorbitantly expensive. This may not be the best use of the signage budget. Is it possible to produce simpler signs that would provide the same information? Directories become quickly out-of-date, so don't install them and forget them. Some libraries have purchased wall-mounted directory cases direct from the manufacturer rather than the sign company. They have decided that since library locations change so frequently, it is better to create their own colorful floor plans, which are much easier and cheaper to update.

Types of signs that are appropriate for libraries include changeable floor signs, hanging and wall-mounted directional signs, room identification signs, and point-of-use instructional signs. As you begin deciding what signs will be needed, consider that signs should respond to the user's need to progress from general to specific information. Directional signs should be provided at decision points. For example, when customers arrive at the top of a flight of stairs or exit from an elevator, they must decide whether to turn left or right. Correlate the size of the sign to the size of the area. For example, large signs with oversize type font or graphics should mark larger areas.

Consider the needs of people with disabilities as you design the signage system. Signs identifying facilities for their use should be visible from a distance. Remember that their mobility may be limited, so make it possible for them to reach their goal with the least amount of effort.

Choosing the Right Words

Sometimes, as readers and writers, we are inclined to make signs too wordy. Signs should present information clearly in as few words as possible. Instructions for using library tools should be located at the point of use like OPAC catalogs and computers that access periodical databases (protected by a Lucite frame, not tacked on a computer desk or study carrel). There is little point to providing such information in a literature rack at the entrance. Customers will not realize they need it until they encounter an unfriendly screen.

Regulatory signs should be kept to a minimum but should clearly communicate smoking, eating, noise, and security policies. Post library rules where people are likely to break them. For example, one sign stating No Food or Drink Past This Point is more useful if customers encounter it as they are leaving the coffee café than half a dozen signs scattered throughout the library. Signs should inform users of fire exit routes, emergency procedures, meeting room capacities, and other information required by law. Other signs, like copyright notices, are posted at copy machines; admonitions to parents to attend to their children limit the library's legal liability. Temporary signs used to notify users of special situations, library hours, and events should follow a consistent format. Just as important, they should be removed when no longer needed.

Good Signage Needn't Be Expensive

Haven't you been in buildings with very handsome, even stylish signs that point nowhere or are covered over with dog-eared paper signs? Those expensive, color-coordinated masterpieces are now useless. They were part of the original capital outlay budget, but locations have changed. Now there is no more money available to update the signs. No one remembers which sign company produced the signs, but it really doesn't matter because the annual operating budget is inadequate to pay for expensive new signs.

Modular signs are a way of making the signs purchased for a new building last longer. They come with bags of different letters that slide into a frame, producing a sign. They look pretty much like other professional ones but can be changed when necessary. Unless you're quite sure that money will be available to maintain your signage system, this is a good use of your capital outlay budget. I do have some reservations here, however. Modular signs will save money and keep your signage system up-to-date if they can be changed easily. However, if nine-year-old boys can also change them easily, then they may not be a bargain. Although individual letters that slide in and out may be handy, they can be extremely frustrating if your more creative patrons make a habit of rearranging the letters or losing them altogether. Be sure the system you choose does not encourage this kind of creativity. In addition, you should be able to remove a sign from a wall and place it in a new location without an expensive house call by the installer.

I've been visiting libraries lately to gawk at their signs and have come to some unexpected conclusions. One library in particular interested me; this is a library that has done a lot of things right. What professionally produced signs they have are modular. However, the majority of their signs are homemade, and I was amazed to discover that the homemade signs are really better. Because the library had a very limited budget for signage, it could afford to purchase only small, rather boring ones. You'll see the kind I mean if you take a look at most library supply catalogs. They're all right, but they will never really attract customers' attention. In fact, many of the etched call number signs attached to end panels are so tasteful and inoffensive that they can't be seen more than a few feet away. Thus, the commercially produced signs I noticed in this library were neat, tidy, and professional looking, but they had none of the eye appeal of a large bookstore's graphics.

Fortunately, the library ran out of money before it could buy more than a fraction of the signs needed. I say *fortunate* because their homemade signs, in contrast, were a delight to see. A small group of staff members was charged with the responsibility of creating the rest of the signs needed with their own hands and imaginations. Researching the subject of signage, they came upon most of the basic rules listed above. However, they added an element all their own—fun! They made their signs with markers and tempera paint, then attached them to foam board. For larger signs, they used Masonite, and all signs were carefully laminated when appropriate.

Although it was obvious that the signs were not commercially produced, few bookstores could boast more attractive ones. Staff really unleashed their creativity. Rarely will you find such unique and imaginative graphics, but they were all coordinated. There was no sense of clutter. Even though the library's carpeting and furniture were rather boring in color, the signs gave the library a decorator look, complete with the trendiest color combinations. Unlike commercial signs, these homemade treasures were also meant to entertain. They couldn't help but tickle the funny bone, especially in the young adult area. Yet these talented staffers had done their homework, and their signs provided the information customers needed in precisely the form that they could most easily use it.

All library staffs, of course, cannot boast outstanding graphic artists. Such unique signs may not be an option in your situation. However, consider whether your signage budget is large enough to purchase signs big enough and prominent enough to attract the attention of your customers. Professionally produced outdoor signs are probably essential since they must be able to withstand the elements for many years to come. However, your parent institution, local government agency, or highway department may be able to provide some of these signs free of cost. For indoor signs, however, think carefully about the best use of available funds. Consider using the capital outlay budget to purchase equipment for producing your own signs.

One of the best things about purchasing your own supplies and equipment is that you need not anticipate all the signs you'll need ahead of time. Developing a signage system is best done slowly, and you'll have a much better idea what you need after you've been in the building a while. It is a good idea to delay installation of a professional signage system until you become accustomed to the new setup. On-site sign-making supplies and equipment will give you the freedom to go on making signs as you discover new needs. The library above had no equipment. Their total budget was only a few hundred dollars, but it didn't prevent them from producing good-looking signs. In fact, in the end, I really think that their poverty resulted in more effective signage specially focused on their library's unique needs.

Word Processing and Desktop Publishing Programs

Even if you have no artists on the staff, computers have made it possible to produce your own signs with only a minimal financial outlay. Color ink-jet printers do an excellent job of creating professional-looking, spur-of-the-moment signs. Here are some proven ideas that should produce good results.

Select your sign-making software. Microsoft Word is fine. You may also wish to experiment with Microsoft Publisher or some other desktop publishing program.

Choose the right materials. For smaller signs, purchase white card stock that's thin enough for your printer to handle. For larger signs, card stock alone will probably not be thick enough to keep your signs rigid. Purchase foam board, and become proficient with using the spray adhesive that professional designers use. Just remember that it's pretty toxic and must be used outdoors.

Produce larger signs inexpensively. There's more than one way to get extra-large fonts and graphics. Many software programs allow you to print out your signs in 8 ½ x 11 inch sections, then mount the pieces on Foam-Core like a jigsaw puzzle. Photocopying makes it possible to blow up an original to a larger size, but unless you use a color copier, your output is reduced to black and white. Visit your local copy center and check into the cost of blowing up signs to the required sizes—compared to professional signage, this will probably be a bargain. Then decide which signs must be larger than your printer can handle, and estimate the total cost.

Make your signs last longer. Consider purchasing a laminator since laminated signs last longer. If a laminating machine is beyond your budget, remember that you can always cover your signs with the delayed bond vinyl sold in rolls for covering paperbacks. You can purchase it from nearly all library suppliers. Just be very careful. Creases and bubbles make a laminated sign hard to read.

Touring the Library as a Customer

Take a good look at your library building. Imagine yourself as a customer looking for information or for a specific book. Start jotting down possible places for signs, together with their locations. Ask other staff members and volunteers to do the same. Gradually develop a complete sign list that includes input from several people. What are the unique challenges of your building? What does the user see as he or she enters the library? What is invisible from the entrance? What building design features lend themselves especially well to signage? Where will it be difficult to place a sign? How can you best display information at the point of need? Make notes as you consider each of these questions.

Talk with others about the vocabulary you will use. Select the most readily understood names for rooms and services. Decide once and for all whether you will use the word *magazines* or *periodicals.* Don't change your mind halfway through the project. Decide how you will hang your signs. Fishing line works fine with a dropped acoustic-tile ceiling. However, it's a challenge to keep your signs straight. Invest in a carpenter's level and a good wooden yardstick.

Settle on one very readable type font. If you're using Microsoft Word to produce your signs, experiment with "WordArt," a feature that allows you to enlarge text quickly without manually changing type size each time. Just be sure you stick to basic shapes and readable type. Long skinny signs are hard to read, so condensed type fonts are a good choice. If you prefer more rounded letters, you can always break the line in two. Limit your color palette to two colors unless you intend to develop a color-coded signage system like the "wayfaring" systems that hospitals sometimes use.

Begin making "dummy" signs; in other words, tape pieces of scrap paper together into different shapes and sizes. Experiment with different colors, different type fonts. Use masking tape to position them. Then check to see whether they are visible from the entrance or from other decision points in the library. Conduct on-site tests if possible to see how real customers respond to your dummy signs. If you have access to a light meter, use it to learn how much light falls on a sign. The best-designed sign is useless if it is placed in such a poorly lit area that it can't be seen by your customers. Once your actual signs have been in place for a while, decide whether any should be added or relocated.

Of course, it's always nice to get some input from a professional. Try to enlist the help of a designer in your community on a pro bono or volunteer basis. Ask for advice on graphic standards like typography, colors, and layout. If such a kind soul can just walk through your building, you can get dozens of practical ideas to incorporate in your project.

A Sign System Is a Work in Process

Whether you employ a professional signage designer or make your signs in-house, you have not solved your problems once and for all. Even if your crystal ball is in good working order and you somehow manage to place all the right signs in the right places, this blissful state will not long continue. Libraries are changing at an astounding pace. We librarians seem to spend half our work lives moving things around. One area may begin its existence as a listening area, then be converted to a space for young adults, and ultimately become a computer lab. For this reason, be wary of building directories. They must change as the library changes. Why not produce a map with areas designated by numbers or letters? Then you can list the collection names or subjects on the side. Take a look at the directories in your local shopping mall. They usually have a modular section for the text (names of stores) but leave the professionally produced map unchanged. Theirs are far more elaborate than you can afford, but they have the same problem of accommodating change.

I hope that my ecstasies over the charms of homemade signs above have not left you with the impression that I do not appreciate, even occasionally salivate over, the signage systems designed by professional designers. If you can afford their wares, professionally produced signage can go a long way toward making your library more enticing. However, one problem I've encountered with professional sign vendors is that they seem to go out of business with disturbing rapidity. This can become a major problem when your modular signage components are so unique that they cannot be used with components supplied by another vendor. Think twice if you hear a vendor bragging about a "revolutionary new design."

Signage is yet another example of how the library can emulate the bookstore's marketing strategy without the bookstore's marketing budget. Although professional designers can add much to your signage project, there is never a price tag on creativity. Yet those talented staff members will need time to work their magic, and time is a scarce commodity in a library. Take a good look at their job descriptions and consider how sign making and other marketing responsibilities can be incorporated.

Few tasks have a higher priority in a library than providing good signage. Since customers cannot find the materials they are seeking without good direction, the core values of the library may actually be in jeopardy. In addition to serving this vital information function, signage also makes a big impact on the public's first impression and response to the library, thus serving more than one basic customer need. Considering what a key ingredient signage is to the library's success, don't let it simmer on the back burner. Time spent on signage will never be wasted, so give it the attention it really deserves.

RESOURCES

Bosman, E., et al. "Creating the User-Friendly Library by Evaluating Patron Perceptions of Signage." *Reference Services Review* 25 (1997): 71–82.

Naylor, B. "Just a Minute—." *Library & Information Update* 1 (April 2002): 21.

chapter 11

Marketing Our Wares

Have you ever noticed that librarians have what you might call split personalities when it comes to the subject of marketing? On the one hand, marketing is trendy right now, possibly because library science has been looking to the business world for ideas and terminology. We've embraced modern management theories and experimented with "au courant" practices like cross-functional teams. In fact, we try to run our libraries according to sound business principles. Since marketing is an important focus in the business world, it has become hot in the library world as well.

There's another side of our collective library brain, however, that is not comfortable with the term. We associate marketing with crass commercialism. We are all too aware of its negative connotations, and we want our libraries to rise above shallow materialism. In fact, we sometimes see our libraries as bastions of civilization and reason, too noble to associate with the more tawdry marketplace.

John Workman, of Creighton University, defines marketing as "the process of understanding what your customers want, and then designing and delivering products and services that fit those needs."[1] This definition should present no difficulty for librarians who do sincerely wish to serve their customers better. Maybe the problem lies with marketing's first cousin, "advertising." To those of us who feel besieged by telemarketers and junk mail, *advertising* may mean merely high-pressure attempts to make people buy what they don't need. However, people do need libraries. We know that the resources and services we provide will help people live happier, more successful lives. Since many people in our communities don't know this, we must find ways to tell them. Ultimately, that means that we must advertise. Effective advertising should attract rather than repel. It need not be unpleasant or invasive of privacy. Perhaps the best advertising simply uses the most effective methods of communication to provide information of interest to our actual and potential customers.

Distinguishing between Kinds of Support

Why should the library advertise? Isn't the main thing to provide consistent, high-quality service to our customers? It comes as a shock to many librarians that most of their community hardly ever use the library. Library usage varies with different types of libraries and different parts of the country, but there is ample evidence that the percentage of people who have visited the library, checked out a video, or otherwise made use of its services is probably not as large as you think. Find out for yourself how many people have used their library cards during the past year. Of course, the number looks pretty impressive, but when compared to the total community that the library serves, it becomes clear that library users represent a minority.

Librarians are not usually well trained at statistics and so may claim inflated usership. Data are of little use if you don't know what they really say about your community. Don't mix apples and oranges. If yours is a city library, sample your customers to find out how many live outside the city limits so you can compare city residents with city library users. If yours is a county library and the library system serves the entire population of the county, compare this figure with the number of active customers in all county branches. Active users, however, are not people who signed up for a library card ten years ago and never returned. In looking over tables of reported library usage, I've found many peculiar aberrations, such as a county library that boasts that 178 percent of residents have library cards. This kind of creative use of statistics, in addition to being silly, is dangerous when you find yourself actually believing it. I used to think bookstores were fortunate because they cannot fool themselves in this way. Either they sold books or they didn't sell books. Recent revelations of creative accounting by large corporations like Enron and WorldCom have made me realize that we're all more than capable of fooling ourselves and misleading our customers.

If your library is well used, and reasonable numbers of local residents are taking advantage of your services, why should you worry about the ones who don't? The reason, of course, is that those people who have never entered your portals have as much power over the library as your best customers. To grow and prosper, the library needs widespread support. It needs the approval of the majority of the residents to carry a bond election; it needs the support of the university faculty and administration to build the new addition or successfully oppose a major budget cut. In most cases, when big issues are at stake, it is not your customers who decide them but rather the larger community.

As we all know, however, there are different kinds of library support, and it is entirely possible that a supporter need never have checked out a book. Yet if local residents don't spend time in the library, then the knowledge of what the library is doing must come to them. This means that if you are to reach everyone in the community, some of your strategies must be directed at attracting people to the library itself and others at presenting an image of the library to the outside world.

Let's consider attracting people to the library first. To do this, we must market or advertise the library's resources and services. This means focusing on our dual goal of first bringing customers to the product and then making the product so enticing that they will wish to purchase it or, in our case, check it out. Many chapters in this book, both directly or indirectly, relate to marketing. For example, both effective signage and attractive displays are part of the bookstore's in-house strategy for connecting customers with books. However, the public first must become aware of and then attracted to the bookstore or library. This means we must advertise.

Learning to Use the Tools of Marketing

Bookstores and libraries share a wonderful advantage in this regard. Their products are endlessly interesting. Books are mines of fascinating information, colorful pictures, and enticing jackets that can all be used in the marketing effort. It is not as if marketing is new to libraries; we have long been producing publicity materials like newsletters and brochures. But these are generally activities that take a second or third place to more traditional library activities, especially as funding has dwindled. The bookstore in our comparison, however, cannot survive unless marketing becomes a top priority, so it does not relegate these activities to the back burner. It cannot afford to leave such a key responsibility to chance because that would threaten the old bottom line.

Libraries rarely have a clear marketing plan. Instead, they do a little of this and a little of that. For example, they start a newsletter and then abandon it when staffing gets tight or some other project takes center stage. They produce a brochure with little attention to design principles and fail to notice when it becomes outdated. Stationary is reordered with the old zip or area code left uncorrected. A talented work-study student or library page produces a snazzy website, complete with the latest java script and a dozen spelling errors. Of course, when he or she graduates, no one knows how to update the site, so it continues to advertise last year's program series. All this adds up to marketing gone awry. All this underscores the need for a marketing plan.

Demographics

Most public librarians think they know a good deal about the reading, viewing, and listening habits of their customers. If they're doing a good job with collection development, they keep an eagle eye on the materials that circulate frequently and those that don't. Over the course of time, they develop a picture of local residents based on the kinds of materials that are most popular in the library. For example, they may view the community as largely composed of young families because children's books circulate briskly. They may assume that theirs is a community largely composed of older people since they're very aware of their seniors who enjoy gentler, less sexually explicit, or less violent fiction.

To some extent, the picture of the community that emerges from circulation statistics is valid. In other words, these are the people who are currently using the library. The question is, "Who is not using the library?" Sometimes a cycle develops over the course of time. Books, tapes, and videos selected primarily for seniors circulate well, so the library purchases more of them. Seniors, visiting the library for the first time, find that the library has lots of material that they will enjoy, so they return again and again. This means that circulation rises, and the library buys more materials for seniors.

The strategy of purchasing materials we know will be used is a good one. However, suppose there is another sizable group in the community we have not identified—Generation X, for instance. Unbeknownst to you and your staff, they have visited the library, found little of interest, and decided the library is not for them. There is probably no way to become aware of these people unless you take a good look at the demographics of your community.

Census information is, of course, helpful, but it is also probable that a great deal of research has been conducted by the business community in your area to identify customers and potential customers. Does the library belong to the local chamber of commerce? There are few memberships that are more useful. Issues that affect local business also affect the library, and, of course, the needs of the local business community should be an important consideration when selecting materials. Your local chamber undoubtedly has statistical information that can help you identify the elements in the community that you are not reaching. Their monthly meetings can be an excellent source of informal information about the community. In fact, you will probably discover that businesspeople view the community entirely differently from the way the library sees it, and some of their insights can be extremely useful.

Some librarians feel that they have wasted time and money trying to reach groups that are not really interested in using the library. It is certainly true that some people will never become regular customers no matter what you do. However, it is often the case that a library purchases materials to serve a specific population and then keeps the fact a secret. They expect the targeted group to somehow sniff out these materials and find their way to the library. People need to be told that the library has something they want. For example, a newspaper column can alert them. Tacking up posters in the grocery store is another possibility, a display in the local bank yet another. The point is that if these people don't come into the library in the first place, they will never discover the materials and services awaiting them. Then librarians say to themselves, "I knew that that they wouldn't come, so I'll go back to buying for our real customers." Somehow the library must find ways to reach out to the wider community.

Over time, the neighborhood in which a library is located changes. Once, young families with school-age children filled the library and heavily influenced the development of services. Now those children have grown up and moved away, leaving their parents, who have developed different needs and interests with the passing years. An urban library in a once affluent neighborhood is now surrounded by urban blight. New immigrant groups keep arriving and changing the character of neighborhoods. One wave becomes Americanized and moves out into the suburbs, making way for another wave of immigrants who know nothing of libraries or have different values and interests.

The library that fails to adapt to these changes is doomed. There is really no age or ethnic group, no socioeconomic segment of the population, that can't enjoy more productive lives by becoming active library users. In the case of immigrant groups and minorities, there may be special difficulties in communicating the library's message. The suggestions above may prove useless because members of the group don't speak English or they don't have bank accounts. They may do their shopping at ethnic grocery stores of which you are unaware. How then do you reach them?

Identifying segments of the community is the first step. You may be aware that as you do your errands around town, you are coming in contact with an increasing number of people with Spanish accents, but you don't generally see these people in the library. Who are they? They may be Mexican immigrants, but you do not have enough information to make this judgment. They may have arrived from Central or South America. In fact, you may be mistaking a Portuguese accent for Spanish.

Sources of demographic information like the census and chamber of commerce surveys can be very helpful in obtaining information, but they are often out-of-date and do not always provide a clear picture. If you are a public librarian, it is a very good idea to maintain close working relationships with the other departments in your county or municipality. Immigrants and minorities often have special needs, and the head of the human services department, for example, can probably tell you a lot more about them than any official report. I've discovered that health workers, social workers, public health nurses, and people in similar positions often know where ethnic and minority groups congregate. They know where you can post a Spanish-language flyer inviting people to the library. They know the president of a neighborhood organization who might be willing to give the library a place on the agenda of the next meeting.

As helpful as it is to obtain information from other government offices, it is even better to talk directly with representatives of immigrant and minority constituencies. If any members of these groups are already using the library, introduce yourself to them. Ask if you can sit down and talk for a few minutes. Explain that you want to know how the library can serve the group better. You might even ask your library user if he or she would be willing to become a kind of library ambassador to his or her community.

Discovering Hidden Constituencies

This last idea is a wonderful marketing strategy if you have the opportunity, but there are probably groups in your community who use the library so rarely that you will encounter them only outside the library. That means that you will need to take advantage of the few opportunities you do have to meet them. Maybe you've discovered the joys of Thai cuisine, and your orbit has widened to include a small oriental grocery where you can find coconut milk and lemongrass. Get to know their staff and the community they serve. If business is slow, start up a conversation with the clerk at the checkout counter. You may have discovered, for example, that they sell many items intended for Vietnamese dishes, so this gives you an opening to ask about the Vietnamese community. How large is it? Where do they live? You need not cross-examine the poor clerk; just friendly interest will elicit a surprising amount of information.

One would think that academic and special libraries would know precisely who their community is and be able to target their marketing much more easily than a public library. Theoretically this is true. Academic librarians know that their community consists of faculty, students, and administrative staff, but their image of these potential library customers may be inaccurate or outdated. For example, some academic departments may have grown in recent years, while others have shrunk. The library may be continuing to buy materials and provide services for departments that, though good library users, no longer represent a sizable portion of the community. Student interests are different from what they were ten years ago, and so the way they use the library may have changed as well.

Special libraries tend to see their parent businesses, hospitals, and other organizations entirely through the eyes of the clerks and other support staff who are their usual contacts. Yet it is the managerial staff who control the library budget, and they may be all but invisible. The librarian's challenge is to obtain an inside view of the workings and priorities of the organization. Much as we all like to avoid committees, these can provide opportunities to meet informally with decision makers. A more formal approach would be to set up interviews with managerial staff. Don't try to tell them about the library; instead, ask them about their own needs and priorities.

Developing a Marketing Plan

Marketing is such a complex subject and involves so many aspects of the library's operation that it requires a very organized approach. Business organizations have developed the "marketing plan" to make sure that the entire organization is working together. Again, their bottom line gives them an advantage. Since the bottom line is to sell merchandise, and marketing is essential to achieving this goal, the roles of the different departments fall into place.

Begin with Your Mission Statement

We have already identified increasing community participation in the library as our equivalent of the bottom line. However, when it comes to marketing, it does not provide the same degree of direction as a monetary goal. There are probably thousands of ways to attract people to libraries, but most of them would have nothing to do with the library's mission. Therefore, when the library sets about developing a marketing plan, its mission statement must be at the core.

If your library does not have such a concise statement of purpose, now is the time to write one. Some libraries have created a mission statement as an obligatory exercise. Staff may simply have been going through the motions, and your library's mission statement may contain nothing but platitudes and plagiarized verbiage from other libraries.

If tomorrow you were to hold a brainstorming session, the creative library staff could come up with dozen of ways the library could become more visible in the community. However, they'd also come up with a lot of ideas that would not be worth pursuing. The expenditure in time and effort would detract from other more important projects, and the results would not be worth the investment. How will you know which ideas fit into this category? There's no easy answer, and libraries frequently become sidetracked with less productive projects. However, the library's mission statement can provide a reasonably direct road map for getting you to your destination. That's why it is worth putting the time into a mission statement that really has some "oomph" to it.

Identify Community Needs

Once the mission statement is in place, you will want to do some extensive research on the needs of your community. Again, many of those needs cannot really be met by the library, but it's surprising how many of them can be reworded as a need for information.

As librarians we are accustomed to measuring what we do, in other words, how many books are circulated, how many customers use the Internet. For our needs assessment, we must look honestly at what we are not doing. In the section above, we discussed sources of information about the community like census data and chamber of commerce research. It is helpful to conduct our own surveys, but we must distinguish between those distributed at the library and those intended to reach the broader community. Of course, we want to serve our regular customers better, but our marketing effort should be focused on people who do not fall into this category.

Over the years, I have found focus groups to be especially useful. Getting together a small group, comprised mainly of nonusers, and encouraging them to freely discuss their needs can be enlightening. I've found, however, that discussing the library may be a little like talking about religion. It's a kind of sacred cow that no one wants to criticize. Seek out someone in your community who has worked with focus groups in the business arena. Find out if he would be willing to participate in library focus groups, or, even better, ask him to train library staff and members of your Friends group in focus group–facilitating techniques. If you don't have access to an expert, the books listed at the end of this chapter will provide a wealth of information.

Interviews can also reap a lot of useful information, but they must be carefully structured to be really productive. Again, search your community for a marketing professional. Although we as librarians are especially good at finding answers in books and periodicals, the guidance of someone who has extensive personal experience can be even more useful.

The value of surveys, focus groups, and interviews is that they enable you to learn what your customers want. Deciding how you will respond to this information is at the heart of your marketing plan. How will you define customer service? What elements in the library's current program most clearly respond to these needs? How will you and the staff adapt or change the library in view of what you have learned? Then, once you have fine-tuned the library to respond to these needs, how will you spread the word?

Identify Obstacles to Achieving Goals

How will you set about providing better customer service, and what are the obstacles that will make it difficult to make improvements? You'll probably discover that there are many. There is little point in identifying the goal if you don't really understand why the library has failed to achieve the goal in the past. Most library staffs have always been interested in making their customers happy, but could it be possible that, once again, they have been planning in terms of what they think customers should want rather than their expressed need? Even the best focus groups and interviews will not result in change if, deep down, library staff believe that they know best.

Distinguish between Your Primary and Secondary Markets

Remember that you began the process of developing a marketing plan by focusing on your mission statement. Don't forget to revisit it often. It will serve as your road map and will help you avoid spinning your wheels or concentrating your efforts on less productive projects. Then define your market. Who are your primary customers? What is your real service area? In other words, who are you actually funded to serve? Who are the other people who have come to depend on your services but are not students at your university or residents of your municipality? How supportive can you be of their needs without penalizing your primary target group? It's important to confront this question early in your planning.

Let me give you an example from my own experience. Our state consortium recently upgraded to a new automation system. It makes it possible for patrons to initiate holds, regardless of where in the state a book or media program is owned. Libraries soon learned that their customers were placing their holds just as if the items were owned by their own library. However, much of the time they were actually initiating interlibrary loans. Naturally, use of this service skyrocketed. Postage costs went through the roof. In the end, each library had to take a deep breath and pause to decide whether it could continue to provide this service. Each had to balance the needs of its own patrons with service to other state residents. If no limits were placed on holds, would other services need to be curtailed to cover increased costs? Did the improved interlibrary loan service their own customers were enjoying make up for the increased workload generated by customers outside the library service area? Ultimately, each library made its own decision, and for the most part interlibrary loan remains a booming business. However, each made certain adjustments depending on how it viewed its responsibility to its own customers and to the larger community. In this case, the new system forced the libraries to confront the issue. In other cases, there is no pressure to make decisions, and libraries can inadvertently lose their focus.

Narrow and Focus the Goal

Once these decisions are made, you will know more about your primary market as well as the relative importance of reaching other constituencies. Next consider what broad results you want to achieve. Let's say that the result should be an increase in library usage. Even better, you might begin immediately to think in concrete terms and specify that the result will be a 10 percent or 25 percent increase in library usage. How might you achieve this end? Break this broad result up into component parts that are easier to work with. You might, for instance, establish broad categories like book circulation, Internet use, meeting room use, and children's programs, setting goals for each of these services. Then work with the library staff to further define those aims. List both short- and long-term goals that will contribute to attaining the goal. Then decide which are most doable.

I hate to use that old cliché, but you're looking for ways to get the most bang for the buck. The library lacks both the money and the staffing to carry out the kind of marketing campaign that a large corporation might envision. The secret of success lies in the creative use of the resources we do have at our disposal, including Friends of the Library groups and donations of professional services. Consider what other resources might be available in your community and how you might use them wisely. Discard elaborate plans that will interfere with the library's efficient operation, but remember that the marketing effort is also essential to the library's well-being.

Identify the Competition

Begin organizing both the long- and short-term goals and objectives that have survived this process into a plan. Before committing the library to any of them, investigate each thoroughly. Concurrently, begin conducting your marketing research. Business organizations at this point identify their competition. Libraries too have competition, although it may not be as important an element. As we've already made clear, bookstores compete with the library for customers. Are there other businesses in your community that also take customers away from the library? What about other departments within your own organization? For example, university libraries may compete with academic departments and with the administrative unit that maintains student computer labs or provides tutoring services.

Businesses and departments in direct competition with the library are not the only external considerations. Where does the library fit into the big picture? What is its role in the larger external environment? There are probably some elements in that environment that are actually hostile to the library and other elements that, though not hostile, interfere with the library's productivity. What are they? From where do the library's challenges originate? Of course, we create many of our own problems but not all of them by any means. Consider the attitude of the library's parent organization. How do your county commissioners feel about the library? Do they understand its importance? Are there individuals or possibly administrative departments that seem to have a negative attitude toward the library that affects the achievement of library goals?

Once you have a clear picture of the library's environment, consider the future. Where do you see the library in five years? Ten years? How might the challenges you've identified in the environment affect the library? Consider best- and worst-case scenarios. Then think about how the library's own strengths and weaknesses fit into these scenarios. How can the library maximize its strengths? How might it be possible to either eliminate weaknesses or minimize their importance by pointing the library in other directions?

It's a good idea, once you have a clear picture of the community, to subdivide it into what the business world calls *market segments.* Seniors have different library needs from young singles, and newly arrived Hispanic residents need different services from longtime residents. To bring each group into the library, a somewhat different approach will be needed. Of course, many people fit into more than one group. That's fine. For example, women aren't just interested in women's materials. They also have educational, recreational, and professional needs that may have little to do with their role as women. Just be sure your information is accurate and you are not working with a picture of your community as it was ten or twenty years ago.

Again, consider your secondary markets—those customers who are not in your service area or who can't vote for your bond issue. There are some very good reasons for trying to reach them (like improved attendance figures), but they are not your primary target. Do you think that, over the years, the library has inadvertently targeted its services at these groups? This gets us into the subject of priorities. Your creative library staff will by this point have generated many good ideas—too many actually. You've reached the point where you must prioritize your goals. You can't serve every potential customer and meet every community need. Which strategies will you pursue and why? Which will best enable the library to achieve its goal?

Next, go back to the demographic research you collected, and consider primary markets that you are not reaching. Who are the groups in your community that are not making use of the library? If you haven't already done so, design ways to sample the library's users, and compare the results with what you know about the larger community. Analyze the results, and adapt goals and objectives to focus some of the library's marketing efforts on underserved populations. What new services might attract these groups? How can the library reach them more effectively?

How is your library perceived by the community? Are your customers satisfied with the services you provide? Why don't other people take advantage of your services? This is where the results of those focus groups, surveys, and interviews are important. There is no point in redesigning services and announcing these changes to the community if people don't want or need them. What is it that makes the library unique? What does the library have to offer that the bookstore doesn't? What does the library have that the campus computer labs don't?

Establish a Marketing Budget

Each of your plans has a price tag. What do you estimate to be your direct and indirect expenses? Don't forget to include personnel costs in your budget; when staff are occupied with marketing activities, other jobs may not be getting done. For example, it may be necessary to hire temporary staff or outsource some functions. The library's standard one-year budget cycle is not usually sufficient to achieve major marketing goals. Consider working with a twelve-month planning phase and a twelve-month implementation phase. If you are thinking in terms of making major changes in the library, you will need to plan for at least this period of time. You may even want to think in terms of a five-year plan.

Then decide what you will do if funds are not forthcoming. Remember that when you're planning even two years ahead, a lot of unexpected things can happen, and budget crises are frequent in libraries. If your library experiences an unexpected budget cut, how will it affect the marketing effort? In other words, what is your fallback position? How can you move forward without the funding you anticipated? The reason for dealing with this now is that a budget cut can throw the library into a tailspin. The anger and anxiety generated can cause staff to view all projects as impossible or doomed. Yet the need for a marketing program is never so critical as during a budget crisis.

Establish a Time Line

Next, develop a time line. If you're thinking in terms of the two-year plan above, break the plan up into a series of interim steps. Which ones depend on other goals being achieved first? Remember that, in a sense, you will be planning to plan. The marketing plan is merely a road map, and it is important to have a clear, objective way of establishing that projects are on track. Consider how much time will be required to advance to each step or rung on the ladder and then set a date for each. Can you reasonably expect to achieve the end result twenty-four months from the starting date? If not, you may need to rework your budget, your goals, or your time line. I find it difficult, however, to make specific plans more than two years ahead. So many new issues will emerge; so many participants will come and go. If you find yourself with a plan that seems to go on indefinitely, it may be worth rethinking the plan to fit into a two-year time frame.

After the excitement of the initial planning stage dies down and enthusiasm begins to wane, little things will begin to bog you down. The staff begin saying to one another, "No, we can't do that now because this or that has come up. We'll get back to marketing next week or next month." Eventually, of course, the marketing plan is forgotten. Deadlines are, therefore, important. The first time the library misses a deadline, it should be viewed as a crisis demanding immediate attention. Often it's the failure to reach a decision that holds up a project, so determine when each decision must be made. Outline each phase of your marketing plan, including dates when each phase will be completed.

How will you measure the success of the marketing effort? This must be decided in advance because we have a naughty habit of cheating. In other words, we want to feel successful, and so we pat ourselves on the back for achievements that have little to do with our initial intention. At the beginning of the project, it is essential to establish clear outcome measures. Then, at the end of the period, measure actual results against them. Decide in advance just how success will be measured because, again, there is always that tendency to try to justify your efforts even if they were largely unsuccessful.

Leverage the Impact of the Marketing Plan

As we've developed the library's marketing plan, our emphasis has been on bringing new faces into the library and better serving the needs of both old and new customers. However, we're also aware that there will be many people who, despite our best efforts, may never use the library personally. Some of these non-customers are essential to the library's success. The library must find ways to bring their message to community decision makers. Although many may be regular library customers, you can't count on it. A special effort must be made to reach this community segment because they wield so much power. Thus, a significant part of the plan should involve reaching them. How will a public library change the opinions of county commissioners? How will an academic library convince the dean or president that the library is worthy of more generous funding? As we've already discussed, invisibility to corporate decision makers is a uniquely troublesome problem for special libraries.

The real decision makers may never enter the doors of the library, so other methods of reaching them will need to be devised. Think of them as a special marketing segment that will require highly innovative techniques. In some respects, this is your most important marketing segment, but there are other groups that need special attention. Annual reports and funding requests are the ways libraries most often communicate with decision makers, and both can be used more effectively in the marketing effort. However, your marketing plan should also include new avenues of communication. Is it possible to meet with your decision makers more often? Might some of them occasionally attend board or staff meetings? Be sure that they are on your distribution lists for library newsletters, brochures, and press releases. Let them know what the library is doing to reach underserved populations. Be sure the library's name is everywhere.

Each type of library can use a somewhat different approach. Often, decision makers holding local offices serve in a volunteer capacity. Since they may not be aware of useful sources of information, public libraries can help inform them. Make a point of supplying the mayor or councilmen and -women with reports and magazine articles about problems that concern local governments. Special libraries can attach cover sheets to every article or report they send out. And distribute business cards freely. Academic libraries can become more fully involved with campus activities. These are just a few of the many possibilities. Consider a two-pronged approach. Provide a service that decision makers find useful, and then make them aware of the wide variety of services that are available to the community as a whole.

Schedule the Production of Promotional Materials

Promotional materials pose a special challenge because they always require more time than you initially imagine. When they're not ready in time to support other marketing activities, the result can be devastating. For example, the brochure must be ready in time to be distributed at the library gala. The newsletter must go out in time to advertise the upcoming program, and a whole series of promotional materials must be timed precisely to lead up to the bond election. Consider how the marketing plan is affected by local community events. How will you use each as an occasion to get out the library's message?

Speaking of promotional materials, it is easy to see that bookstores put a great deal of money into their glossy, full-color masterpieces. Yet desktop publishing has made it possible for any library to produce newsletters, brochures, and other publications that come quite close to rivaling the bookstore's. Good design costs no more than bad, but no matter how talented the staff, they cannot produce quality materials if they must borrow bits of time from their regular duties.

A marketing plan should be a written document. However, I am always a little suspicious of written plans. I have had all too many negative experiences with strategic plans that had no impact on the library's operation, and it is too often the case that a formal marketing plan will be similarly filed and forgotten. Nevertheless, the high degree of coordination needed to pull together different departments and groups makes it necessary to have a common reference. Include in the plan a regular schedule of meetings to review progress, and don't type the last period or press the print button until you have set times and dates.

Time must be blocked out when staff can concentrate on a project and get it done. Marketing is not an extra; it is a necessity. In the next chapter, we will delve more deeply into the subject of desktop publishing, and I think you will be amazed at how even small libraries can make a big splash. Like everything else that is important to the library, however, it requires time, talent, and ongoing commitment.

NOTE

1. J. Workman, "Marketing Basics in a Changing Information Age," *Nebraska Library Association Quarterly* 30 (winter 1999): 3–11.

RESOURCES

Block, M. "The Secret of Library Marketing: Make Yourself Indispensable." *American Libraries* 32 (September 2001): 48–50.

Burks, S. "Marketing Your Library, Marketing Yourself." *Arkansas Libraries* 59 (December 2002): 19–20.

Cox, M. A. "Colorado Library Marketing Council: Giving Librarians the Tools to Market Their Skills." *Colorado Libraries* 27 (winter 2001): 37–40.

Creaser, J. "Through a Library User's Eye: The Marketing Images." *PNLA Quarterly* 66 (winter 2002): 7–9.

Cuesta, Y. J., et al. "Getting Ready to Market the Library to Culturally Diverse Communities." *Alki* 18 (March 2002): 6–9.

Fink, D., et al. "Marketing Libraries." *Colorado Libraries* 27 (winter 2001): 5–40.

Lutz, P. C. "Beyond Parallel Universes: Marketing a High School Library Program to the Community and to Students." *Colorado Libraries* 27 (winter 2001): 23–24.

Sass, R. K. "Marketing the Worth of Your Library." *Library Journal* 127 (June 15, 2002): 37–38.

Sutherland, S. "Passion, Practice, Partnership and Politics: Marketing the Future of Public Libraries." *Australasian Public Libraries and Information Services* 15 (June 2002): 61–69.

chapter 12

Creating Promotional Materials

Let's return to our bookstore tour and take a look at their promotional materials. At the entrance, the service desks, and the literature racks throughout the store, we find a variety of printed materials. All the larger chains publish a newsletter or magazine highlighting new services and promotions. True, they are usually much glitzier and more expensive than most libraries can afford. However, careful perusal will make it clear that such publications are the result of applying basic design principles to documents produced with standard desktop publishing programs. Although your library may not be able to afford full-color printing and high-gloss paper, it can achieve a very credible version with a talented staff member and a less than state-of-the-art computer software program.

The Growth of Desktop Publishing

Central to any library marketing effort is desktop publishing savvy. Whether it's an annual report, an advertisement for an upcoming library event, a fund-raising brochure, or even a lowly bookmark, most of the printed materials we produce require a basic knowledge of desktop publishing. A few years ago, the library was in good company when it circulated mimeographed circulars and produced hand-lettered announcements. Before the arrival of personal computers, all but the largest businesses did the same. Most local stores did not have the money to hire professionals to design their publications, and local copy shacks had not yet made their appearance.

Today, many libraries continue to produce essentially the same kind of materials, but they are no longer in good company. Sophisticated word processors with desktop publishing features, as well as specialized programs like QuarkXPress, PageMaker, and InDesign, have made it possible for almost anyone to create professional-looking promotional materials. Patrons accustomed to reading graphically sophisticated annual reports and responding to eye-catching fund-raising materials may take one look at the library's boring attempts and toss them aside.

Like the bookstore, the library produces a wide variety of publications. Here are some examples of publications that your library may be currently producing or that could make the library more visible to the community.

- Annual reports
- Business forms
- Accessions lists
- Bibliographies and reading lists
- Brochures
- Flyers
- Posters
- Letterhead stationery
- Notepaper
- "Thank-you" cards
- Business cards
- Advertisements
- Newsletters
- Labels
- Presentations (e.g., PowerPoint presentations)
- Booklets
- Manuals
- Signs
- Proposals

Isn't It a Lot of Work?

You might ask why it's worth putting staff time into desktop publishing. For example, why should you consider desktop publishing when you are writing an annual report? Isn't the main thing just to get the darn thing done, distribute it to your board of directors, and then forget it? Definitely not; the annual report is an opportunity to brag about your library's accomplishments. It is potentially an excellent marketing tool but not if no one wants to read it. The same is true of the library's strategic plan. Share it with your community. Allow them to be full participants in the library's hopes and dreams. How many people have read your library's mission statement? Nothing sells the library better than your brief or abbreviated mission statement printed on stationery, in the brochure that lists your hours and services, on flyers, and in newsletters.

Your attention to design principles can help focus the reader's attention on the library's accomplishments. Design can make important information stand out and catch the eye of the reader. It's no longer difficult to use tables and charts to present statistics in a way that makes it easy for the reader to understand what's really happening. Color can also keep readers interested. It focuses their attention on the positive achievements you want to emphasize. You might even consider condensing the report into a brochure and making it available to the library's customers. Don't hide your light under a bushel. You and the library staff have spent the past year serving the community and developing new services. This is your opportunity to make sure people know about them.

Competing for Your Customers' Attention

Since the advent of desktop computers, as well as relatively inexpensive word processing and graphics programs, it seems as if everyone is sending out snazzy newsletters and other publications. You may be wondering how the library can compete with such professional-looking productions. In fact, you may be feeling that the library simply can't compete. Maybe you think that there's far too much work to be done to divert staff energies to anything as nonessential as impressive marketing materials. Unfortunately, the truth is that you're already in competition. Your library is competing for the attention of people who have become accustomed to well-designed materials that are arriving daily in their mailboxes, eye-catching magazines, and elegant business stationery. If your library's publications look amateurish and unprofessional, that may well be the impression that you're giving your customers of the whole library.

Since your library owns at least several computers, you already have the equipment you need for successful desktop publishing. Your word processing software is probably adequate to produce satisfactory newsletters, brochures, and flyers without any additional expenditure. What is lacking is probably the expertise to use your software's more sophisticated features.

The Basics of Production

The essentials of desktop publishing are few in number. They are page layout, typography, graphics, and printing. All of these are skills that you are already using if you depend on a word processor for your correspondence. The next stage, however, is incorporating them into an effective design. There is probably someone on the library staff with an interest in art and design who would be more than willing to become the library's desktop publisher. There are also a number of small businesses that specialize in this kind of work and that will, for a price, produce very attractive materials for your library. The question is where do you begin?

In my own personal experience, I've found that many people have a knack for design. Sometimes they're the ones who spend hours deciding on their draperies and moving their furniture around. Sometimes they're hobbyists and crafts persons. Finding someone willing and able to learn the rudiments of desktop publishing has not generally been difficult. I have learned, however, that some people can produce a quick flyer in an hour, while others seem to make one brochure their life's work. This difference is so deeply rooted in an individual's personality that I've had little success in changing anyone. If the library staff includes a treasure who can produce acceptable work without worrying over every small detail, then you are in business. The library budget, however, probably cannot stretch to a full-time desktop publisher, no matter how talented. Consider the actual cost to your library in terms of time and materials.

Explore Both In-House and Outsourced Options

You may find that it is preferable to contract out your library's publications if you cannot produce them cheaply in the library. The problem here is that it becomes much more difficult to update information if the master file does not reside on a local computer. In your negotiations, request that the library be given a copy of the files used for the publication. If the business is unwilling to do this, you might want to reconsider, since the cost of paying to redo the publication from scratch each time changes are needed effectively puts a damper on the best of intentions.

Some libraries have had extraordinarily good luck with publications produced by high school pages, college work-study students, and volunteers. Just make sure that they finish their work, not leave it in limbo when they depart for Christmas break or get a new job. In addition, be sure they turn in copies of all word processing documents and graphics files that they used. Young people may be extraordinarily talented, but they move on with their lives. They are not always the most organized of workers and may not view spelling as a high priority. Proofread their copy carefully.

Although commercial businesses and student workers may solve most of your publishing problems, it is always better if a staff member can produce good, spur-of-the-moment publications. You yourself may be able to fill this role. Just remember, however, that you may be the kind of person who spends hours trying to get it just right; monitor your own time carefully.

Getting Started

If you'd like to give it a try, start with a template. A template is a pattern that either you or someone else has already created. That means you don't have to start from scratch. The template may include margins, type fonts, and graphics. Microsoft Word includes many basic templates, including newsletters, stationery, brochures, flyers, and even business cards and labels. MS Word also allows you to save your own additions to the template (you save them as ".dot" rather than ".doc"), so you can add boilerplate text like your mission statement and library contact information, and you need not retype or reformat this information when you create your next publication. Other libraries, however, may be your best source for templates. If you notice that a nearby library produces an especially nice newsletter, ask if you might have a copy of the file. The word processing file from which the newsletter was produced serves as a template since you can delete the actual text and retain the margins, columns, type fonts, and other formatting.

Fonts

Fledgling desktop publishers tend to go overboard. They see that Microsoft Word provides dozens of different type fonts, and they decide to use them all. It might be fun to try them out, but one or two type fonts are plenty. Restraint is essential for a professional-looking product. Remember that each font can be used in different sizes and can be boldfaced, italicized, or underlined to add variety.

Graphics

Just as all the different type fonts can be tempting, so can the hundreds of clip-art files that came with your word processing program and are so easy to find on the World Wide Web. Beginners almost always clutter up their publications with annoying clip art. Yet most people have seen those same images dozens of times. They are not impressed with yet another hackneyed graphic. There is another type of graphic accent that is often used in desktop publications. Most of us have discovered Microsoft's "Wingdings" and have had fun producing rows of things that look like this—☙❧☙❧☙❧❦❧❦🗐☏. Used judiciously, they can add interest, but once again, don't get carried away. A really well-designed page need have no graphics at all. The thoughtful use of type, as well as simple borders and boxes, can create a perfectly satisfactory product that attracts rather than annoys.

Photographs are much more appealing than clip art, but they can be difficult for a beginner. We've all seen newsletters in which photographs are nothing more than dark, blurred rectangles. The type of file, paper, and copying equipment all affect the quality of photographs. Before you build a publication around them, make sure that the final product will be clear and crisp. Otherwise, use another way to make your publication interesting. Remember too that one large photo or graphic is usually much more appealing than several small ones scattered around a page.

Paper

Next, you'll need to think about the kind of paper you'll be using. Paper can be terribly expensive so plan carefully. If you're going to use photographs frequently, then you'll probably want to choose a paper with a glossy finish. Consider whether you really want to spend that much money. Also give some thought to the weight of the paper you'll need; a brochure, for example, needs rather heavy paper. If you are printing on both sides, then you'll also need heavier paper so that ink does not bleed through. Certain types of paper are better to use with a laser printer than for offset printing. A commercial printer will recommend other papers for special projects.

Alignment

Alignment is a term you'll often hear among desktop designers. Every element on the page should align with or relate to everything else. You will therefore want to become familiar with the grids and rulers that are part of your word processing or publishing package. You might want to use a pencil to rough out blocks of type and other elements. Occasionally, a photo or block of text placed off the grid can attract attention, but more often it tends to be simply confusing.

Margins

Margins can add interest to a publication. Don't make the left, right, top, and bottom margins all the same size. For example, the eye of the viewer prefers a slightly larger margin on the bottom to ground the page. If your publication has one fold in the center (called a facing-page document), the margin nearest the fold should be smaller than the one away from it. The general rule is to make the inside margin the smallest, the top margin a little bigger, the outside bigger yet, and the bottom margin the biggest, large enough to hold down the page. Experiment with the space between columns and around photos to decide what looks best.

It's a very good idea, as you're planning a page, to divide it in thirds. You can do this with pencil and paper or you can do it in your head. You'll find that you'll have a more visually appealing layout if you place your type and graphic elements within each third. In addition, it is only common sense to decide what is the most important information you want to get across or which photographs are most interesting, then make those elements larger. Using larger and smaller type, and thicker and thinner lines, adds interest. If you know in advance which elements you want to emphasize, you can eliminate less important ones when you don't have enough space.

Getting into Print

One of the most exciting aspects of the desktop publishing revolution is the availability of relatively inexpensive printers that can produce a professional-looking product almost instantly. They allow you to produce quick, colorful signs, flyers, and other public relations materials on the fly. For example, if you have a template for advertising library programs, you can use the same design over and over, deleting out-of-date information and inserting only the specifics about the upcoming program. With a ready-to-use template and a color printer, you can create dozens of signs or advertisements in ten minutes or less. However, do-it-yourself printing is not always the best or least expensive choice, so it's a good idea to know about all the options available to you.

Make the Right Printing Choice

Budget is usually the main consideration that determines how you produce a publication. For example, if funds are not tightly restricted, color laser printers produce results that are almost undistinguishable from professionally printed materials. Ink-jet printers, however, are more than satisfactory when you need only a small number of copies. For example, if fifty copies of your library's holiday letter will suffice, then you can produce a full-color ink-jet masterpiece complete with Santa, holly, or whatever holiday graphics appeal to you. Color laser printers are faster, but their toner cartridges can be very expensive. Color photocopy machines require similarly expensive toner cartridges, so large-volume printing runs may be best left to professionals.

Get the Most Effective Publication for the Lowest Price

If you are thinking in terms of a thousand or more copies, then you will want to investigate the cost of offset printing. It never ceases to amaze me how far apart two different price quotes for printing services can be. Although one printer may be consistently less expensive than another, they may also be quoting on different processes and different papers. It is essential to get several cost estimates whenever a substantial amount of money is involved. It is also helpful to become more familiar with printing terms so that the estimates you receive are for the same products. Don't produce your publication on your own computer, print it on your desk jet printer, and then go to the printer and ask the cost of reproducing it. Instead, find out how much a publication would cost printed in only black ink, with the addition of one or more colors, and, if you're feeling unusually affluent, in full color. If you know ahead of time how the publication will be printed, your design will be more effective.

It is helpful to collect some of the more attractive advertising pieces you receive in the mail, especially the ones that don't depend on glossy paper and a lot of expensive full-color photos. This will give you a better idea of how different types of paper and the number of ink colors affect the finished publication. Produce an original that allows you some flexibility. That way if you find that you can save money by eliminating an ink color or resizing the publication, you're free to do so. Anything that makes your publication more difficult to produce will add to the price, so ask about ways to reduce the labor involved in printing.

While you're at the printer's, find out exactly what they will want from you. Will they produce the publication from your file or from your paper master? You should be aware that some software programs squeeze everything—all the elements of the publication—into one file. When you use publishing programs like PageMaker, however, a single publication usually has many files, including complete type fonts and separate graphics files. Some print shops, however, don't want to deal with your files. Instead, they prefer "camera-ready" copy, in other words, a master that is exactly as you want the finished publication to look.

Make It Perfect before Printing

Most of us have had the experience of bringing a box of brochures or bookmarks back to the library, delighted with their attractive colors and effective graphics, appreciative of the satisfying tactile experience of good paper. Suddenly we gasp. There in the midst of our beautiful creation is a typo. We proofread the copy again and again, but somehow we missed that one foolish misspelling. If the error is a particularly embarrassing one, we will have to have the publication reprinted at additional cost. If it is fairly small, we will feel obligated to let it go and distribute copies of the publication until the supply runs out. However, each time it is handed to customers, we will hold our breath, wondering if they see our mistake, wondering if they are deciding the library staff is illiterate. Ask several staff members to proofread a publication before it goes to the printers or before you photocopy a large quantity of copies. This works much better than having one person proofread a document several times. Different people will notice different things.

Sometimes the problem is not a word misspelled but a faint mark that we were sure nobody would notice. Now looking at the finished product, the offending mark seems to stand out, much clearer and more noticeable than it looked on our original copy. Experienced designers will tell you that if you don't want something to show up, it will inevitably be twice as obvious once printed.

Protect Precious Files

No matter how efficient and organized you may be, publications take a long while to produce. It is not uncommon for a printer to lose files and hard copy, so be sure you have made provisions for backup. Even if your originals are not lost, you don't want to have to start from scratch each time a change is needed. That means you will need to save the document files in a safe place.

Establish a library policy that important publication files don't reside on just one staff computer but are shared with several other people. It's a good idea for all the staff on your publications team to swap finished projects back and forth, maintaining archive folders on several computers. Crises are not uncommon. Staff members retire or resign from their positions, and no one remembers that an important publication resides only on their computers. Other staff upgrade their computers and forget to transfer all the files. Hard drives crash, viruses disable, and other tragedies assail unwary computer users.

The Joy of Scanning

Inexpensive desktop scanners have become common in libraries. At this time, you can buy a satisfactory scanner for about ninety dollars, and there probably is no single add-on that will do more to improve the quality of your publications. With a scanner, you can reproduce anything you see. Although you must be ever mindful of copyright laws, a scanned image can be easily modified to make it your own. Once you start looking, you'll find design elements everywhere. Just don't get carried away. More is not better in desktop design.

Desktop scanners allow you to scan an image at varying resolutions from about 200 dpi (dots per inch) to 1,200 or more. Higher resolution is not better if you will be printing the scanned image. Most laser or ink-jet printers can't print pictures at the higher resolutions. Unless you have quite an expensive printer, 300 dpi is usually as good as they can produce. What you can end up with is not a better photo but a very large file that is difficult to manipulate and may cause your computer to crash. Your printer will simply ignore or discard the information it cannot use.

Investigate Desktop Publishing Programs

Once you've begun producing publications for the library, you may become frustrated with your word processing program. Word processors were not really intended for this function, and they can cause a lot of annoyance. Text blocks jump around, and a photo that was perfectly positioned moves unexpectedly to the next page. At this point, you will probably begin pining for a more sophisticated program. In my own libraries, I've found that Broderbund's very inexpensive program PrintShop fills a gap between word processors and more professional desktop publishing programs. Although it lacks their flexibility, it is extraordinarily easy to use. Even better, the program includes samples of almost every publication you are likely to need. In an hour or two, you can choose a completed brochure, substitute your text and your graphics for the ones provided, and it's done.

When you're ready for the next step up in terms of sophistication, the programs most often selected are QuarkXPress, PageMaker, and InDesign. These programs, however, are expensive and time-consuming. Most people find that although they can produce more professional results with such programs, they spend a lot more time doing it. If your library is churning out a number of publications and someone on the staff is interested in becoming more proficient, one of them may be a good investment. If your publications are not all that numerous and staff time is limited, it might be best to learn to live with the limitations of word processing programs and inexpensive desktop publishing software.

Creating a Promotional Blitz

I recently discovered a public library that seemed to have an outstanding marketing department. It was a natural assumption, since I encountered their publications all over town. When I went to the bank, I found a flyer announcing their book discussion groups. I found their newsletter in the grocery store and their brochure among the Welcome Wagon handouts. Within the library itself, the signage system was up-to-date and well designed, as were announcements of schedule changes and upcoming events. I could not help but imagine an entire department devoted to library publicity.

When I finally met the director, I discovered that there was no such department. The library used the same five or six templates over and over. One staff member was responsible for keeping abreast of the library's calendar and new services, regularly pasting new information into templates, and printing out a small pile of colorful documents once a week. If nothing out of the ordinary was happening that week, a specific library service like the large-print collection or "books on tape" might be spotlighted. Other staff members regularly picked up the week's output before leaving work in the evening and dropped them off when they were doing their personal errands. Often, they simply removed last week's flyers and substituted new ones. The entire process for routine announcements required almost no time at all. Once the pattern was set and the publicity machine was in motion, it became almost automatic. Newsletters and special publications, of course, were more time-consuming, but templates and a well-established distribution routine considerably reduced the amount of time needed.

This list of basic steps will help you get started on your promotional materials.

Decide what kind of document you want to create.

Do some brainstorming. Consider what information you want to communicate. Think about imaginative ways to do it.

Select a template if you plan to use one.

Adjust your word processor to the correct page size and margins.

Set up columns if you plan to use them. If not, check to see if your word processor can display a grid for positioning elements.

Create a rough draft that includes your text and space for the graphic elements you want to include.

Be sure you can see the entire page on the screen. Experiment with making different elements larger and smaller to get a feel for the overall look of the page.

Decide on your colors. By this point, you should know how much color you can have for the price you're willing to pay.

Choose your type fonts. Decide whether you want to create a formal or informal impression. Text designers tend to use serif fonts for blocks of type and san serif fonts for headings and accents. Don't exceed two fonts per publication.

Choose your images. Scan photos, search the Web, and consider editing clip art. Use a photo software program to increase brightness and contrast. If you don't have a graphics program, Microsoft Paint is surprisingly useful.

Experiment with different arrangements. If you're not satisfied, look at some magazine advertisements. They usually incorporate state-of-the-art design.

Give pages a consistent look. Create boxes and rules, headers and footers.

The World Wide Web is full of helpful information about desktop publishing. One of the best introductions I've found is "Super Simple Self-Publishing: Start-to-Finish Book Publishing in an Hour or Less," provided by Okidata (http://my.okidata.com). At this website, you are shown how to produce a simple miniature book. You are even able to download the finished product as a Microsoft Word file so you can use it as a template for your own projects. The About.com website also offers a number of links to how-to information, graphics, and templates.

Unlike libraries, bookstore chains have large central departments that do nothing but produce publicity materials and other publications. By applying the techniques described above, the library can produce promotional materials that are not so very different in quality from the bookstore's. The library, however, cannot afford to hire a group of people who do nothing but produce publications. While the bookstore department works with a schedule and turns out materials week after week, month after month, library staff must complete a project and move on to other more traditional library duties. That means that newsletters are sometimes begun and then forgotten; brochures might be distributed long after the information they contain has become outdated. Just as important as desktop publishing savvy is a real commitment to an ongoing marketing program. Short-lived enthusiasm is not enough. Just as bookstore executives know that marketing is an integral part of their business, libraries must make a similar commitment.

RESOURCES

Boosinger, M. L. "Using Desktop Publishing to Create Newsletters, Handouts, and Web Pages." *Journal of Academic Librarianship* 24 (March 1998): 180.

LaRue, J., et al. "Writing the Library Newspaper Column." *Colorado Libraries* 27 (winter 2001): 29–31.

chapter 13

Serving the Library's E-patrons

If you were to ask many people to name a single bookstore, the one most often mentioned might not be a bookstore at all in the conventional sense. It is really located in cyberspace on the World Wide Web. Few people are unaware of the spectacularly successful Amazon.com. Although it started out selling merely books, the site now seems to peddle just about everything. Nevertheless, Amazon calls itself the largest bookstore on Earth with good reason. The Internet has made it possible for businesses like Amazon to become extraordinarily successful even though their customers never enter their front door.

Libraries too have established their presence in cyberspace. One of the most unusual developments in recent years has been the emergence of a group of customers who use the library's resources but may never enter the library building. These are the people who are encountering the library online. Websites have become fairly standard for libraries, and we no longer think of them as unusual or exotic. Library sites appeared in the Telnet era and have been going strong ever since. Of course, there are still some libraries that do not yet have websites. If yours happens to be one of them, consider taking the plunge into cyberspace. Library customers find that getting what they need online is empowering. They have the option to access virtual resources when it's convenient for them, not when the library happens to be open.

A World of Information Providers

Just as honesty compels us to see ourselves in competition with bookstores, we also have to admit that libraries and bookstores are not the only online information providers. We are now in competition with a wide variety of commercial and nonprofit enterprises. Our potential customers can go shopping on the Net and visit a fascinating assortment of virtual libraries, commercially sponsored sites, and nonprofit organizations. Just the other day, I was surfing online, looking for information about the towns on Long Island where some of my ancestors once lived. I was overwhelmed with chronologies and time lines from historical societies, newspaper articles from the late 1800s, and more enticing clues to my heritage than I could possibly investigate. Yet, just a few years ago, the only place where I might have sought help with my project was the library.

Since this is the way contemporary people seek out information, the library should be in the forefront. As the premier information providers, we should be out there with the best. Not only should the library have an online presence, but it should be highly informative, service oriented, and just plain fun. Otherwise, the library's website will fail to attract surfing patrons. Both the design and the content of the library's site must immediately halt the surfer in his or her tracks and say, in effect, "This is where you want to be. This is the site where you can find what you're looking for." Big business is currently putting millions of dollars into their websites, and, of course, libraries can never hope to do the same. However, the Web is an environment that values creativity over money. As we all know, teenagers produce some of the most eye-catching if not informative websites. Anyone, old or young, can learn basic web skills, and it is even possible for talented people with more imagination than money to create the very best sites.

Creating the Library Website

So how do you create a website that lures customers both to the site and to the library itself? What arc the secrets that successful webmasters know? Probably your first consideration should be making your site an effective marketing tool. In a sense, the site becomes an advertisement for the library. It is, therefore, essential that surfers come to recognize the library's page and know how to return to it again and again. Remember too that people who visit the library's website are real library customers, so you will want to keep track of usage statistics and present them with your other data in whatever statistical reports the library produces. Website traffic can help you justify both budget and staffing requests. Don't look on it as just a little trendy frill worthy of scant attention.

For your site to be successful, you will need to tell people about it. That means listing the URL or web address on all your publications, including stationery, brochures, bookmarks, business cards, flyers, newsletters, and pamphlets. It's a good idea for staff to include the web address in their e-mail signatures and on any promotional giveaways like pencils and magnets. Even bumper stickers can be printed with the address in great big letters.

Newspaper articles about the library should emphasize that the website means the library is open twenty-four hours a day, seven days a week. Emphasize that the site is a real extension of the library. I remember that the Internet Public Library used to have a really great graphic of a library reading room complete with reference librarian. A click on the various humorous drawings sent visitors to the reference collection, travel section, and other traditional library locations. In other words, your own site should be viewed as an integral part of the library.

You might think in terms of providing different links and web pages for the children's department, the YA area, and the local history section. Some of the resources listed on those pages will probably be created by the library staff, some will actually be links to the databases to which the library subscribes, and some will take the surfer to sites on the Web. Nevertheless, they should all be perceived as part of the library's virtual collection. Consider putting together a bulletin board or display that highlights the attractions of the website. Conversely, the site itself can emphasize the services and resources found at the "bricks and mortar" library. You might even want to hold a workshop demonstrating the resources that can be found at the website, and when you or your staff are giving presentations to local community groups, be sure to mention it. If you're using a PowerPoint presentation, it's easy to include a screen capture slide that shows the site's homepage.

Building the Site

Well, OK, so the website should invite customers as well as enhance and support the library. Let's get down to specifics. What should be included? The first and most obvious answer is the library's hours. Of course, you will want to include library events, loan policies, street address, staff and department phone numbers, and access to the library catalog. These are the essentials, but they're not really likely to generate any devoted e-patrons. If this is all you can do, it is certainly better than nothing. Even if your library is too small and financially challenged to purchase the automation system module that brings your catalog to the Web, the site is still useful. If you have a high school student who can create such a simple site and—very important—update it regularly, your library at least has a presence in cyberspace.

Let's hope you don't have to stop here, however. Such a limited site will at least tell your customers when you're open, and if the catalog is available, customers can find out whether the library has the book they're looking for before coming over. But there's much more to be done if you really want your site to be a popular and informative presence on the Web.

The first additional feature I would strongly recommend is remote access to periodical and reference databases. It is usually not much more difficult or expensive to make the databases to which you're already subscribing available from your website. Of course, database vendors will probably insist on your limiting access to your own card-carrying patrons, but that's yet another opportunity to encourage your user community to register. Many databases have a feature that allows patrons to e-mail articles to themselves—in other words, to their home or office e-mail account. Some libraries make their e-book subscription available online, thus providing a real traditional library, complete with books and magazines.

Another recent innovation is the virtual reference librarian. Many library websites encourage questions submitted either by e-mail or using a form provided on a web page. The online public access catalog (OPAC) often includes the capacity to place holds on items online and to renew materials. A few libraries offer a "real-time" reference service that allows customers to participate in a "chat room"–type environment and communicate with a librarian. This is an expensive service to provide since it ties up a staff member who must await the arrival of information seekers, but it may be possible to provide the service for an hour or two a day.

The problem with initiating such services is that the library may not be really committed to them. When the web developer suggests them, the response is, "Of course, sure, that would be great." However, no one is really assigned to monitor incoming messages. E-patrons send off their messages and wait and wait and wait. The library staff tend to forget what is on the web page. The "Coming Events" page continues to list programs that took place last year. Telephone numbers are not changed, and unchecked links send visitors to nonexistent sites. Once you make a commitment to maintaining a website, it must become part of the library, and staff must understand that they have an obligation not just to the customers who walk in the door but to their e-customers as well.

Local history has always been the special province of the community library, and genealogists are usually enthusiastic library customers. Now that desktop scanners are so very inexpensive, the Web can become an extension of the historical collection. Photos and documents can be easily scanned, and inexpensive software programs allow you to include explanatory text with images.

One project that a number of public libraries have tried with great success is the creation of an online index to local obituaries. Sometimes the index links to scanned images of the obituaries. Images of local death certificates and marriage licenses have also been hugely popular. I mentioned earlier finding local history time lines online. These can bring genealogy to life, creating, together with local photographs, a vivid picture of the way residents lived in earlier years. Libraries that house archival collections are also digitizing their finding aids and putting them online. Building some web pages around a specific theme is another good way to attract attention. For example, you might collect resources for Black History Month or Banned Books Week, and try to come up with a local slant.

My own library is currently considering online book clubs. Community members sign up at the library's website. A commercial vendor sends book club members the first few chapters of selected books via e-mail and provides online message boards for discussion. To be successful, the library must make a commitment to purchase enough copies of the selected books to satisfy demand. The service is free to customers and has the advantage of "hooking" your e-patrons and bringing them into the library.

Website Design Principles

If you've done much surfing, you've discovered that there are a lot of unattractive, disorganized, and frustrating websites out there, some of which, unfortunately, are maintained by libraries. To be successful, your site must be easy to navigate, informative, and appealing. It must be designed to attract customers and to communicate an amusing yet professional image of the library. This requires careful attention to design principles. It also means that you and the staff need to use the site on a regular basis. Otherwise, you will fail to notice the embarrassing misspelling or the link that goes to the wrong page.

At some point, you've probably found yourself at a site you couldn't identify. It may have been showy and professionally created but failed to provide some basic piece of information you needed. Be sure that the name, address, telephone number, and e-mail address of your library are displayed prominently on every page. Don't assume that everyone arrives at the front door. Web surfers sometimes reach your site by searching for a keyword in a search engine. When they arrive, they may be plunged deep into one of your site's inner pages. By the way, you too can use a search engine to help web visitors find what they're looking for. Site maps also make it easier for them to navigate to the section that most interests them.

Your library undoubtedly has one or more books about basic design, and it is likely that you have at least a few manuals specifically on designing web pages.

Armed with these tools, it is not difficult to avoid the shoals of bad design and make your site both easy to navigate and visually appealing.

Remember too that you are designing your site on a particular computer using a particular web browser. Your online visitors are coming to you via different computers on which they have loaded different software. They may have older, slower computers, so your web pages need to load quickly. Large photo files can be extremely frustrating for the person who couldn't care less about your exciting visual but merely wants to get to the catalog or the magazine database. Sound and video files can be fun, but be sure that they are options for the visitor who is really interested.

Don't forget that your site should be accessible to people with disabilities. E-patrons with visual impairments should be able to use their speech synthesizers and screen-reading software. The inability to perceive certain colors should not make it difficult for other customers to find their way around the site. You've probably seen the graphic of a London Bobbie with the "Bobby Approved" certification at the bottom of some web pages. The Bobby site, found at http://bobby.watchfire.com, states, "Bobby was created to help Web page authors identify and repair barriers to access by individuals with disabilities . . . Bobby tests Web pages using the guidelines established by the World Wide Web Consortium's Web Access Initiative (WAI), as well as guidelines from the Architectural and Transportation Barriers Compliance Board." You can submit your own site files to them for evaluation.

Make Routine Maintenance a Priority

What most of us find frustrating is a site that has not been regularly maintained. Apparently, the webmaster has forgotten about it and moved on to other interests. No time is being spent checking the site, so we encounter broken link after link. Libraries seem to be particularly vulnerable to this problem. One summer, a high school page volunteers to create a website. The staff contributes ideas, and voilà! The virtual library is up and running. Come fall, however, the page goes back to high school and has too many extracurricular activities to maintain the website. No one on the library staff really knows what to do with it, so they just forget about it. This is an all-too-effective way to generate bad publicity. If your software doesn't already have a link-checking function, you should have no problem finding freeware or shareware link checkers at software download sites like PC World and Software.com on the Web. They are not hard to use, but someone must remember to do it. If the library staff never has reason to use the website themselves, they will not notice how badly it looks with other web browsers. These cross-platform problems are all but inevitable if the website is not viewed as a real part of the library.

Applying Library Skills to Cyberspace

Since yours is a library site, you can bring to bear much of the expertise you have acquired in the course of your library education and your career as a librarian. For example, just as you select books and media programs for the library, you can select high-quality websites that you think would interest your e-patrons. Just as librarians provide readers' advisory services, it is helpful to provide customers with lists of outstanding websites. The Web is a mixed bag containing many treasures, it's true, but also stuffed with a lot of trash that simply wastes time. Encourage staff to keep track of websites they visit and write brief reviews of the ones they find most helpful. You can provide links to these sites and even classify them by subject.

As long as you're reviewing websites, why not review some of the books and programs that have recently arrived at the library? You may want to create an online newsletter or simply have a web page devoted to reviews. With your desktop scanner, you can easily provide images of book jackets, publishers' blurbs, and tables of contents. Earlier in this book, we discussed Amazon.com's sophisticated site, which provides not only basic bibliographic data about the books it sells but also all of the above features as well as several sample pages. Although this sounds complicated, it really is not beyond the technical skills of the average webmaster. Again, this helps your e-patrons to understand that the library is not a building but a sophisticated network of services and resources.

Now that so many people use e-mail for much of their personal and business communication, you may want to consider sending e-mail notifications that requested items are available or even e-mailing overdue notices to people who prefer to be contacted this way. E-mail can also be used to advertise upcoming library events, and sending out a monthly program calendar can greatly increase participation. As described above, online book clubs are also becoming more common in libraries. Some clubs continue to meet regularly at the library, but members also communicate via an electronic bulletin board accessed through the library website. Other groups have completely relocated to cyberspace, using not only the library website's bulletin boards but also e-mail lists and chat rooms.

Using the Website to Achieve Library Goals

Once you have determined that your library should build a website as an extension of the library, how do you go about making the kind of decisions that are needed? To begin with, it's important to see the site as a marketing tool and apply marketing principles. This means that it is not just a matter of learning a little HTML and deciding on resources. Effective marketing is more complex. First, of course, is deciding who your customers are. Once you have made that decision, you can move on to determining their needs and then, finally, developing a site that will meet those needs.

This should not be that difficult, since we are accustomed to working with customers and striving to meet their needs. Yet we must also find ways to attract the attention of our cyber customers and make them aware of us. Remember that the Web is crowded. There are millions of websites that a customer can reach just as easily as he or she comes upon our site. We must find ways to focus on the community of users we identify, make them aware of our site, and bring them to it.

Attracting Customers

One excellent reason for developing a website is to attract customers who should be part of the library's community but who somehow have not availed themselves of the library's services. For example, the Web is extremely popular with young people, especially teenagers. You might want to target them specifically and design web resources that will interest them. Businesspeople might be another group that is underserved by your library and might be reached through resources specifically aimed at them. Earlier in this book, we discussed ways to learn more about the library's community. These same techniques can be used to decide how best to use the library's website. For example, you might involve the library in local activities, encouraging the use of the library building for community events. Talk to the people who participate. Make library questionnaires available. Think of the library staff as ambassadors to the community, and assign them the task of talking informally with as many people as possible who are not regular library customers.

Give some thought to how your community is changing. Has a large employer recently moved into town? Maybe this new employer is attracting diverse groups of people who are still unknown to the library. Maybe an employer has left town, leaving behind a large number of unemployed residents. You might think about web resources that would be useful in finding a job, for example, help with writing a résumé or preparing for an interview. Census reports can help you determine whether yours is a community that is attracting young people or senior citizens. Not only will this information help you provide resources for targeted groups but it will also help you with design issues. While young people respond to high-tech, glitzy sites, seniors may prefer simpler, more straightforward pages that are easier to navigate.

Meeting Customers' Cyber Needs

Once you have a clear picture of the customers the website will be serving and the needs it will seek to address, consider how you can make the experience of surfing the site as easy as possible. Develop a logical organization that gets customers to the resources they seek without sending them to half a dozen unwanted web pages. Be sure your pages are well organized and attractive in appearance. Too many pages are so cluttered that one has difficulty just figuring out what is available and how to get to it. Create groups of clearly labeled choices. Word them in such a way that their meaning is immediately obvious to different kinds of people. In other words, avoid library jargon. If you think of the site's home page as a gateway or front door into the library, you can plan visitors' journeys from starting point to the object of their quest. Try to imagine what they might be looking for. Ask some of your face-to-face customers how they might use the website. Then either provide those resources or provide links to other sites, especially other library sites, where they can find what they need.

Learning from the Yahoo! Model

Take a good look at a large information provider like Yahoo! You may not think of Yahoo! as a library, but look at the way they manage to clutter their homepage with advertising and yet efficiently send visitors to the resources most often requested. Take a close look at their "Website Directory." It's organized by broad subject areas. The most commonly accessed categories are there on the home page, so they can be accessed directly. However, clicking on the broad subject heading takes you to a much larger list of subcategories as well as a list of top resources. Visitors have the option of narrowing the focus of their searches until they are quite specific or choosing more general resources after only one or two clicks.

"Yahoo! Picks" is an especially interesting feature and one that can be imitated by libraries. If you've never clicked on this wonderful resource, you're missing a most enjoyable experience. Each month, the staff reviews the best new websites. Then, after they have been showcased, they are placed in a directory with what Yahoo! considers the best of the last few years. Checking these out is one of the best ways to fill an hour that I can think of, since they are both entertaining and highly informative. Your website might do the same, reviewing new materials and then archiving the reviews in a list of past picks. By the way, not only can Yahoo! give you ideas about organizing resources on your site but you might also provide links to some of their reference listings like phone books, maps, and dictionaries.

While you're surfing, take a good look at the organization of a bookstore site like Amazon.com or Barnes&Noble.com. There are many features that you can imitate without spending the huge sums of money these big businesses expend on their supersites. Some OPAC programs, for example, allow customers to put books and other materials into a shopping cart, just as they do at the Amazon site. If you have a web page or newsletter devoted to book reviews, be sure that you include links directly to the catalog so that customers who want to borrow one of the books listed can find out whether it is available.

As your community's premier information provider, you will want to make it easier for your customers to locate important community resources; you might think about devoting one or more pages just to community services. These could include municipal and county departments, schools, and key phone numbers for obtaining services. What does a new resident need to know? Organize this information in such a way that the most important and most frequently used community resources stand out and are not lost in long lists.

The Website as a Group Effort

Maybe by now you're feeling inspired to create a library presence on the Web, but who will do it? It really depends on what kind of site you're planning. It's not difficult for a staff member to learn to use one of the easier software programs. They've become so user-friendly that it's no longer necessary to know how to code HTML. Another possibility is to hire a web consultant who maintains sites for local businesses. A committee of staff members is chosen to work with the consultant, providing ideas and copy that will be incorporated into the site. The consultant provides the technical and design skills.

If you choose this option, always remember that unless you commit to a monthly fee, the consultant will probably not be there when the site needs to be updated, and a good site needs almost constant maintenance. While the outside consultant is creating the initial site, one or more staff members must get ready to take over. Maybe they can take a beginning course at the local community college to rev up their web skills. Even more important, they should spend lots of time with the library consultant, learning how each section of the site is put together and how each can be modified. Even for an experienced web designer, it's hard to work on someone else's project. If the library doesn't have skilled website creators on the staff, the consultant should be cautioned against sophisticated scripting that is beyond the ability of the novice to maintain. In fact, a good consultant will show staff exactly how to make changes and limit fancy web work to elements that needn't be changed.

For some libraries, the only option may be a high school or college student who creates a website as a part-time job. I've had some incredibly good and incredibly awful experiences along this line. In general, I would hesitate to recommend it unless other members of the library staff are fully involved in the project. Even if the design of the site is entrusted to a student, the content must be determined by the library staff. The staff must also give final approval before a site goes up on the Web for all the world to see.

Young people have often created their own sites and so have the technical knowledge for the job. They may lack an aptitude for design, however, and so their pages may be cluttered and disorganized. In addition, they will soon move on. This means that someone else on the library staff must take over the site, and young people are not usually skilled teachers. They may disappear suddenly with none of their work documented. If you've ever tried to make sense of someone else's work with nothing to go on, you'll realize that it's like being a detective on an extraordinarily difficult case.

Some libraries have experimented with having their teen advisory board build and maintain the site. This generally works pretty well if all the work does not fall on one person. Of course, group members may tire of the project, or key site creators may go on to college, but the library still has a longer window of opportunity to accommodate such transitions. One key to success is making sure the group understands that the site must meet the library's goals. Site builders may be given more freedom on their YA pages, but the library should not project the same image as a teen fan site.

Creating Web Pages for a Larger Site

If the library is part of a larger organization like a college or county government or law firm, it may be possible to simply copy the basic design of the parent body's website and insert the library's own information. You might even borrow the site developer as well. Being part of a larger site has many advantages, like not having to work directly with an online service provider. However, it may also make it more difficult to make small changes. Occasionally, high schools and colleges have had good luck working with an instructor who assigns the library's website as a class project. The problem, of course, is keeping it up, but if a library staff member can take the same course, then you can have some assurance of continuity.

Whoever is chosen to develop the website, it is essential to have firm, written guidelines about who determines content. Many librarians report that somehow they can never seem to get their information posted on the library's website. The webmaster never seems to have time to add the requested section. Maybe it's a matter of student workers who do not really understand that library programs must be advertised in a timely manner. Sometimes the problem lies with staff members who always manage to find time to update the pages that reflect their own interests but not those of other departments. Larger libraries may assign the task of maintaining the website to a computer technician who knows little about the library. The goals and priorities of the website must be made clear to all the people responsible. When there's a conflict between substance and glitz, substance must always triumph.

Selecting Hardware and Software

Compared to the cost of labor, the cost of hardware and software to develop the site is quite low. Nevertheless, the library will need to make some investments. Web authoring software ranges from free to several hundred dollars in cost. At the time of this writing, the program Dreamweaver seems to be the program of choice, but new programs are appearing constantly. The most important consideration should always be the skill and experience of the staff who will be creating the site. There are many easy-to-use programs that do not require sophisticated skills or knowledge of HTML. In fact, there is no need for staff to spend endless hours trying to master the bells and whistles of a complex program. The library's goal of an attractive, informative site does not require advanced skills.

In addition to an authoring program, you will also need some web browsers. Only one is essential, but it is very helpful to see how your site looks on both Microsoft Explorer and Netscape. If you can get hold of some of the earlier versions of these browsers that some people may still be using on older computers, you will have additional opportunities to check the impact of the site. Even though web browsers are either free or provided with the Windows operating system, they have heavy RAM memory requirements, and so, as computers age, owners tend to stop updating their browsers. To minimize memory requirements, some users choose the Opera browser because it's so speedy and economical in terms of space required. If you're interested, you can find the Opera browser at http://www.opera.com.

Also needed is file transfer protocol (FTP) software if you send your website files to a host. Hosting companies load your site on their large servers, protect it from hackers, and make sure it's available twenty-four hours a day. Your own parent institution may provide these functions, but generally only large libraries have the resources to do their own hosting.

Another software program you may wish to invest in is PhotoShop, a very sophisticated program for manipulating photo files. It's expensive, however, and you may wish to look for a less expensive alternative. PhotoShop Essentials is a scaled-down version of the program that comes by itself or packaged with some computer peripherals like scanners and graphics tablets. It includes nearly all the features that novice web designers might need. A number of other programs are available priced as low as twenty-five dollars.

Basic Hardware

When it comes to choosing hardware, a fairly up-to-date desktop computer equipped with a scanner and a CD read-write drive (burner) is the first requirement. Websites include large files, so RAM memory must be sufficient to accommodate them. However, if a computer is being purchased especially for website maintenance, be sure that it is compatible with other library computers. Web developers occasionally have strong feelings about Macintosh or PCs, but mixing platforms in a library can create endless compatibility problems.

Scanners

Webmasters find the desktop scanner one of the least expensive and most useful gadgets ever invented. Anything you see on paper can be transformed into a graphics file and appear on your web page with almost no hassle. Once you get started thinking of possibilities in the library, you will be overwhelmed. For example, your entire collection of historical photos can be scanned and made available. Old letters and other documents scan beautifully as well. You probably have a publicity file with lots of photographs of the library taken over the years. All can be easily scanned and made available online. Considering that a scanner usually costs about one hundred dollars, it's the best investment in the high-tech arena. There are many brands, but perhaps the most well known is Hewlett-Packard's ScanJet, which comes with its own software program.

Digital Cameras

As wonderful as scanners are for creating graphic images, it's also a good idea to invest in a digital camera. The great thing about digital cameras is their immediacy. An event occurs in the library, someone snaps a few pictures, and within minutes the event can be shared on the website. If you are simply thinking of the website, an expensive camera is unnecessary. Digital cameras priced under a hundred dollars will probably provide more than adequate photos as long as they come equipped with a flash. However, it's a good idea to integrate your digital camera into your overall marketing strategy. Since files used on the Web must be small to load quickly, you don't need a camera that can provide high resolution. But press releases are an important part of a library marketing plan, and photos should almost always accompany them. Newspapers may require higher quality, and so it may be worth the cost to invest in a better camera.

Another nice feature to consider in a digital camera is the ability to create a brief video clip. A very talented staff member in our library children's department recently created a full-size Chinese New Year dragon. The sight of the children hiding under the dragon's voluminous body and wending their way around the room was something to behold. The still photos we took just didn't capture its charm. Too late, we got around to reading the directions and discovered that our camera actually includes a video feature.

Most digital cameras save the file to a chip inside the camera and require a cable to send the file to a personal computer. The disadvantages of this type of camera are that you must stop when the storage chip is full, and the cable effectively limits you to one computer. To share photos, you must download them via cable and then send them as e-mail attachments to the library staff. Some cameras offer floppy-disk storage, though the trend seems to be moving away from this type of camera. Floppy-disk storage cameras make it easy to share files without searching for the camera cable. Another advantage of this type of camera is that you can keep taking pictures endlessly as long as you have a pocket full of floppies. The downside, as I have found out to my sorrow, is that the floppy drive within the camera is scaled down in size and prone to jamming.

Many digital cameras come with image-editing software that makes it possible to correct simple problems like photos that are too dark or need to be resized. In fact, there is no shortage of free or inexpensive image-editing software, and some editing features may be built into website development programs, web browsers, and even word processors. Although these programs will do the job if necessary, they cannot compete with more sophisticated software like Adobe's PhotoShop.

Graphics Tablets

Although there are many other peripheral components that would enhance your system, they are not necessary. Your website development budget may well be overspent by this point, and there's no real need for anything else. However, I have become very attached to a clever innovation called a graphics tablet. It consists of a pad or tablet about eight inches square that looks a little like a rigid mouse pad. But it can do some amazing things. Both a cordless mouse and a pen or stylus usually come packaged with the tablet. The ease of enhancing a graphic with a pen instead of a mouse will spoil anyone creating a website. While the mouse is clumsy to manipulate, the stylus can be used almost as easily as drawing with a pencil on a sheet of paper. If you happen to be in the market for a new mouse, the graphics tablet, at a cost of approximately sixty dollars, becomes more affordable since both mouse and pen are included.

Finding a Host

Once you have a site ready, you will have to find a service provider to serve as host. As briefly described above, this is actually a computer server on which your web pages are stored. It must be a computer that is linked directly to the Internet twenty-four hours a day, seven days a week. As web surfers, we are all aware that when we type in the URL for a website, web pages are transmitted from a server somewhere out there in cyberspace to our own computer. That is the function of a host.

There are many different ways to find a host. For example, Internet Service Providers (ISPs) are companies that provide computer storage space and web server facilities for other organizations. They normally charge a fee or make their profit adding extensive advertising to their customers' pages. In exchange, they provide the equipment, software, and technical staff needed to keep the server up continuously. They usually provide webmasters with a limited amount of technical support either by phone or by e-mail. Sometimes it is possible to obtain free website hosting from an ISP that the library already uses to provide e-mail and other Internet services. This free option, however, is usually limited in terms of storage space and bandwidth available. Smaller sites will probably experience no difficulties, but if you plan a large and sophisticated web presence, you will very likely have to pay for it.

The library's parent organization may already maintain a website, and the library's pages might become a part of it. If you are responsible for maintaining only a small part of a large site, you can count on hardware, software, and technical support. Yet you will also probably have to sacrifice a certain amount of control over your site. Your county or university, for example, may insist on a uniform look and feel to the site. You may not have the option of designing more interesting features, and your pages may not be updated if another project takes priority.

Only larger libraries can serve as their own hosts, dedicating a server to this purpose round the clock. Since there are many pitfalls lurking out there, considerably more technical expertise is needed, and the job of webmaster usually becomes much more complicated. Security is by far the most worrisome problem, and firewalls can be tricky, blocking what you don't want blocked and welcoming intruders. Firewall maintenance requires a competent technician or at least a very savvy staff member. Hardware also becomes more complicated and costly. For example, the website may be loaded on a small minicomputer like a Sun that runs the UNIX or LINUX operating system. Any powerful server that is constantly available on the Web poses a huge temptation to hackers, who, without your knowledge, may use your site for their own illegal business operations. Extensive firewall protection is, therefore, needed. As you can see, this is a real commitment in terms of time and money that is beyond the reach of most libraries. Fortunately, with so many service providers out there, it is rarely necessary.

A library website is one of the most effective and least expensive ways to market the library's services. With the new generation of user-friendly software, almost anyone on the library staff can become a webmaster. The Web provides a wonderful opportunity to even the playing field and compete with bookstores on the library's own terms. Most of the skills needed for creating websites are applicable to many other software programs as well. There is a great deal of overlap between web publishing and desktop publishing, so most skills are transferable. There is so much to be gained that even the smallest library should consider making its presence known on the Web.

RESOURCES

Brooks, M. D. "Web Page Design." *Library Mosaics* 12 (March/April 2001): 8–11.

Brown, S. W. "Test, Edit, Repeat: Steps to Improve Your Web Site." *Computers in Libraries* 22 (November/December 2002): 14–16, 18, 20–21.

Lubans, J. "Building Brand Loyalty: Using Your Library Web Site to Promote Return Visits." *Illinois Library Association Reporter* 18 (December 2000): 7–8.

Lugg, R., et al. "Deconstructing Earth's Largest Library." *Library Journal* 125 (August 2000): 44–47.

Pace, A. K. "Redefine the Experience, Not the Library." *Computers in Libraries* 22 (October 2002): 47–49.

Puacz, J. H. "Catching (and Keeping!) E-patrons." *Computers in Libraries* 22 (January 2002): 12–14, 71–72.

chapter 14

Generating Publicity for the Library

When a bookstore decides that it needs to attract more customers, what does it do? It advertises! When its marketing department reaches the conclusion that there is a segment of the population who are not fully availing themselves of the bookstore's services, the department directs its advertisements toward that group. Millions of dollars may be spent on an advertising campaign, but if it is successful, the bookstore will reap several times that sum in sales.

In a previous chapter, we discussed the development of a library marketing plan. A key element of that plan was to identify population groups that are not being fully served by the library. Once the library has identified these constituencies, what does it do? If one takes a good look at the track records of many libraries, the answer, unfortunately, is not very much. As a profession, we tend to be quite good at writing reports. We have excellent research skills and count many English majors among our ranks. We may have difficulty finding the time to write a marketing plan, but if we are somehow able to slip it into our schedule, we will probably do a very credible job. Then what?

Reaching New Customers

Thus far, we have discussed ways to make the library more attractive, appealing, and responsive to our customers. What about those people we have identified who are not yet our customers? Like the bookstore, we must advertise. The problem, of course, is that we have no advertising budget. True, we have a little money to print flyers and brochures. Maybe the printing budget can be expanded to include a newsletter. But that's probably about as far as we can go. Few libraries have the money to hire big-name ad agencies to produce television commercials or full-page newspaper advertisements.

Just as we must become our own visual merchandisers, webmasters, and interior decorators, we must also become our own advertising agencies. As was the case with those specialty areas, there are skills we can learn. Though they will not place us on a par with professionals in the field, they will make a profound difference in our libraries.

Attracting Financial Support

Although it may sound facetious, an excellent way to become effective advertisers is to let someone else pay the bills. Boston Public Library, for example, launched a campaign that included five television spots as well as 100 billboards, public transportation posters, and print ads. With help from an ad agency and local media, they did all this with almost no budget.[1] These were not merely public service announcements that ran at 3:00 a.m. Instead, they included full- and half-page ads in the *Boston Globe* and the *Boston Herald* and TV spots on prime-time news. Although the effort was costly in terms of time and energy, circulation statistics rose 10 percent.

With the help of professionals, the library learned the language and basic principles of marketing. They employed solid marketing strategies like focus groups with library users and nonusers that led them to target the twenty-five to forty-five age group as one that the library was not fully serving. Their research indicated that this group would best respond to a "hip" message, and so the campaign was built around this goal. Product placement was used in both TV and print ads to attract funding from commercial sources. A new logo that could be easily recognized on press releases, billboards, and print advertisements made a great finishing touch. It appeared on everything from Boston Transit Association trains to the library's newly designed website. Its bright colors were prominently displayed on AT&T-funded street banners that blanketed the city. Even better, the campaign was no one-day wonder. It was continually reinvigorated with new programs, emphases, and merchandising materials.

Creating a Publicity Machine

Stories like this one make it clear that with help from the business world, librarians can function nearly as well in the marketplace as the pros. The problem is that this type of concerted campaign can be extremely time-consuming. If you are contemplating a major fund-raising effort, it will be well worth the time. If, however, you just want to make your community more aware of the things the library is doing, the answer may be creating what I will call for want of a better term a quick and dirty *publicity machine.* Let's say the library is sponsoring a political forum, during which candidates for local political offices will speak. How do you get out the word? You want a good turnout, but you and the staff have little time to devote to publicity.

The answer is that you put your publicity machine into high gear. I use the word *machine* to emphasize the need for procedures that become almost automatic. You use the same well-developed procedures each time you need publicity, and each time they get smoother and speedier. For example, you have a to-do checklist, together with specific information about local media. Since your press release will fall on deaf ears unless it gets to the right people in plenty of time to make an impact, your publicity machine streamlines the process. A template on your computer allows you to produce a news release in just a few minutes. Ready at your fingertips are the names, fax numbers, and e-mail addresses of newspaper reporters who consider the library part of their beat. The same information, slightly modified, can be sent to the news and programming directors of local radio and TV stations (the text of a brief public service announcement can be included). Just a few changes and the press release is ready for the home page of the library's website.

When you're creating your publicity machine, consider how else you can get the word out. Quickly produced flyers will need to be distributed immediately. A ready-to-roll plan that includes a list of designated staff and volunteers who will distribute them and at what locations makes the process easier and much more dependable. What about the chamber of commerce? Can you include an article in their newsletter? Will they tuck in your flyer too and distribute it for a small charge? When is their deadline? All this information should be codified and stored in one place.

One colleague, who has been enormously successful at getting publicity for her library, tells me she now has it down to a science. She has obtained the publication schedules of all local newspapers, newsletters, and shoppers. She knows the submission requirements for each publication and has learned ways to make the same information slightly different for each targeted audience. She has the names and phone numbers of the program chairs of all the local civic clubs. She has identified library staff who have the "gift of gab" and can be quickly dispatched to fill in when a club speaker cancels unexpectedly. She has cultivated radio and television talk-show hosts, who know they can depend on the library when they need an extra guest. Every few months, a volunteer contacts each media outlet. He verifies that the library is sending its publicity to the appropriate person, that the fax number has not changed, and that no new policies have been imposed. He uses the opportunity to learn more about their needs, so the library can better tailor its publicity to its audience.

Bookstore chains centralize their public relations departments at corporate headquarters. The library has a big advantage in that it is an integral part of the local community. The library's customers will know of still other opportunities to spread the message, and they may have personal connections with local media. These are opportunities that bookstores, depending as they do on directories and other sources of information that become quickly out-of-date, may never become aware of.

Getting into Print and on the Air

A press release is the most common way of communicating with the news media. Perhaps the most important thing to remember is that it must get to the right people in the most useful form. Check with your local newspaper as well as radio and television stations in your area. Find out who handles news about libraries. You may discover that no one has been assigned this task. For news purposes, the library may be completely invisible. In that case, you'll have to talk with the editor or program director to find out who would be the most logical person to cover library news. In all probability, the staff member who has the education beat is the best choice.

Next, give each of the people you've identified a call. Find out what kind of news they're most interested in. How do they want it presented? How long are their typical articles? How much lead time do they need, or when do they go to press?

Successful librarians have learned that their news is far more likely to get attention if they make it as easy as possible for the media. One of the most important points to clarify is how to submit your press release. Increasingly, the preference is for electronic submission. Especially in the case of newspapers, the text can be imported into news articles without retyping. If yours is the easier story to write, it makes sense that it is more likely to find its way into print. Sending copy via e-mail may also be in the library's best interests. After some painful experiences with spelling-challenged young reporters who can't remember names, I much prefer them to copy and paste my text.

Find out if your media contact would like you to submit digital photos with the press release. In my experience, it is always best to have a professional photographer come out and take pictures, but any photo is better than no photo at all. What resolution do they require? What file types can they work with? Should you save your photos in gray scale? Full color?

As you get to know your contact persons for different media, you will probably discover that they have quite different needs. This means that you will probably want to write separate news releases for radio and television. Broadcast media work on a very tight schedule but may be willing to send a camera crew to the library if you can convince them that there will be something interesting for them to shoot. Broadcast media usually prefer short words and short sentences that can be quickly communicated and understood.

Crafting the Press Release

I find that it's important to come across to the media as being a professional. Your news is more likely to be taken seriously if it comes from an organization that knows the ropes. That means that observing accepted conventions is important. If you're submitting a news release in hard copy, always use white 8½ x 11 inch paper. Leave wide margins all around so there will be plenty of room for editing. Use only the front side of the paper, and double-space the text.

On the upper-left-hand corner of the first page, type the name of the contact person as well as the library name, e-mail and street addresses, and phone number. Most of the time, you'll probably want the news story to appear as soon as possible. In this case, type "FOR IMMEDIATE RELEASE" in caps under the contact information. If you are planning ahead and want the media to hold the story until shortly before an event is scheduled, type "FOR RELEASE THE WEEK OF __." As you get to know your media contacts, you'll gradually learn whether this is a safe strategy. Experienced media staffers will put the library on their calendar, and your publicity will appear when it can be most helpful. Inexperienced media newbies may pile your press release on the stack on the back of their desk and only discover it months later when they finally get around to clearing off some space.

Begin with a headline that clearly communicates the point of the story. Make it brief and pithy. Your first paragraph is called the *lead.* It too should be short and straightforward. If you take a look at some articles in your local newspaper, you'll discover that paragraphs often consist of just a single sentence. Don't embroider or elaborate, because it must catch a busy reporter's attention. Don't include anything at all complicated in the lead, but begin answering those famous five questions: who, what, when, where, and why. Continue communicating basic information in the second paragraph. Don't hyphenate words at the end of lines, use bullets, or include other formatting that could create problems when the text is imported into another software program.

Don't use the press release to demonstrate your clever writing style. The place for that is in the column we'll discuss later, not in the press release. In this case, you're not the one writing the article, and your prose is simply the raw material the reporter will use. State the facts as clearly and simply as possible. Then organize the rest of the information you want to include according to its importance. You have no way of knowing how much space has been allocated or what the reporter will cut, so follow the "inverted pyramid" rule. The most important information is placed at the top. Make sure the article can stand on its own if the last paragraphs are eliminated. If you can get all the information on one page, type "-30-" at the end. If the press release occupies two or more pages, type "-more-" at the bottom of the first page and interim pages. Include an abbreviated version of the headline at the top of the second and subsequent pages.

The Library as the Media Sees It

Meeting deadlines is really important. As you can imagine, the library is not viewed as "red-hot news," so your story will be squeezed in when more important assignments are not pressing. You're more likely to get the news out if you give the media as much flexibility as possible. It is in your interest to entice the media into spotlighting the library as often as possible, so good communication is essential. Many library activities can provide two opportunities for publicity. The first is the announcement of the upcoming event. The second opportunity for publicity is to invite the media to cover the event themselves. In this case, you might want to specifically invite your media contacts. A phone call or e-mail message, in addition to the press release, might be in order.

Try to see the library event from the media's point of view. What would make a good story? What would provide a good photo opportunity? I've found that reporters sometimes have so little experience with libraries that they don't know what to expect. Put on your thinking cap, and come up with a human-interest angle that will entice a reluctant reporter. Then, each time you are successful in getting a story on the air or into the paper, express your appreciation to the people who made it happen. If they fall down on the job, don't react in anger. Ask what went wrong. What might you have done to bring the story to their attention or make their job easier?

Sending Out Digital Photos

Nothing enhances a newspaper article more than a photograph, and libraries just naturally provide many "photo ops." A photograph of a young child reading a picture book or listening with rapt attention while the children's librarian reads a story will almost always be welcome. Digital cameras now make it possible for you to photograph an event and send it to a reporter's computer within minutes. Even this, however, is not always fast enough.

If there is one single factor that determines success or failure when working with the media, it is timing. If you miss a deadline, your story will probably be ignored. Newspapers, however, are sometimes unable to accommodate material even when it comes in shortly before the deadline. Once their pages have been set up, only a very important, late-breaking story is worth the effort of rearranging them. Let's say that you'd like to get a photograph published in your local newspaper. Let's also assume that the newspaper will probably not consider it worth their while to send a photographer to cover the event. You or a staff member can take your own photograph with a digital camera and e-mail it to the newspaper immediately.

Since a photograph is an excellent attention grabber, you'll want to accompany a press release with a picture whenever possible. The problem is that while a press release can be sent out before a newsworthy event, you can't take a photograph of something that hasn't happened yet. This may require using your imagination. For example, since you want publicity for your book sale, send a photo of volunteers getting ready for it. You may need to stage the photo using piles of books and empty boxes as props. If you know that you'll be cutting it close, send out the press release several days early. Then let your reporter-contact know when you'll be sending the photograph. If you've established a good relationship, he or she may be willing to hold a spot for the picture if the story looks like a good one.

The Library Newspaper Column

For many libraries, a weekly or monthly newspaper column is a wonderful way of revving up community interest. Although the bookstore must pay to publicize its wares in newspapers, libraries are actually invited to tell their stories. Many local newspapers are delighted to publish a library column as long as the library understands the paper's needs.

Have you ever written a newspaper column before? It's really not very difficult. In fact, there's a tried-and-true formula that will help you construct a pretty good column with a minimum of effort. Begin with a personal detail. Ask the staff for stories about patrons who have said funny or touching things. Stories about children in the library are always good attention grabbers. The point is that readers are attracted by "people" stories. We always enjoy little personal details that make other people seem more human, but be careful about embarrassing anyone. The one person you can freely make fun of is yourself, so if you can think of something humorous that happened to you recently, readers will probably enjoy hearing about it.

Once you have a good opening paragraph, lead into a message about the library, letting readers know about new services and resources or even existing ones that they may not be aware of. Using humor effectively throughout the article is a good way to keep your readers with you. As a profession, we still must cope with the stereotype of the boring library and librarian. You will want to convey the feeling that the library is a delightful place to be and you and the staff are utterly fascinating people.

Sometimes it can be frustrating trying to think up a theme or topic for an article on deadline. Don't wait till the last minute. As you're talking with staff and customers, keep an ear out for a new angle, a different take on the library. If you should ever run out of ideas, you have thousands of them sitting on your shelves. When you've had a dull week, a quick overview of some newly arrived books or media programs is always appreciated.

Keep your audience in mind. They will give you just a few minutes to tell them about the library. Then they'll be moving on to the sports page or the comics. What you write must relate to them personally. It must in some way speak to their lifestyles and interests. That means your goal is first to entertain, then inform. If you're in doubt about the best approach, read some other columnists who write for the local paper. Which ones do you enjoy? Take a more in-depth look at those columns and try to discover precisely what it is that gets and keeps your attention. If the newspaper is focused on one particular segment of the community, consider how you can slant your article to appeal more to their interests.

Play by Their Rules

The newspaper editor will tell you how many words are needed. It's up to you to produce a column of almost exactly the required size. Since the newspaper holds a space for your column, you will be causing the staff additional work if your column does not fit the space. As with the press release, it's always a good idea too to put less important thoughts at the bottom of the column. That way, if it's been an eventful week and there's more news than expected, your column can be shortened without ruining your important points.

Newspapers operate on deadlines, and you will surely lose respect if you repeatedly miss the deadline. Most editors agonize over late-breaking news stories, which inevitably occur just as the paper is going to press. Your column should never be the source of headaches. It should arrive on time week after week, and the editor should come to see the librarian as somebody he or she can count on.

Much of what you learned creating the press release is applicable to the column. For example, it's a good idea to send your column electronically. If you send it to the editor's e-mail address, it is less likely to get misplaced. The text is already in digital form, so it needn't be retyped. It is actually in your own interest to send a computer file because an editor is much less likely to alter it. If the whole thing must be retyped, the temptation to change a bit here and there is much greater.

Be sure the column you submit has been carefully proofread. That means you've carefully checked for spelling errors, not just run the spell-checker. You've asked another staff member to check for grammatical errors. You've asked other people to read your rough draft to make sure that your writing flows easily and clearly. If your week isn't full of twelve-hour days, write the column ahead of time. That way some time can elapse before you give it a final edit. It's amazing how a day or two allows you to see errors that earlier were completely invisible. Silly errors can be terribly embarrassing when you first discover them in print.

Content Dos and Don'ts

Your column is not the place to voice complaints about local government or the library's inadequate budget. Make sure your tone is always upbeat. Remember, if you are a government employee, you can't encourage your readers to vote for the library bond issue, but you can clarify the issues at hand. Tell people all the great things the library will be doing with the money. If you use the column as an opportunity to talk about the library's future, you can encourage readers to respond with ideas of their own. Make it clear that the library is really interested in their needs and wants to hear from them.

Don't get angry if the column you see in print is not the one that left your word processor. Newspaper editors will inevitably make changes, and they have every right to do so. They will always put their personal stamp on your writing, and for the most part, it is only your ego that suffers. If it seems to you that important information is lost, talk with the editor, but don't criticize. Ask what you can do to make the column more acceptable. Explain that you don't think you're getting your points across and would like to enlist the help of a professional. That way you don't alienate a much needed friend.

Becoming a Public Personality

Although bookstores use newspapers to sell their merchandise, the bookstore's message is often communicated to the public by golden-throated radio and television personalities or, even better, celebrity spokespersons. Libraries need spokespersons too, but we lack the resources to attract Hollywood stars for the job. So who can be the library's spokesperson? You! You and other members of the library staff are the ones who must spread the message.

You may be fortunate enough to have a customer or member of your Friends of the Library group who is skilled at media relations and would be willing to help. For the most part, though, that burden usually falls on you. You are the library's spokesperson, and to be effective, you need an audience, a big audience. This means scheduling appearances on local radio and television programs as well as inviting yourself and your PowerPoint presentation to Kiwanis meetings and other community gatherings.

For librarians, this kind of exposure is difficult. Don't we, as a group, hate public speaking? There is a good reason why few organizations have as low a profile as libraries. As a profession, we tend to be publicity shy. Yet to lead our libraries into the spotlight, we must turn ourselves into public personalities. How can this be accomplished?

Although it is true that there are people who just naturally have a gift for public speaking, most of the basic techniques can be learned. It is a skill that can be mastered, one step at a time. Central to achieving those skills is finding a way to control our fear. If you are like many of our colleagues, you panic when you are asked to give a speech. Perhaps the first thing to realize is that help is at hand. Many librarians endorse Toastmasters (http://www.toastmasters.com), which has chapters in most communities. The Dale Carnegie organization (http://www.dalecarnegie.com) is another good source of information. Workshops and courses that promise to make you a confident public speaker in a matter of days abound. However, they are expensive. You can also learn the basics on your own, seeking out less threatening opportunities to try your wings.

Preparing for a Speaking Engagement

Let us imagine that a group has asked you to give a presentation about the library. The first thing you should ask yourself is why? Why is this group interested in the library, and what can you bring them that will really relate to them? Your approach will be different if your audience is composed of businessmen than if it is mostly academics. Consider the age group as well since people of different ages have different frames of reference.

It's a very good idea to practice a speech beforehand. Get a feeling for your pace and timing. Consider your posture. You will want to stand straight and talk directly to the audience. You may have a screen or blackboard, but it's the audience you are talking to. In fact, move your focal point so that you are talking to everyone, not one group or one section. If you're not speaking in the library, arrange to visit the place ahead of time.

If you're bringing a laptop computer or other equipment, check the power outlets and data jacks. Plug in your equipment to be sure the outlets are "live." If you're using someone else's equipment, get comfortable with it. Check the microphone to get a feeling for the right sound level. In fact, bringing someone with you who can listen from the back row is a very good idea. Nothing can throw you for a loop like having people continually shouting, "We can't hear you."

Having to ad-lib while you're plugging and unplugging, flipping switches, and pressing buttons can be one of the most agonizing experiences you'll ever live through. Equipment that worked flawlessly yesterday invariably becomes temperamental when there's an audience waiting expectantly. A common problem is incompatibility between your own equipment and that which you'll be borrowing. For example, you have no trouble plugging your laptop into the library's projector, but this one requires a different cable. Check it out ahead of time. Allow time for a "technical" rehearsal. Make sure that your audience will not only be able to hear you but will also be able to see the slides in your presentation. Although a room doesn't actually need to be darkened for the audience to see your presentation, direct sunlight can wash out the brightest of images.

Even after a technical rehearsal, your equipment may decide to self-destruct, so be sure you have a backup plan. If the computer projector won't project, the same presentation slides can be printed on transparencies for use with an overhead projector. If the program depends on accessing the Internet, capture the most important web pages using the Print Screen key on your computer. That way if the Web is slow or no phone jack is available, you're prepared.

Write out a list or inventory of everything you'll need for the program: extension cords, computer cables, microphone, flip chart, notes or index cards, lectern, white board, felt-tip pens. You might even include a glass of water to deal with dry mouth. Then shortly before the talk, check off each item on your list. Finally, load your presentation software, web browser, or whatever computer programs will be needed. By the time everything's ready, some members of the group should be arriving. Start up a conversation. Now that you know everything is in order, start getting to know your audience. It will lower your stress level, and you will be giving your talk to people you know, not strangers.

Before you begin speaking, take a moment to relax. Take several deep breaths from the diaphragm. Deep breathing calms you, and shallow breaths heighten tension. Shrug your shoulders to relax your muscles and maybe even roll your head a bit if you can do so inconspicuously.

Becoming a Speech Writer

As you plan your speech, remember to make it entertaining. Of course, you're communicating information, but audiences expect to be entertained by a speaker. Ask your host how long you should plan to speak. I find that although I dread making a speech, once I get started, I tend to go on and on. Find out how much time you have, and take a tip from Goldilocks. Outline a talk that is not too long, not too short, but just right. Decide which parts can be easily eliminated if you're running out of time and insert them toward the end. Keep an eye on your audience's body language, and when they become restless, it's time to quit. Allow enough time for people to ask questions. Decide what information you will present and what you will keep in reserve for questions. Don't throw it at them all at once.

Some public-speaking experts recommend that you write down your thoughts, main points, and key phrases on index cards, allocating one thought per card. Then put the cards in order and number them so they don't get mixed up. I personally have trouble with index cards because if I ad-lib for a few minutes, I forget which card I'm on. Then I become flustered trying to find the right card. What works better for me is a single piece of paper that is just a very brief outline.

Don't write out your entire speech, whether on cards or paper. You've undoubtedly suffered through speakers who simply read their message from beginning to end. They look up only occasionally, apparently to check that the audience is still there. Your audience does not want to listen to you reading. All the spontaneity is gone. If you are looking down at your text, you are not looking at them. It is as if they don't exist. You're just trying to get through the words, phrases, and paragraphs you have written.

A colleague tells me she uses a box of props. She finds a way to work the box into the first part of the talk and then pulls out objects. Each object triggers her memory to recall a basic point she wants to make. The audience becomes fascinated, wondering what object will next emerge from the box. Just as long as the audience does not become more interested in the objects than in the points they correspond to, this is an excellent technique.

Again, experts differ on the way to begin the speech. It's probably best not to start out by thanking people. The person or persons being thanked, of course, appreciate it, but most of your audience is left out. Don't talk about the weather or other standard topics that are nothing more than starting points. It is vital to connect with your audience immediately.

Many speakers begin with a joke to warm up the audience. Others claim that only an accomplished comedian can do this effectively, and it is better to begin with a personal experience that casts the speaker in a humorous light. Audiences do like to laugh, so intersperse lighter elements throughout the speech. I think we have all been imbued with the principles of political correctness, but be extra careful that your jokes are not offensive. Poking fun at yourself is, therefore, sometimes the safest way to go. Another advantage of the personal experience is that the audience does not know what's coming. All too often, we anticipate the punch line of a joke long before the speaker has arrived at it. Another big advantage of a personal anecdote is that you don't need notes.

Use some aspect of the story to lead into your talk. However you choose to begin, make sure you have memorized the opening thirty seconds of your speech and have it down cold. Of course, you'll need to have a clear idea where you'll go from there, but having a strong beginning establishes your relationship with your audience and also helps relieve your own tension.

Next, move into the body of the speech. Put your basic points in a logical order. Consider including a question or two. A question near the beginning makes the audience feel more involved. A question near the end wakes them up and refocuses their attention. New cordless microphones allow you to move around comfortably. You can walk toward the projection screen to emphasize a point or walk toward the audience to establish a closer relationship with them. Some professional speakers do unconventional things like sitting on the edge of the stage, but do only what's comfortable for you. Throughout your speech, remember that your audience wants you to succeed. Even if you lose your place or make an error, it's not the end of the world. You can keep your audience with you and maintain the rapport. They don't expect perfection.

Just as experts differ about using a joke to begin a speech, they also argue about whether you should sprinkle jokes through the presentation. For one thing, it depends on how well you can tell a joke. If you're the kind of person who usually forgets the punch lines, this is probably not your forte. Again, the personal anecdote may work better for you. It's certainly true that audiences need a break from the business at hand; they need to be entertained or their attention will soon wander. However, you're the best judge of how to achieve that change of pace.

Although it's hard to remember when you're feeling stressed, try to avoid saying "ah," "uh," or "um." There's nothing wrong with a pause while you collect your thoughts. In fact, it can add drama and focus the audience's attention. Are there certain words that you tend to repeat as fillers? Some speakers insert "like" into every sentence.

Give yourself time at the end to summarize your points and make it clear what you'd like the audience to do in response. For example, you might invite the audience to make better use of the library or contribute to a fund-raising campaign. Make your ending memorable; give your audience some words that they will take home with them—maybe an inspiring success story. Thanking the audience at the end is a nice touch, but convey the sense that you are speaking directly to individuals. Thank them for something specific, not just getting their bodies to the program.

Forget the Orations of the Past

One very useful thing to remember is that people are easily bored listening to speeches. Think about your own reaction to someone who stands in the front of the room and talks at you. Think about how you respond when you're with an acquaintance who just can't stop talking. Most of us quickly become bored. And yet you have a message that needs to be communicated. How will you keep your audience involved? How can you create the illusion that you are just having a conversation with each member of the audience individually? Try to use the same tone, the same body language, the same posture that you might if you were just talking with two or three friends. Forget the rhetoric of the past. Make your speaking style more human and more communicative. Relax.

Of course, this is easier said than done for a librarian who dreads speaking engagements as much as a trip to the dentist. If you're talking with friends and you momentarily forget the point you were making, you admit it and probably turn it into a joke. You can do the same with an audience since they will respond in very much the same way as your friends and acquaintances. It takes a Franklin Roosevelt or a Winston Churchill to succeed in capturing an audience with a traditional oratorical approach, so don't try it yourself.

Most speakers have a great deal of trouble deciding what they will do with their hands. Then, after the speech, they realize they did exactly what they tried to train themselves not to do. It seems that when you become conscious of your hands, trying to use them effectively, the movements tend to look awkward and forced. For an apprentice speaker, it is probably just best to forget about your hands. If there's something useful you can do with them, great. For example, a laser pointer serves a useful purpose and keeps at least one hand busy.

When planning a speech, we tend naturally to make use of library reference sources. We look up definitions in dictionaries as well as quotations from famous people. Unfortunately, these frequently serve no useful purpose. They don't entertain; they don't address the topic at hand. They're just fillers. If there are really terms that should be defined, then use your own words. Quotations are no more interesting. If you're just looking for an authority to back you up or give you moral support, it's not going to work. Your audience isn't impressed, just bored. I've often thought that if I had to hear that "it was the best of times, it was the worst of times" one more time, I'd have to restrain myself from hurling rotten tomatoes.

Fillers like these not only distract the audience's attention from the points you are making but they reduce the emotional content of your talk to zero. To win your audience, you must feel passionately about the subject and communicate this passion. What you're saying must matter very much to you. At that moment, you are wholeheartedly involved, and your enthusiasm is beamed out to your audience.

When looking for help with public speaking, I continually run into the same dubious advice. For example, you've undoubtedly heard that you should picture your audience in their underwear. Do speakers really think that by imagining their audiences as ludicrous and humiliated, they are going to give a better speech? Neither is it wise to try to impress your audience with your knowledge or importance. Never pretend to be an expert when you're not. Imagine your own reaction to a friend or colleague who continually toots his or her own horn. Think of your audience as peers who you enjoy being with. And remember when you're with your peers, you look at one another; you smile and laugh and enjoy one another. You don't keep your eyes glued to a sheet of paper.

Finally, when the speech is over, relax, take a deep breath, and then spend some time mingling with your audience. Speakers often refer to "working the room." Use this time to get to know people and make your points in a one-on-one situation. For the last half hour or so, you have been bringing the library's message to a group. Now you have the opportunity to establish a personal relationship with individuals in the audience. This has the effect of making the message especially relevant.

Radio

Once you've become accustomed to speaking to a group, it's time to consider becoming a media personality. Painful as the thought may be, you and key members of the library staff and board will find that you can reach more people over the air than at individual public gatherings. When plunging into the fearsome sea of media appearances, it's best, if possible, to start with radio. That's because all you have to worry about is your voice. You needn't concern yourself about what you wear or the funny way your mouth twitches when you're nervous. So ask around to find out which radio stations in your area do some of their own local programming and produce community-focused talk shows. Once you've identified them, become a regular listener.

Almost every community has at least one radio station located nearby. It is usually possible to get yourself invited to appear on a locally produced program. Such stations are almost always in need of local people, who chat companionably with a program moderator for half an hour or so. Often several community people will be invited to the same program. You sit around a table and tell listeners about exciting, upcoming events. Few experiences are as likely to strike terror into the hearts of most librarians.

As you twirl the dial, you'll discover that you are most inclined to listen to the relaxed speakers, the ones who sound just as if they are sitting in their living rooms, chatting with friends. Their voices don't sound forced. They laugh often and give the impression that they're having a lot of fun being with you and with the program's host. They sound as if they're speaking completely off the cuff, and there's no evidence that they are reading prepared text. When the host asks an unexpected question, they're able to change topics quickly and probably have a humorous story ready to pop into the conversation.

You'll generally find that experienced radio personalities speak in a conversational voice. They don't sound as if they're trying to project their voices. Even very small radio stations have high-tech microphones that can be centrally positioned and then ignored. They allow you to almost forget that you are being recorded, making it easy to talk in a normal voice. The only problem I've ever found is that you need to be aware of how loudly or softly the other participants are speaking and adjust your own voice to theirs.

Speaking of other participants, don't let them overwhelm you. You may be partnered with highly verbal people who will scarcely let you get a word in edgewise. Sure, you want to ooze charm and appear to be fascinated with what they have to say; however, you're there to talk about the library. Don't try to monopolize the conversation but don't let the discussion move away from the library. Keep bringing it back to the topic you came to talk about. Some librarians find they have a natural gift for the kind of casual, relaxed chatter that seems to work best on the radio. If the moderator of the program is impressed with your gift of gab, you may be invited back. If this works for you, it's a wonderful opportunity. It's even possible that you could be scheduled weekly on a radio program and find something new and interesting to say about the library every week.

Television

Once you've mastered radio, television can be your next challenge. It depends on the station and the locality but chances are that you can get invited to an early morning program. These shows usually involve a group of people sitting around a living room set, drinking coffee, and chatting about the day's events. Cable programs may be broadcast at any time of day.

An alternative is the local news clip. A local television camera crew sets up their equipment outside (or inside) your library and interviews you about your fund-raising campaign or an upcoming library-sponsored event. The interview is shown on the evening news broadcast. Since news programs reach a large number of people, they can be your most effective opportunity to enlist support. However, the interview may be edited down to less than sixty seconds, and the final segment that the public sees and hears may have a very different impact from what you intended. Occasionally, the station is looking for a local reaction to a national news story. If, for example, you spot an Associated Press article about libraries, suggest to the local station that they may want to follow up on it.

So what do you do when you find yourself in front of the camera? First, of course, don't panic. Imagine the people beyond the lens. In fact, you might imagine yourself talking to one or two individuals. Remember that you're reaching these people in their homes. Imagine them at the breakfast table or relaxing in lounge chairs with their feet propped up. Television creates the illusion that you're there with them in their living rooms, so your approach must be informal. If they're at breakfast, then you are a guest who has joined them. Imagine yourself sitting across the breakfast table.

One of the main differences between television and this cozy face-to-face environment is that the camera sees more. In a close-up, awkward gestures are all too visible. If you were really sitting across the living room, you would be looking right at your companions. To create this illusion, you have to look right at the camera lens. It's easy to forget and look at the people who are with you in the studio. A guest in fuzzy bedroom slippers would not deliver a speech. Therefore, you do not want to give the impression of being overrehearsed. Neither do you want to be constantly looking down at your notes. For the same reason, you don't want the viewer to be aware of a teleprompter or cue cards. This type of program always works best if there is a strong element of spontaneity.

Once in a while, you might be in the uncomfortable situation of being interviewed by someone who isn't there at all. That TV camera crew may be all set up in front of your library, but the interviewer is back at the station. Maybe the library spot isn't seen as important enough to make it worth the trip, or another crew is shooting elsewhere. Questions come to you through a small device in your ear. Since you can't appear to be having a conversation with yourself, this means that you must imagine the interviewer behind the camera lens. All too often, you encounter technical problems like feedback from your own voice. Throughout the ordeal you must continue to smile charmingly, appearing not to notice the problem.

Many of us, when invited to appear on television, immediately wonder what we should wear. We've all heard that the camera adds ten pounds to our appearance. Next time you watch the show, notice the color of the background and choose a color that is harmonious but doesn't make you fade into your surroundings. Choose clothes that don't have busy patterns. If the set is a busy one, don't wear any pattern at all. Since jewelry catches the light in unexpected and sometimes irritating ways, always keep it simple. There is special makeup made just for TV, and it should be applied professionally. Local stations do not often have makeup artists, so if you must do your own makeup, concentrate on avoiding shine and gently emphasizing your better features.

Coping with Controversy

Whether you're appearing on radio or television, you may encounter an anchorperson who wants to liven things up with controversy. He or she is quite sure that viewers would rather hear an argument about Internet filters than an announcement about the upcoming Friends of the Library book sale. This means you'll have to be prepared. Consider what controversial library-related issues have appeared recently in the media. Any topic could be fair game, so watch the program as often as possible to find out if the host commonly employs this tactic. If he or she enjoys skewering a guest, then be prepared with a response.

Even though it will be uncomfortable, use controversial questions as opportunities. You will have your audience's undivided attention so take advantage of it. Don't apologize; don't hem and haw. Just answer the question and move the conversation back to the subject you're there to promote. One way to keep the conversation on topic is to chat with the host ahead of time. You'll be surprised how little he or she knows about libraries. You may be able to suggest questions that will not only lead into a discussion for which you're well prepared but your interviewer will look more knowledgeable as well.

If you're fearful that your local media personality fancies himself or herself a hard-nosed investigative reporter, you might enjoy Michael Wessells's article "I Faced Dr. Laura—and Survived!"[2] Wessells writes that he thought it was a practical joke when he found a message from Dr. Laura's producers on his answering machine. He was being asked to appear on her show to discuss libraries and pornography. If you've ever seen Wessells in action, you'll know why he was invited. He has the unique distinction of being both a librarian and a Pentecostal minister. This was apparently too much for Dr. Laura to resist. Well, Wessells quivered in his shoes for a week wondering what he would say. His first and best thought was to call ALA's Office for Intellectual Freedom. They can give you a tremendous amount of help when you're defending the library's position or facing an intellectual-freedom challenge. Wessells writes that "after a half-hour with OIF director Judith Krug, I was ready to tackle an army of hyperactive grizzly bears."

In the article, Wessells makes a distinction regarding the difference between print and television. While thoughts can be presented in a logical order in print, he likens television to a pogo stick jumping between sound bites. This means that you need to limit the number of points you plan to make. Be sure that they're short and snappy. Just in case time crawls too slowly, you may also want to have some extra points ready. In this kind of on-screen environment, questions fly fast and furious. You don't have time to think, so Wessells suggests a mock interview during which someone grills you, throwing one tough question after another at you. Don't break down in tears if the interviewer makes some devastating point at the end and breaks to a commercial before you can reply. That's just the way the game is played. Be sure you've made your points before the ax falls.

No matter how terrified you may feel, practice making a cool, relaxed impression. If you've had any experience in amateur theater, imagine yourself playing a part in a play. In fact, since you've become a media personality, have some fun. Sink your teeth into your role and do it right. Keep clearly focused on the points you want to make because your time will be up long before you realize it. Try to keep an eye on the clock or bring a pocket watch if you can check it inconspicuously. Then when your time is almost up, you will have an opportunity to make one quick, clean jab just before the camera cuts to another guest or to your host for closing remarks.

Let Your Product Speak for Itself

Whether you decide to become a newspaper columnist, a television personality, or just a good all-around publicist for your library, always remember that you have one huge advantage over the bookstore's marketing department. You have a product that you really and truly believe in. It can't help but be obvious to a reader or to a radio audience that your purpose is not to transfer money from their coffers to yours. Of course, you depend on your salary, but that isn't really why you're there. You are there because you are supporting a cause you believe in. And no, you don't have the dollars that the bookstore can lavish on its marketing campaign, but you have the greatest marketing tools of all—commitment and sincerity. If you can just relax and reach out to them, they will not only sense but share your commitment.

NOTES

1. C. Shier, "Thinking Big: Boston Public Library's Hip Media Ad Campaign," *Shy Librarian* 2 (spring 2002): 5.
2. M. Wessells, "I Faced Dr. Laura—and Survived!" *American Libraries* 31 (November 2000): 56–57.

RESOURCES

Bartheld, E. "Tips and Techniques: Promoting an Academic Research Library." *Indiana Libraries* 20 (2001): 24–26.

Brodie, C. S. "Add Some Pizzazz!!! Ideas for Promoting the School Library Media Center." *School Library Media Activities Monthly* 18 (May 2002): 34–35.

Miller, P. *Reaching Every Reader: Promotional Strategies for the Elementary School Library Media Specialist.* New York: Linworth, 2001.

Russo, M. C., et al. "Something for (Almost) Nothing: Public Relations on a Shoestring in an Academic Library." *Library Administration & Management* 16 (summer 2002): 138–45.

Schank, S. K. "'Hey Look at Me!' or, Five Easy Ways to Promote Your Library Media Center, Your Services, and Yourself." *School Library Media Activities Monthly* 18 (June 2002): 28, 39.

Spencer, D. B. "Boosting Libraries at University Orientations: Designing Promotional Booths." *College & Research Libraries News* 63 (June 2002): 418–19.

Van Riel, R. Getting Past G: Measures to Promote Public Library Usage." *Library & Information Update* 1 (August 2002): 38–39.

Wang, J. "Promoting Library Services to Campus Administrative Offices." *College & Research Libraries News* 62 (February 2001): 193–97.

Wilczewski, K. E. "When the Media Calls—." *Indiana Libraries* 19 (2000): 32–34.

Yutzey, S. D. "Promoting Teen Read Week." *Book Report* 20 (November/December 2001): 34–35.

chapter 15

Food and Drink in the Library

For many years, eating has been considered anathema in libraries. Signs stating No Food or Drink have been posted in every reading room, and pity the patron who surreptitiously sneaked in a candy bar or Coca Cola. Although such rules do not sit well with patrons, libraries defend them by invoking the gospel of preservation: food attracts pests, and pests damage books. Many of us remember the graphic evidence our library science instructors brought into the classroom to demonstrate this truism. There were books that had been chewed on by ambrosia beetles, others tasted by buprestid borers, and still others that were the domicile of bostrichid bugs. They were the stuff of librarians' nightmares, and we never forgot them.

Yet there is something very congenial about the pairing of snacking and reading. In fact, curling up with a good book and a cup of tea or coffee is one of life's simple pleasures. As the media keeps making painfully clear, libraries are going through a period of transition. It is a precarious time when there is a reasonable possibility that at least some types of libraries will cease to exist or evolve into a form that we would not now recognize as libraries. We must admit that the transition in some disciplines to exclusive dependence on databases, storing vast quantities of journal articles, legal cases, corporate reports, and other documents, poses a very real threat to libraries.

Clarifying Our Identity

Early databases were not easy to use, and we imagined that there would always be a need for mediators to assist customers just as librarians have always done. More recently, these programs have become so much more user-friendly that it is actually easier to find information in an online service than to locate books or journals in a traditional library. Research can also be done from any location, so the library has no special claim. Academic and special libraries that depend more heavily on databases are feeling a high degree of discomfort. Anthony Grafton, professor of history at Princeton University, believes that some types of libraries may even be becoming dinosaurs. Interviewed in the *Chronicle of Higher Education,* he recalls that "the library was probably a part of everyone's experience at one time, and now my sense is that you can get through as a very high-achieving science major without ever having to set foot in the library."[1]

The Library Is a Place

As we try to define our identity more clearly, one thing that comes up again and again is that despite our ventures into cyberspace, a large part of our identity lies simply in being a place. Libraries have always been the place where people could go to find a world of quiet comfort and where they could find materials that entertained and informed. They could lose themselves in the world of ideas or travel in their imaginations to castles in Spain.

You may remember that public libraries of the past did not lend books. Lending is actually a rather new innovation. When most of the old Carnegies were built, the books were intended to reside permanently in the library. People came to the library to read and often stayed for hours. Those old Carnegies were truly elegant places in their time, and simply being in them was an experience.

Carnegies were not unique, however. Throughout the years, all sorts of libraries provided an opportunity for people to get out of the house, go to a quiet yet sociable place, and lose themselves in books. Academic libraries have a similar history. My own college library was not only a place to prepare for the next day's classes or study for exams but it was also a place to get away from the dorm room, see friends, and flirt with the opposite sex. Libraries have always provided an experience for their users, and it may be this role that guides us safely through the twenty-first century.

Since "a place to be" is an important function of the library, it should be an inviting, enjoyable place. It should be a place where the temperature is moderate, the chairs comfortable, the lighting cheerful, the books and other media enticing. In short, it should be a place that gives pleasure to the senses. We have already discussed ways of making the library visually appealing at some length. We mustn't forget, however, that human beings have other senses, two of which are taste and smell. If you were to ask many people to describe a favorite pastime, they would picture themselves curled up in a large, cozy armchair, possibly by the fire, with a good book and a favorite hot drink. In other words, libraries check out books to people who take them home and enjoy them in just such an environment. To make matters worse, they are likely to read them with breakfast, lunch, dinner, and snacks. If we're honest, we must admit that we do the same thing ourselves. It is really impossible to keep books and food apart unless we never let them out of their hermetically sealed environments.

Learning from Bookstores

Like libraries, bookstores are packed with books, but their cozy cafés are thriving. True, bookstores are not planning to keep their books for decades, but then libraries generally plan to replace most of their materials within a few years. Public libraries, especially, prefer to stock recent books that circulate frequently and withdraw them when public interest wanes. Each library has a small collection that it prizes and plans to keep indefinitely, but except in the case of research and rare book collections, this is quite a small group of items. Is there a way, we wonder, to keep these treasures safe from the cockroach and the silverfish while at the same time entice customers with espressos and biscotti?

Figure 15-1 An attractive railing and a few steps separate this Barnes & Noble café from the rest of the store.

Librarians should not imagine that bookstores are content to have hot chocolate poured over their merchandise. They too are concerned about the damage that edibles and drinkables can do. But modern bookstores are looking for ways to make their customers stay longer and buy more. The café strategy has worked well for them. Is this a strategy that could also be successful in your library? To answer this question fully, it will be necessary to do an extensive analysis of your library, its customers, and its staff. Some libraries have tried it and agree that a café or coffee shop brings in customers who would otherwise be unaware of the library and its services. Others have had disastrous results and have quietly decided to abandon the idea of food in the library. How is it possible to successfully introduce food into the library? What is it that the successful libraries have done right? If you are presently trying to weigh the pros and cons, here are some points to consider.

Collections

If you are thinking about a café, one of the first questions you will probably want to answer is whether the library's collections can peacefully coexist with a food-service establishment. For example, if a sizable proportion of your library's collection consists of rare books and manuscripts, then the answer is, of course, a resounding no! In most libraries, however, the answer is not so clear-cut. You probably have some valuable books and some not-so-valuable ones. You have a few collections that you do not plan to discard for many years, and you have popular sections that are (or should be) weeded every year or two. In general, public libraries have found that collection issues need not prevent them from having some sort of food service in the library although careful planning is required. Most of the collection should be weeded out every five to ten years, and only a major pest infestation would noticeably affect the collection within this time frame. Community and four-year colleges also find it is usually possible to accommodate a café. In large research libraries, the big question is where are the more valuable collections located? If, for example, a large collection is housed on its own floor, then food may pose few problems. If such collections can be found throughout the library, then it may be impossible to completely segregate areas where food is permitted from areas where it is forbidden.

Location

At the start of the project, successful librarians have taken a good look at their buildings. Where would they locate a café? Is there a space that is not currently being fully used? Is a new building, building addition, or renovation in the planning stages? Ideally, the area chosen should be as far from the book collection as possible. It should be large enough to include a preparation area and a space for tables and chairs. Remember that you want your customers to remain here and drink their lattes or finish munching their bagels before they enter the library proper. This means that the space needs to be large enough to accommodate sufficient tables that they will have no trouble finding a place to sit.

The preparation area needs to be large enough and sufficiently well equipped to meet local food-service regulations. There should be enough space to stow supplies like paper cups, napkins, and plastic spoons. Food storage may require locking metal cabinets and refrigerators.

Like the library meeting room, it will be more successful if its hours of operation do not depend on the library's hours. Most cafés are built around coffee, and coffee is drunk mainly in the morning. Your café will be more successful if it can open at 7:00 or 8:00, long before most public libraries are open for business. Therefore, a separate entrance is desirable. The more extensive the library's hours, the more likely that a café without a separate entrance could be successful.

Successful libraries generally try to keep food in a clearly identified area. Therefore, it is helpful if there are natural barriers between food and books. A separate floor, wing, or room is preferable, but simple solutions like wrought-iron railings will work too. Many libraries find basements to be a good place to put a café if it is not too difficult to bring wiring up to code and make provision for fire safety. For example, if yours is an old and grungy basement, you can create a darkened, coffeehouse atmosphere that will be the perfect spot for poetry readings and impromptu entertainment. Almost all it requires in the way of interior decoration is dark-colored paint to cover walls, ceiling, unsightly pipes, and ugly fixtures. Before you become too enthusiastic about your project, talk to your local fire marshal. If your basement was never intended for public use, it may not have enough fire exits.

A Café May Be a Cooperative Endeavor

Libraries are usually part of a larger organization and may be unable to make a decision about a food-service operation without approval from above. Cafés are, of course, not unique to libraries, and, occasionally, you will actually find yourself in competition with another department that is already providing this service. For example, on a college campus, the library may be perceived as being in competition with the student center, or there may be a full-scale food-service department that believes it has an exclusive monopoly.

It may require considerable skill and tact to convince the powers that be that a library café does not pose a threat to their profits. For example, it may be possible for one of the student center's vendors to handle an expanded operation with an additional location.

Whether or not a university outsources its food-service operation, there may be an opportunity for collaboration. Since the reasons why the library is considering a café have little to do with money, it probably does not matter if the food-service vendor takes most of the profit. Just as long as bureaucratic conflicts are eliminated and the library covers its costs, your ends can be achieved.

What the library does care about, however, is retaining some control over the actual operation. Since the idea was conceived as a way of bringing additional customers to the library and enhancing the experience of its existing clientele, that goal must be achieved. Therefore, the quality of the items sold must meet high standards, and the operation must not interfere with the library's other activities. This will require extensive discussion with the appropriate department, culminating in a written agreement. Since it is important that the library maintain good working relationships with other departments, the library café should not become a source of conflict.

Sometimes it is simply a matter of educating your county commissioners or city manager concerning recent developments in libraries. They may have a very traditional view of the library and its services that just needs to be updated. Take advantage of their experience and learn from their mistakes. Providing food service is a surprisingly common function of government, and whether you are talking to someone who is involved in serving food in the local jail or for an early childhood program, he or she can provide a great deal of basic information about local regulations, space needs, and other important considerations. They can also put you in touch with others in the same business, and, gradually, you will amass a wealth of useful information.

Legal Issues

The introduction of food brings up a host of health and sanitation issues that must be fully investigated. The first thing you will want to do is find out what government body regulates and inspects food-service operations. If your library is part of a large organization like a state university, the parent body is already operating cafeterias and snack bars. There is probably an office on campus that regulates such operations. If yours is a county library, maybe the county provides a lunchroom for staff. Check with the manager and ask who you should contact for regulatory information. If, however, your library is not part of an organization that has experience with the food-service business, you will need to look further afield. In most localities, restaurants must display a certificate verifying that they have met sanitation requirements. The certificate includes the name of the responsible agency.

Before you do any serious planning, you must find out whether the space you have in mind can be made to meet local regulations. For example, coffee cups and other dinnerware require commercial dishwashers that can maintain a higher water temperature than your home dishwasher. This means a greater electrical load, so you may need to upgrade the library's electrical service to accommodate such equipment. Think about espresso machines as well as refrigerators to keep coffee beans fresh and store milk and cream. A nearby sink will probably be required for washing hands and cleaning out equipment. As is the case with the dishwasher, the water must be hot enough to kill germs, so a new hot-water heater may need to be added to the plans.

Another important consideration is insurance. Before making any commitments, find out what the addition of a café would do to your library's insurance premiums. In most cases, the increased cost can come out of the money the vendor pays to the library. In other situations, however, an insurance provider will flat-out refuse to permit the café or will raise premiums well beyond the library's ability to pay. It often depends on the nature of the operation and the kind of food preparation that will be taking place. A deep-fat fryer, for example, like the ones found in most fast-food restaurants, considerably increases the likelihood of fire or injury.

Complexity of Operation

When you and the library staff first begin thinking about food service, you are probably just envisioning a good cup of coffee. You are thinking, "What could be simpler?" Staff make coffee every morning. You're just extending the opportunity to your customers. Gradually, however, the project becomes more elaborate. You have to have goodies with your coffee, don't you? That means bakery items. When you begin talking with prospective vendors, they are likely to suggest sandwiches, soups, and desserts. Bit by bit, what was at first a very simple operation becomes a full-fledged restaurant. If your project is going to be successful, you will need to get it quickly under control. Each additional menu item needs more equipment. Each means escalating the objections your insurance provider is likely to raise.

Begin with the simplest operation possible, probably just a coffee cart where customers can get drinks and a few pastries baked off the premises. I'm a big fan of coffee carts, and most vendors like them too. They're very sophisticated, self-contained units that provide most of the essentials for running a simple coffee operation. Even though they're costly, they're a good investment for vendors since they can take them to another location should the library café prove unsuccessful. However, even this simple operation will involve some building modifications and some complex planning.

Sending Out an RFP

Most successful libraries with cafés have learned that the library shouldn't even consider operating it by itself. Librarians have no experience with food service and will undoubtedly make a mess of the project. Sometimes a Friends of the Library group hosts a café to raise money for their projects. As long as this is a very simple, small-scale operation limited to coffee in paper cups and prebaked sweets, the café can be fairly successful. However, even such a limited endeavor is far more labor-intensive than most people would expect. In all probability, you will want to contract with an outside vendor that is already engaged in the business and has a successful track record. You will, therefore, be working with your parent organization to develop a request for proposals (RFP), and it is this step that can make or break the project.

If the library has had little experience preparing RFPs, it would be a good idea to get help from your parent organization. There's probably a purchasing agent or other administrator who does this on a regular basis. He or she can provide a file cabinet full of boilerplate language that will save you expense and legal hassles in the future.

What will you include in your request for proposals, and how specific will you be? What will you insist on now, and what will you leave open for future negotiation? You don't want to box yourself in and lose what might potentially be a good opportunity. On the other hand, you want to include stiff-enough requirements that you can eliminate from consideration any vendors that are either financially unstable or otherwise have a poor track record.

What will you require of the vendor, and what will you offer to provide? Will the space be rented for a flat fee, or will the library get a percent of the profits? Who will be responsible for cleanup costs?

Most of the issues discussed in this section need to be included in the RFP. Since it will be important to include all the restrictions specified by the insurance company and health department, all your research and meetings should have taken place before you begin drafting this document. For example, if you don't want a vendor bringing deep-fat fryers onto the premises, then now is the time to make that clear. An acceptable range of menu items should also be specified. So that potential vendors can accurately assess their chances for a successful business operation, you will need to provide specifics on the available space and equipment, including a floor plan with the water supply and electrical supply clearly marked. Including typical library attendance figures helps the vendor predict how much business can be anticipated.

Most successful libraries do not initially plan to make a profit on their café operation, but they do want the proceeds to cover their increased expenses. Some charge a flat rent. Others negotiate for an escalating percentage of the gross receipts. It is important to the library that the chosen vendor be successful and that the café becomes a thriving establishment. Otherwise, the library will be left with a space it has modified for a food-service operation and no vendor to run it. Negotiating for a second vendor will be time-consuming and expensive. If one vendor was unsuccessful, it will be harder to sell the idea to others. Therefore, extracting a lot of money during the start-up period is not a good idea. If the business becomes very successful, the library certainly has a right to profit from it.

It is a good idea to do everything possible to get the café off to a good start. You may wish to begin with an agreement that requires the vendor to invest a certain amount of money in the facility itself. For the first year or at least six months, the library might not receive any money at all, but the vendor would be required to add an electrical circuit, install a hot-water heater, or make other modifications in the space. If this is the route you take, be sure the contract the library negotiates with the vendor makes it clear that the work must meet all city or county regulations and that the library has the right to inspect and approve the work.

Decide in advance how custodial duties will be handled. Often, the library is responsible for heavy-duty cleaning, the café for keeping things neat and tidy. If possible, avoid carpeting in the café area. Untreated coffee stains can spell disaster for carpets, so café staff must be ever vigilant. A stain that is treated immediately is much easier to remove than one that sits for days. Make it as easy as possible for the café staff to maintain their area.

Evaluating Proposals

Let us say that your library has written an excellent RFP with help from your parent organization and possibly legal advice from the library's attorney. You have identified coffee shops and other similar establishments in your own and neighboring communities. To each of these, you have sent an RFP. Included in that document should be a compulsory meeting at which you provide potential vendors with additional information as well as a tour of the proposed space. This will give you an opportunity to talk with vendors individually and see the project from their points of view. You will also be able to see how much interest there is in your project and identify any possible problems before they get out of hand.

Bids are opened on a certain day at a certain time. The people evaluating the bids should be as knowledgeable about the project as possible. You probably won't be inundated with proposals, and you may not get exactly what you're looking for. In my own experience, the smaller, hungrier vendor worked out better for my library than the larger corporate entity. Nevertheless, *hungry* does not mean totally lacking in financial resources.

If the café is outside the security gate, books and other materials will need to be checked out before they are taken to the café. That's a good idea because it will give the staff an opportunity to take notice of their condition when they are returned. If food and drink are served within the library proper, try to establish a buffer zone between the café and the library's more vulnerable materials. Arrange displays of popular but more expendable materials near the café. You might even include some shelves or bookcases containing unneeded magazines and book donations that customers are free to peruse or take home with them.

Coffee cafés are just one way in which libraries are trying to make themselves more attractive to customers. They may not work for every library, but the goal is valid for all. Increasing the number of people who use the library must become a high priority. If a café doesn't seem to be a workable strategy, ask yourself what would work better in your environment. It might be a weekly movie night complete with popcorn or possibly a new lounge area or a meeting room with compressed-video capability. Somehow, if your library is to survive and prosper, it will be necessary for the library staff to become more innovative. New ideas must be tried and evaluated. The status quo will probably not see your library through the twenty-first century.

NOTE

1. S. Carlson, "The Deserted Library," *Chronicle of Higher Education* (November 16, 2001), http://www.chronicle.com/infotech (accessed February 4, 2003).

RESOURCES

Kloberdanz, K. "Speak Softly and Carry a Big Mug." *Illinois Libraries* 78 (spring 1996): 75–76.

MacLeod, L. "Bestseller Blend: Starbucks and Library." *Public Libraries* 37 (March/April 1998): 102.

———. "Lattes 'n Libraries." *Bottom Line* 11 (1998): 97–100.

Masters, D. C., et al. "Café Gelman: An Innovative Use of Library Space." *Journal of Academic Librarianship* 19 (January 1994): 388–90.

Reese, N. "Café Service in Public Libraries." *Public Libraries* 38 (May/June 1999): 176–78.

chapter 16

Finding the Time and the Money

Even though the strategies suggested in this book are usually inexpensive to implement, there is always some cost involved, whether for staff time or materials. If your transformation strategies are successful and result in more patrons, more checkouts, and more Internet use, library operating expenses will also rise. In general, as a library achieves greater visibility, its budget will increase, and the effort will more than pay for itself. However, in the early stages, when rapid change is occurring, your budget may be stretched to the breaking point. To get through such a crisis period, you are going to have to find ways of increasing and expanding available resources or sit back and allow entropy to set in. If you don't want your library transformation to come to an ignominious halt, where will you find the resources to achieve your goals?

Focus on Resources, Not Money

Remember that the term I'm using is not *money* or *staff* but *resources.* A wide assortment of resources can help you achieve your goals if you use them effectively. Too often, librarians look at their budgets, especially in a year when student enrollment is down or the economy is sagging, and despair. They assume that they're going to have to tighten their belts, curtail services, and just endure until good times return. Such an attitude almost inevitably leads to a downward spiral. As services decline, so do attendance and circulation. As library use drops, so does library visibility, and, ultimately, the budget drops again. Every library has hard times, but they needn't spell defeat to your vision. The trick lies in substituting available resources for the ones that have dried up. This requires a three-pronged attack:

1. Reallocate the monetary resources you still have so as to affect public services as little as possible. In fact, consider whether a readjustment of priorities could actually support expanded public services. This way, the library can emerge from the crisis with its customer-support base intact.
2. Supplement paid staff with volunteers wherever possible. Simplify routine tasks to allow a volunteer to perform them effectively.
3. Give the library a fresh look. Use the same skills bookstores and other retail businesses have mastered to give the library a look of affluence and excitement. Identify those changes that can be wrought with the least time and money.

Establishing Priorities

Despite tight budgets, libraries can usually expand their services by focusing on priorities. Like bookstores, libraries have adopted modern technology and even embraced it. Yet librarians may fail to understand how technology has changed staffing needs, processing procedures, and a host of tasks involved in running a library. Because, unlike bookstores, they have no clear bottom line, they may not realize that some procedures and services are no longer needed.

The Public's View of the Library

As a profession, we inherited a nineteenth-century library model, remnants of which are still with us. This was a highly labor-intensive model that is no longer appropriate. Consider whether your library is really using staff and financial resources to support twenty-first-century priorities. If attracting users to the library and meeting their information and recreation needs are the goals, then why isn't this where time and money are concentrated? Bookstores have been successful in melding the old with the new, in shedding their nineteenth-century mustiness while at the same time treasuring the customer service and cozy atmosphere of an earlier time. Libraries too can take the best from their past and enhance it with sophisticated marketing strategies.

A while back a poll was taken to see how John Q. Public felt about a variety of careers. I can't find my dog-eared clipping, but the results so surprised me that they are engraved forever on my memory. The average American, it turned out, thought that librarians had the least stressful job on the list of careers surveyed. If I know anything about the views of librarians, I believe we would say with one voice that we've got news for John Q.!

Although our work is both satisfying and rewarding, libraries are nevertheless experiencing hard times. Heartbreaking tales of public library closings and slashed academic library budgets abound. Federal funding for libraries has been cut, and real poverty is not uncommon. Most librarians who have been in the profession any length of time will recall a succession of catastrophic budgets, and few libraries have ever had money to burn.

Money is not the only source of stress. Parent academic institutions, corporations, and government units often have little understanding of the needs of libraries. They can unknowingly create an environment in which it is extremely difficult for the library director or staff to function. Such continuing trauma inevitably takes a sad toll on libraries.

Are there experienced librarians who haven't at least once discovered on their first day at a new job that they are faced with a first-class library disaster? This goes for research giants, church libraries, public branches—almost every genus you'd care to name. When you get right down to it, there aren't very many libraries in glowing good health.

What John Q. hasn't thought much about (or library boards, school principals, or college presidents, for that matter) is that libraries are very labor-intensive and expensive institutions. Despite clichés about hallowed halls of learning, libraries are usually only minimally funded. They are even sometimes seen as the "low-man" in their organizations. Faculty members and garbage collectors (no relationship between the two implied) are seen as indispensable, while the library can limp along without endangering the public safety or the faculty-student ratio.

It is most unlikely that any librarians have succeeded in accurately conveying to their funding agencies the enormous expenditure in labor necessary to catalog and maintain a collection properly. How delighted are the powers that be when circulation statistics rise. Yet it never seems to register that each of these volumes will return like the swallows to Capistrano, and each must be checked in and shelved and dusted along with the flocks that were merely leafed through and abandoned. Computer data require similarly extensive effort to remain current and accessible.

Do any of these tales of woe sound familiar? The inventory is years behind. The computer system has more glitches than bits or bytes, and some MARC records have mysteriously disappeared into the ether. Staff morale is low, and tech services isn't talking to circulation. The mending mountain looms ominously, and the periodical list is out-of-date. Worst of all, the great ideas you had when you arrived are gradually dying on the vine because there's never enough time. Granted, money is the root of at least some of these evils but not all by any means. It must be written in the stars somewhere that libraries are supposed to be poor. To make things worse, we can't win. If we're doing a good job and making our patrons happy, we're going to need more books, more databases, more staff, and more space to handle increased demand.

Accentuating the Positive

Though the library world may look grim and every librarian has her personal tale of woe, most libraries can usually function more efficiently. It's all a matter of deciding what comes first: what will eventually glare and what can safely be swept under the rug. Although it may sound a bit shocking, lots of good and worthy projects can be swept under the rug, and no one will be the wiser. What often holds us back and makes us ineffective is our inclination toward perfectionism. I've occasionally imagined conducting a study proving there are more perfectionists per capita among librarians than in any other profession. For our own psychological well-being, we should probably abandon libraries en masse. They neither are nor ever will be perfect places, and we'll continue to wallow in unending frustration if we don't face facts.

If the guilt twinges have not become too painful, let's consider what can safely be swept under the carpet. Most dysfunctional libraries have at least one thing in common. They haven't set any priorities. There is insufficient money or staff to do all that needs to be done, so we do a little of this and a little of that. Our library-school education remains with us still in the form of a perpetually uneasy conscience. We learned how things should be done in the best of all possible worlds. For some reason, the librarian's eternal longing for professionalism occasionally expresses itself in making things as complicated as possible, in embroidering details until they become works of art.

First Things First

It is essential to look objectively at the resources at hand and decide what can reasonably be done with them. Librarians, in their angst over their libraries' inadequacies, feel better if they can do just a few things right. They can take pride in these islands of order when depression threatens. My mother had a friend who was an absolutely dreadful housekeeper. You had to clear a path to get from one room to another. She had, however, the most beautifully organized kitchen cabinets you ever saw. They must have comforted her when she got to musing over her housewifely inadequacies. Since her home was never condemned by the board of health and her family remained robust, no great harm was done.

Obviously, the "kitchen cabinet" approach can have much graver consequences in a library, but is there really a better way? The one absolutely essential thing a library must do is serve the needs of its patrons. Of course, the computer system must be tended, the books cataloged, the periodicals checked in, and the bills paid, but remember why the library is there in the first place. Your library was established to serve the information needs of your public, and it's that public who evaluates the effectiveness of your library. You and your staff are judged on their expectations. Don't ever underestimate them because they know so little about libraries. If you are not meeting their needs—and I mean what they tell you they need, not what you think they should need—you are failing. Establishing priorities, however, is not quite this easy. The next time you are attempting to decide on the importance of a particular action, ask yourself the following questions:

Can you weigh the impact of the action against the other alternatives? Will it really make a difference? Will the impact be really noticeable?

How is the action connected to the library's mission? How well does it relate to the strategic plan?

Can you rank your options based on how much they contribute to the library's service goals?

Will library patrons see an immediate change if the action is taken? Will staff experience an improvement in morale or working conditions?

Does this action represent the most timely and cost-effective way of achieving the goal?

Is it urgent that this action be taken immediately, or do you have time to assemble more complete information?

Are you the right person to take this action? Should you leave the decision to a staff member or to your own superior?

When you begin listing priorities, ask yourself how your public would react if this or that task on your "to-do" list never got done. A cutback or improvement in services would have immediate impact. Backroom operations take a while longer to filter down. If an activity never filters down, never makes a significant difference in the way your customers use the library, then maybe you don't need it. Maybe it can be swept under the rug and safely forgotten.

Achieving Visible Results

Much of the essential work in libraries, like maintaining the catalog, is seemingly endless. Hours of staff time must be spent on interminable yet invisible tasks. However, these efforts are largely unseen by your customers. They may eventually notice a full-blown crisis, but you'll never be showered with compliments for superior bibliographic control. Though a lot of staff time must inevitably be consumed in such invisible labors, many projects requiring very little staff time can have a major impact on customers.

When you establish priorities, it is important to put a "price tag" on each item on your list. In other words, it is necessary to evaluate each goal in terms of its cost in both staff time and money before making any binding decisions. Of course, you're going to have several items at the top that absolutely must be achieved no matter what, but keep this group small. Give yourself some flexibility. Look for impressive achievements, which provide a sense of momentum at relatively little cost to you and your staff. Don't think I'm encouraging you to abandon the straight and narrow path. If you've ever inherited a library where standard library practices were apparently unheard of, the mere mention of bibliographic control may inspire you to place hand on heart.

Think about this. Top priorities should be the tasks, activities, projects, services, and so on that make the most difference to your patrons. If you can manage to get those things done, you'll have happy customers who'll sing your praises, write nice letters, vote for the bond issue, and generally make your life ever so much pleasanter. Tell that library school conscience to look the other way. Sure you've got to maintain some professional standards, but stifle the urge if it starts getting out of hand. If your patrons are happy, you had "darn sight" better be happy too.

Dealing with Crisis

As this book is being written, articles are appearing in both library journals and in the popular press about the impact of the enfeebled economy on libraries. In an article in the *Washington Post* entitled "Libraries across U.S. Are Scaling Back," reporter Jason Straziuso writes, "Libraries across the country are cutting staff and services because of a budget crunch.... The problem stems from tight state and local budgets. When cuts need to be made, libraries are hard-pressed to compete against, say, fire and police protection."[1] As evidence of the crisis, he cites the main library in Erie, Pennsylvania, which will soon begin closing on Sundays; the Denver Public Library, which will double its fines to twenty cents a day; and Cincinnati Public, which planned to close five branches until a loud public outcry convinced library administrators to reduce staff and services. Elsewhere in the nation, he notes that in New York City, service will be reduced at sixty-seven of the system's eighty-five branches to five days a week; the Berkley Public Library in suburban Detroit will cut hours and lay off its children's librarian; and Seattle closed down its libraries for a week in August and December.

Reducing Hours of Operation

During the past year, I have spent a lot of time talking with librarians who are considering restricting library hours. Most, like those above, have experienced repeated budget cuts. They have tightened their belts over and over again until they've reached what they consider the end of their tether. It may be that the decision to reduce library hours was made only after every other option was explored. It may also be the case that repeated budget cuts have resulted in so many cost-cutting measures that there is no alternative.

Yet most of these librarians also believe that they cannot allow the library's budget to continue to be hacked to bits without making a very forceful public statement. The public must be made to understand that the library cannot continue to absorb these revenue cuts without a corresponding reduction in services. They view the decision to close the library on certain days or during certain hours as an anguished cry for attention. It is a way of saying, "Take notice! Look what's happening to your library!"

When these librarians imagine the outcome of such a decision, their reasoning goes something like this: if people come to the library and find it closed, they can't help but notice. If they are forced to notice, then, hopefully, they will respond. The message of the library's poverty will be conveyed much more effectively than if the library simply uses traditional channels to communicate its plight.

Although the decision may be a calculated effort to bring the financial crisis to the public, one can't dismiss the possibility that, deep down, these librarians are reacting to the situation with personal hurt and anger. They are in a sense saying, "If you [the powers that be] won't give my library the funds it needs, then you will be punished. If we can't have what we want, then you'll be sorry." This is a childish response but perfectly understandable in the circumstances. The problem with such a response is that it can do incalculable harm to the library.

When you close the library, most of the people who will notice will be your regular customers. The fact that the library has sustained repeated cuts indicates that the number of regular customers is not large enough to sway political opinion. It is true that your regular patrons should be encouraged to become more politically active. However, in general, if library usage were higher, funding would follow.

If you reduce the library's hours, you are also reducing usage. This means not only reducing the opportunities that regular customers have to use the library but also making it less likely that new customers will happen to discover its services and become library supporters. For these reasons, reducing the library's hours of operation tends to set in motion a downward spiral. If the library is already in a slump, then reduced hours will exacerbate it, making it nearly impossible to halt or reverse the momentum.

Paving the Way for Recovery

Yet, for these libraries, the fact remains that each year brings increased financial stress. Such libraries cannot continue to provide the same services at the same levels that they did during good times. Cutbacks are most assuredly needed. A clear sense of priorities is needed now more than at any other time. The budget cuts chosen must not prevent the library from recovering from the crisis. They must be carefully planned so as to retain the tools and resources needed to pull the library out of its slump. Surely, near the top of its list of priorities must be placed the goal of developing a large, articulate, and politically effective customer base. This means establishing stronger relationships with your present customers while at the same time attracting new people to the library. These new arrivals must be quickly brought into the fold and converted to the library's cause as swiftly as possible.

Certainly, new customers cannot be expected to discover the treasures and delights that await them at the library if the library is closed when they happen to encounter it. If the bookstore in our comparison finds that it needs to sell more books, it doesn't cut its hours. Reduced hours will mean reduced cash-register receipts. Instead, they must reduce costs, and libraries must do the same. True, the time may come when there are no other alternatives, when every other option has been tried and red ink still flows copiously.

Creating an Effective Volunteer Staff

Although a successful library is the result of its many components working in harmony, no underfunded library can succeed without an army of committed, well-trained volunteers. Bringing a troubled library back to life is a very time-consuming endeavor and requires not only the efforts of paid staff but the talents of diverse volunteers, each of whom can bring a special gift to the library's program. Although you have probably realized that you are going to need more help to achieve your goals, you may erroneously believe that your goals will be achieved once you have recruited a sufficient number of warm bodies. These new arrivals will be of little use, however, unless they are truly committed to the library's mission and trained to perform needed tasks accurately and efficiently. If training is haphazard, little work will be accomplished, and much of what is done will have to be redone. Your paid staff, instead of revitalizing the library, will be busy undoing the mistakes made by the volunteer staff.

If new recruits are not kept fully informed about what is happening and given a voice in decision making, they will become passive and uninterested. Their work must satisfy some personal need of their own or they will soon drift away and move on to other activities they find more interesting and fulfilling. One of the main reasons volunteers become involved is that they need to be needed. They must be made to feel that they are a part of the library and their work is fully appreciated.

All of us need to know that what we are doing is worthwhile—that our work and expertise are essential to the group effort. We need to know not only that we are doing a good job but that others are aware of and appreciate our work. Everyone who takes on a volunteer job is motivated in part by the desire to do something fulfilling, something that satisfies the need to be needed.

If volunteers are to be successful, they need jobs and job descriptions just like paid staff. The duties outlined in their job descriptions fall into two basic categories. First, you will be identifying tasks that are currently being done by paid staff. Using volunteer labor will free paid staff to become involved in the effort of transforming and revitalizing the library.

Second, you will be seeking out skills that the library staff may not possess. For example, you may need more accomplished writers to produce the publications that you've planned. You may need an artist to produce the graphics or a website designer to create a library presence on the World Wide Web. These tasks are not currently being performed, so you will have less information about how they are to be fitted into the library's operation.

It has been found throughout the business world that those organizations that have well-written, comprehensive job descriptions for all active participants function more effectively. Those in which responsibilities float casually from one individual to another accomplish less and achieve fewer goals. Get together with staff members to discuss the specific library tasks that are going to need to get done and try to put groups of tasks together in a logical way.

Expanding the Role of Library Volunteers

In most libraries, volunteers can wear more than one hat. They can make public presentations, solicit donations and perform copy cataloging tasks, or they can create displays and process paperbacks. Their job descriptions will become complex. However, it is best that each have a single supervisor or staff mentor. This way a relationship is established between paid and volunteer staff. They become an integral part of the library team. The following list is just a sample of the kind of job descriptions to be written:

Fund-raiser

Book-sale volunteer or coordinator

Landscaper

Painter

Woodworker

Cataloging and processing volunteer

Website content provider and designer

Public relations

Ice Cream Social (or any other event) volunteer or coordinator

New book display coordinator

Local history coordinator

Library historian

Video inspector

Responding to Change

As your plans develop, tasks will change too, so new job descriptions will need to be written. One phase of the effort will become less time-consuming, and new needs will emerge. It may be necessary to redesign existing job descriptions to take these changes into consideration. You and the staff may be performing a kind of juggling act, delegating the new responsibilities and keeping your antennae attuned to volunteers who may have little to do or be on the verge of dropping out. At the same time, make sure other volunteers are not overloaded with work.

Since there should be no queen (or king) bees in your organization, each job description should include some tasks that traditionally carry a higher status, some that are especially enjoyable, and some that are downright unpleasant. No job description should be an amalgam of all the jobs that no one else wants to do, and necessary tasks should not be left out of job descriptions merely because no one wants to do them.

Customer Service Training

Perhaps the most important thing that volunteers can do is to give your library customers the kind of personal, individualized attention that harried staff may be unable to provide. Elsewhere, I described an information desk in the entrance to the library that was staffed entirely by volunteers. Each customer was greeted personally and each asked about his or her library needs. This made an enormous difference in the public's perception of the library and cost almost nothing.

Volunteers, however, need formal training in customer service. Since it is essential that all staff—whether paid or volunteer—meet the same high standards, a training program is absolutely necessary. Just because volunteers are donating their time to the library, it does not mean that they can put less effort into developing public service skills than if they were being paid a salary. Your customers will not usually know who is a volunteer and who is a paid staff member. They will hold the library responsible for any slights or aggravations they endure at the hands of a volunteer just as they would in the case of a staff member.

Reviving a Library on a Zero Budget

To be truthful, the title of this section is a little misleading. A library must have a budget to really meet the needs of its users. Donations of materials and services are great, but if you want to have more than a used-book reading room, some money is necessary. However, there are times when no ready money is on hand. Let's say you have a fund-raising program in place, but it has not yet begun to yield results. Enthusiastic volunteers are coming onboard, and you want to keep them involved and active. There are many things that can be done now to invigorate a dormant library. With nothing more than inexpensive supplies and a lot of hard work, your library can begin to come alive again. If you need some new ideas, here is a baker's dozen to get you started:

STEP 1

Remove out-of-date signs, announcements, old calendars, and cast-off paintings from the walls.

Take down any decorations that look dusty and dreary. Do you really need a plastic bust of Shakespeare? An old globe that doesn't show recent political changes? Remove anything that's creating clutter but serving no useful purpose.

Streamline your space. It's truly amazing what people give to libraries. Don't allow would-be artists to seek immortality for their work or board members to assuage their guilt and rid their own homes of granny's bad taste. If you must, remove these eyesores in two steps, moving them first to a storage shed. If you hear no outcry, then you can send them to the dump.

STEP 2

Paint everything that's paintable.

Get some guidance from a professional decorator, select two somewhat trendy but harmonious colors, and go to work. Most volunteers will have no difficulty painting walls with inexpensive latex paint. Long-abused wooden furniture takes somewhat more skill, and painting plastic and metal requires some previous experience (don't forget the primer). Old, smelly carpets can be pulled up and floor paint or polyurethane varnish applied. Give some thought to what will be happening to this space when money becomes available in the future. Will it be professionally remodeled or renovated? Be careful that you make no changes that will result in more expense later.

STEP 3

Weed obsolete books and other materials from the collection.

This includes any items that have not circulated in years. Get rid of vinyl records, beta videos, 8 mm films, and other long-gone formats for which equipment is no longer widely available. Remove each book or media package from the shelf. Then, if you really want to keep it, dust it and mend it. Remove stains and other gunk with a wet paper towel. This will not be anyone's favorite job, but it's amazing what a difference it will make to the look of the collection. While materials are off the shelves, clean the bookcases or stack sections. Paint them too if needed.

STEP 4

Become a regular at the town dump.

Make as many trips to the dump as needed. Get rid of the boxes of old books piled up along the walls. Cart off that ancient equipment donated by a local business but never used. You don't need equipment "just in case." It takes up too much room and is too expensive to repair.

STEP 5

Make new signs.

Use the techniques we've discussed to print signs in colors that harmonize with your new look. Even if these signs will be temporary, now is an excellent time to begin analyzing ways in which signs can make the collection more accessible.

STEP 6

Make the library lighter and brighter.

Replace burnt-out lightbulbs and fluorescent tubes. Make better use of sunlight. Wash the windows. Get rid of old, dingy curtains. Once the curtains are gone, decide where solar glare is a problem. Purchase inexpensive miniblinds if you really need to control glare from particular windows, but you don't need a blind for every window. Lighten rooms by using white paint for the ceiling and overhead pipes and fixtures. Experiment with different types of fluorescent tubes to achieve a warmer, more natural environment.

STEP 7

Create a children's nook.

Go wild with wall color. Ask a local dealer to donate colorful carpet remnants. Sew large floor pillows to go with it. Use bright plastic crates for seating and surfaces. Paint worn furniture in primary colors.

Figure 16-1 Norfolk (Va.) Public Library's Teen Advisory Board helped to remodel this colorful children's room.

STEP 8

Attract new users.

Plan book talks, book club meetings, and other adult programs to make use of library space after closing. Schedule story hours and other children's programs before the library opens. Use volunteers to expand library programming.

STEP 9

Become a bargain hunter.

Find inexpensive sources for furniture, library materials, and equipment. Check with your school district, county, or municipality to see how they dispose of surplus furniture and equipment. Institutional furniture is usually well made but dreary-looking. A coat of paint does wonders, but make sure you can really use what you get. You don't want the library to start looking like a secondhand furniture store.

STEP 10

Take a sniff.

How does the library smell? Does it seem damp and moldy? You're going to need to invest in some dehumidifiers. They're relatively inexpensive and can make a big difference if your problem is not a serious mold infestation. Are you breathing in a lot of dust? After you've given the whole library a really good cleaning, change all the filters in your HVAC system and experiment with home air purifiers. Run them for a week or two, then move them to other library areas and start them up again. Maybe there's just not enough fresh air. Open windows and use fans to expel stale air and introduce fresh outdoor air. Do this even in winter since modern climate-control equipment sometimes does little more than recycle used-up air. It is amazing how smell affects our attitude toward a place. Patrons may literally turn up their noses and think poorly of a library just because it doesn't have a pleasant odor.

STEP 11

Look outside.

Spruce up the entrance to the library. How about designating a Saturday for library cleanup? Bring rakes, shovels, and trash bags. Weed the lawn, prune trees and bushes, and plant some new perennials. Painting the outside of a building is a major project, but if yours is a small building, then it may be a possibility. Otherwise, consider repainting the trim. It can make a big difference.

STEP 12

Create a publicity blitz.

Write press releases for the local media. Place articles in your local newspapers. Write book reviews. Put up posters in shopping malls and community centers. Make attractive displays of books, nonprint media, and donated items. Change them frequently. Create a new bookshelf. Print out lists of new books. If your library is visible from the street, use the area out front for activities that will attract attention. Children's events are especially colorful, and fund-raising events benefit from balloons and large signs that are easy to read from a distance.

STEP 13

Expand services.

Use volunteer help to extend hours. Have talented volunteers put together an imaginative display or newsletter or both. In school libraries, assign volunteers to work with individual teachers to design more productive visits to the library. In public libraries, assign volunteers to work with homeschoolers and other groups that can profit from customized services.

Only the smallest libraries can function without money, and there's no question that funding has a huge impact on the success of a library program. Nevertheless, the library has other kinds of capital it can expend. Perhaps the most precious of these assets is public goodwill. Think about the thousands and thousands of concerned people who volunteer in libraries, serve on library boards and foundations, and raise money through Friends of the Library groups. These are priceless human resources on which bookstores cannot call. When we are fretting about all the money and all the staff and all the expertise that bookstores can bring to bear on their operation, we must remember that libraries are rich in other ways.

NOTE

1. J. Straziuso, "Libraries across U.S. Are Scaling Back," *Washington Post Online* (December 30, 2002), http://www.washingtonpost.com (accessed March 17, 2003).

RESOURCES

Driggers, P. F., et al. *Managing Library Volunteers: A Practical Toolkit.* Chicago: American Library Assn., 2002.

Linke, L., et al. "The Librarian's Understudy." *American Libraries* 31 (June/July 2000): 78–81.

Macksey, J. A., et al. "Pitch In: Why Volunteering Helps Everyone." *Information Outlook* 6 (February 2002): 30–35.

McCune, B. F. "Marketing to Find Volunteers." *Colorado Libraries* 26 (fall 2000): 40–41.

Thelen, L. "Volunteer Magic: Finding and Keeping Library Volunteers." *School Library Media Activities Monthly* 18 (November 2001): 22–25.

Vaughan, J. B., et al. "Community Service Volunteers in a University Library." *Library Administration & Management* 15 (spring 2001): 91–97.

"Who Is Mrs. K. Allen?" *Colorado Libraries* 27 (winter 2001): 47.

CONCLUSION

Many more years ago than I care to admit, I was a work-study student in my liberal arts college library. To be perfectly truthful, I wasn't terribly successful. It's true I was pretty good at working on the circ desk, and I enjoyed tracking down information for my fellow students. However, I was a terrible typist and an indifferent filer. In those days, any library staff member who possessed those skills was seen as a treasure, and a keyboard-challenged student like me was a liability. That was because of the mountains of Library of Congress cards that needed headings and the order forms that had to be painstakingly typed for every single book. We student workers joked that we needed a PhD in filing rules. The librarian in charge of the card catalog rarely dropped the cards below the rod without caustically informing me that once again, I had forgotten to file "Mc" as if it were spelled "Mac."

It wasn't long before I discovered the reference librarian shared my lowly status. Even though I thought she was truly amazing when she tracked down the most esoteric topics, she obviously did not enjoy the esteem of her colleagues. They thought of her as the grasshopper in the fable, and they were the worker ants. They had a point because when the cataloger caught the flu, everything came to a halt. OCLC was in its infancy, and catalogers still had shelves piled high with original cataloging. Every record was maintained manually, and looking back, it's unbelievable how numerous they were. As I recall, the book order form had five different carbon copies, and each had its own file.

It was true that all those files might not have been necessary. Some librarians, in their quest to organize materials and processes, seemed to lose control and to make each task much more complicated than it needed to be. Once these procedures were codified and became part of the library bible, no untrained person could do them properly. Professional librarians were then hired, not because of their education or expertise but because only they understood the rules.

Changing Library Needs

Nevertheless, most of the backroom jobs were needed, or the library would have sunk into chaos. There was no escaping the mountain of work that waited in the inner sanctum, far from the public reading rooms. It was that pressure that drove the library, and it was no wonder that a reference librarian and an untalented work-study student were not highly regarded. Those days are gone forever, but librarians have not fully adjusted to the fact. Smaller libraries no longer require professional catalogers, and library automation systems have reduced both the quantity and the complexity of clerical tasks to the point that almost anyone can do them. Those mountains of work no longer burden libraries, and the skills that were valued when I was a student worker have long since become obsolete.

Even in those bad old days, librarians did not perceive these tasks to be ends in themselves. They saw them as a means to an end—the loftier goal of serving their communities. The trouble was that the work was so overwhelming that, somehow, service took a backseat. Computers have greatly simplified the work of operating a library. They have eliminated much of the drudgery, but we must not forget that, in another sense, they may threaten our very existence. As we've already discussed, computers and other recent developments have put us in competition with other information providers. Although bookstores are not our only competition, they must be taken into consideration as we define our twenty-first-century identity.

Facing the Uncertain Future

Although I don't want to sound like an alarmist, I think we all must face the fact that libraries are in danger. The more traditional academic libraries are emptying out rapidly. True, they contract with database providers and make these resources available online, but an administrative assistant or business office clerk could do the same. It's hard to view high database usage as an indication of the library's success. Public libraries are doing better, but as local governments look for places to make budget cuts, libraries are high on their hit lists. Since statistics indicate that most residents don't use libraries, it's difficult to make a very compelling case for better funding.

If libraries are in danger, we as librarians must look around for successful role models, and bookstores provide one such model. Obviously, not everything a bookstore does is better than a library, and we are right to see their materialistic aims as being out of line with the goals of library service. Nevertheless, on a more superficial level, they are doing a great many things right. One of their chief discoveries is that although looks aren't everything, looks really matter.

Few of the people the library serves are scholars, and even scholars don't especially enjoy sitting on hard chairs, breathing in dust, or working in a dreary environment. Most of us prefer to spend our time in a comfortable, attractive space where our sensory needs are considered. When people read an announcement of an upcoming event, they are naturally attracted to the colorful, well-designed flyer or brochure. Similarly, they are repelled by the boring, badly designed photocopy. Most customers, whether scholars or bored students, businesswomen, or custodians, are attracted to a place where they can find a good book and relax with a good cup of coffee. It's hard to think of any reason why dirty wallpaper, flaking paint, broken tiles, or scuffed floors would be preferred to a bright, clean, and inviting space.

Reexamining the Bookstore Model

It's also hard to accept the fact that the service one receives in bookstores is often superior to the service in libraries. Librarians usually give outstanding service to their customers, and no one bends over backward to please like a reference librarian. Library files are stuffed with the letters of grateful customers who relate the extraordinary lengths to which reference librarians have gone to find the answer to a question. The problem, of course, is that most library patrons are almost unaware of the services of the reference librarian.

Bookstore corporate headquarters assiduously control what they view as the "bookstore experience." Maybe we need to place the same emphasis on the "library experience." When the overall experience of our customers becomes our focus, the picture changes. It doesn't matter what marvelous resources we have if customers don't use them. It doesn't matter how skilled the reference librarian is if customers don't ask reference questions. It doesn't matter that we sincerely want to serve immigrant groups if no one on the staff speaks their language.

Building on Our Strengths, Confronting Our Weaknesses

If our strengths are invisible to or ignored by our customers, they aren't really strengths. If our weakest, least knowledgeable staff member represents the library to them, then that is their library experience, not the achievements we laud in our annual reports. Today, few people are required to spend time in the library. Students can get their articles from online databases, readers can find their best sellers at Borders, patients can find their medical information on the Dr. Koop or PubMed website, and couch potatoes can get their movies at the local video rental store. Though we are reluctant to admit it, they can manage pretty well without us. Since we're no longer the only game in town, we've got to be the most attractive choice.

"But we're free!" we cry. Sure, that's an attraction, but it's not enough. Free or not, people won't spend time in a library unless the experience contributes something to their day. It must satisfy social needs, for example, a pleasant exchange with a staff member. It must lift their spirits and meet their expectations with regard to space and cleanliness.

Librarians are fond of saying that the library should be the center of the community. To make this more than a glib cliché, the library must find ways to appeal to a broader spectrum of users. Bookstores too want to find ways of attracting new customers so that they will have more opportunities to sell their books and media to the larger community.

Both libraries and bookstores have found that they can reach more people by becoming a venue for community programs. Bookstores, for example, often provide live music, like a jazz group that performs in the café on Friday evenings. Bookstores also try to generate excitement by scheduling book-signing events and book talks by local authors. Providing a wide variety of services and playing host to many different activities, however, can be compared to being a juggler, who must keep several balls in the air at once. Just as one ball too many can cause all the others to clatter to the ground, becoming overextended can spoil the impact of all the library's programs. Some services and activities are more suited to the library environment than others. For example, noise must be contained in designated areas, or readers will go elsewhere. Expanding library programming is also time-consuming and can distract administrators from the library's traditional responsibilities. Collection budgets become fragmented when we purchase a little of this and a little of that.

Being all things to all people is not possible. Yet the rewards of expanding and enhancing the library experience can be great. The secret is balance. Ours should be a more diverse customer base than the bookstore's, and we cannot favor the "haves" over the "have-nots." We can't be all things to all people, but we can leverage our resources, selectively choosing services that will change lives. Although our resources may be limited, we have our communities behind us. No, we can't call on the professional expertise that can be harnessed by the superstore. Yet we have a product that will sell itself with a little help from our friends. And speaking of friends, we have many. They're out there, willing and able to help us. Our job is to extend the invitation.

INDEX